BEHIND THE COCKPIT DOOR

With best wishes
Arthur Whitlock

BEHIND THE COCKPIT DOOR

Arthur Whitlock

ARTHUR WHITLOCK
Robertsbridge, E. Sussex

All pen and ink drawings by the author

Casebound edition first published in Great Britain, 1991
Reprinted 1992 and 1994
This paperback edition published 1996 by Arthur Whitlock

British Library Cataloguing in Publication Data.
A catalogue record for this book is available from the British Library

ISBN 0 9530230 0 1

Printed in England by Orchard & Ind Ltd., Gloucester

DEDICATION

To my betters and peers, who instructed me in the lore of the air and the aeroplane. To my old friends and new, who flew with me across many skies and remembering too, those whose luck deserted them, often with fatal suddenness. To the fellowship of the air.

MAN, THE SERVANT OF MACHINES

Remember please the law by which we live,
We were not built to comprehend a lie,
We can neither love, pity or forgive,
If you make a slip in handling us: you DIE!

Kipling

INTRODUCTION

With the end of World War II, Civil Aviation entered a new phase. Thousands of war surplus transport aircraft were on the market and with them came a mad scramble among wartime aircrews to find employment in the hundreds of post-war airlines mushrooming into existence. The lucky ones were taken on by the State Corporations and National Airlines throughout the world, while the others had to make do with jobs in what were then referred to as Charter Companies. Supply exceeded demand, and the remaining wartime pilots had two choices (if they wished to stay in this exciting profession that had got into their blood) either go overseas in search of work, or give up flying altogether. Some, of course, hoped never to see an aircraft again, let alone pilot one for a living!

Having just finished school at the end of World War II, I first took to the Indian skies myself, and served my apprenticeship as co-pilot with veterans of a wild breed: RAF pilots who had squeezed Dakotas into 600-yard-long strips behind the Japanese lines during the Burma monsoon, their only defence against Zeros being machine-guns fired from the passenger door and holes in the windows; Americans who had flown the worst air route in the world, the notorious 'hump' into China; and many more who all had hair-raising tales to tell to an impressionable youth.

It was a decade full of growing pains for Civil Aviation; fatal accidents were commonplace, and the prime cause, to put it bluntly, was the lack of regulations governing aircraft operations. It was only after many bitter experiences and much loss of life that different forms of control were introduced. Periodic training and tests were made compulsory for aircrew, safety standards were tightened, flight time limitations were introduced along with improvements and new equipment both on the ground and in the aircraft themselves. However, all this was a slow process with the way strewn with casualties. I had been fortunate enough to enjoy an aviation career spanning only peacetime years, and yet within the first twenty-five years well over a hundred pilots, whom I had known personally, had met their deaths in aircraft accidents; while within the next fifteen years none at all, so dramatic had been the improvements in safety.

This then is an account of progress in Commercial Aviation, from free and easy bush flying and charter operations to strictly regulated scheduled passenger airline flying on the wide bodied L.1011 'Tristar'.

VT-CFS
VT-CXH

CHAPTER 1

High above the desert, the dawn sky was lightening perceptibly. Hanging majestically in the chill air of the substratosphere was a most beautiful flying machine, its bulging wide body perfectly proportioned and capable of seating up to four hundred passengers. The aircraft's pedigree was impeccable, a long string of classics had gone before her — Orion, Sirius, Lightning and Constellation were but a few.

This aircraft was huge, passengers sat ten abreast, row after row; it was more like a flying township. A telephone system linked all sections, and lifts served from the galleys below floor level. It weighed two hundred tons, could fly at six hundred m.p.h. and yet was capable of landing blind in the thickest fog. It was the climax of a career that had spanned four decades — what a far cry from when I had started flying.

The Lockheed Tristar's dolphin-like nose was pointing steadily northwards as she was steered towards Cairo. Far behind, the sweltering dust of Khartoum had long since settled back into the darkness after the huge machine's night take-off. Now, the first rays of the rising sun were already beginning to glint on her in full flight, and aboard passengers were stirring. Up front on the flight deck, the crew, somewhat jaded through lack of sleep, operated the airliner's navigational, radio and other systems.

Meanwhile, the cabin staff were busy; an appetizing smell of breakfast being cooked drifted forward from the galley. The co-pilot was quick off the mark as usual when the stewardess popped her head round the door, "Bacon, egg and toms please luv," he quipped cheerily, "mushrooms too, if you have any spare."

He was a genial colleague, the product of quite a different era of aviation; hand picked from among thousands of hopefuls, academically supreme, perfectly at home among the computers of today and, happily for me, not one to hold a grudge for long. I even felt a little guilty for I had spoken quite sharply to him on the previous sector into Khartoum, when it had been his turn to fly. He had brought the aircraft on to the parking area with the taxi lights blazing full into the eyes of the awaiting ground staff. "You young buggers lack airmanship sometimes. How about more consideration for others!" I rebuked, snapping the lights off as those below raised their hands to shield their eyes. But now all that was far behind as the stewardess

AGE 16½ YEARS, FIRST SOLO FLIGHT IN D.H 82 'TIGER MOTH'
FIRST JOB WITH A CHARTER COMPANY AGED 19, NO UNIFORM OF COURSE NEEDED BUSH FLYING IN ASSAM, ASIA AND AFRICA....
ENGLAND, PROUD WEARER OF FIRST UNIFORM.... DC3 FIRST OFFICER AGE 22
AGE 24 NEWLY PROMOTED JUNIOR CAPTAIN DC3
← 310 lbs. THRUST....... 154,000 lbs. THRUST →
CHANGING HAIRLINE AND THE CREEPING DEMISE OF IRRESPONSIBILITY.
THE BEGINNINGS OF THE SERIOUS WORRIED LOOK...... HARASSED RESPONSIBILITY......
SENIORITY LIST..... PENSION ?.....

came forward and placed a tray cloth on each of the three crew members' laps. The breakfast trays soon followed with silverware, gold crested bone china crockery and crisply laundered linen, the food being served from the airline's full first class menu. Why! one of those old aeroplanes I had flown might not have got off the ground with all that extra weight aboard. As I raised the glass of fresh chilled orange juice, my thoughts drifted down to the desert far below.

Down there, somewhere, lay the dreadful spot where over thirty years previously my friends had perished after a forced landing in one of our company's Dakotas. The sky around seemed almost haunted. Here we were, high above that same dreaded Nubian desert in air-conditioned comfort. The sun's rays, which streamed pleasantly through our tinted cockpit windows, would very soon be turning that sand waste far below us into a terrible searing cauldron. What would my old friends have given, as they staggered, driven mad by thirst, to their end, for just one sip of this cooling orange juice I now held? They had fallen victim to the inadequacies of aviation at that time, lured off course in the dead of night by a radio beacon whose frequency had been changed. Glancing across the Tristar's spacious flight deck at the first officer munching his mushrooms, while the aircraft was steered automatically by computers linked to Inertial Navigation, perhaps he would never know the stony pathways that aviation had travelled.

"Brian, over on your side, can you, by any chance, see the remains of an old Dakota lying in the sand?" — a facetious remark — for, from this height, one would have to be looking at the exact spot. Foraging nomads must, long ago, have picked the wreckage to pieces, and shifting sands covered it.

A puzzled expression prompted me to explain, "Friends of mine who didn't make it — they were buried at Wadi Halfa up ahead."

Just coming into sight on the horizon, the great loop of the Nile was curving in to meet us at the Egyptian border, where the city had once been. It had lain these many years submerged below the waters of Lake Nasser and Lake Nubia, formed by the Aswan High Dam. We would soon be in Cairo. I took a last look downwards at the melancholy spot and remembered my old friend, Manohar Singh, the bearded Sikh radio operator. We had been through many adventures together in the past.

Above this very same African continent, as a co-pilot only just twenty years old, he had rudely awakened me when the Dakota, which I was supposed to be flying, plunged earthwards out of control. That had been in the year 1951, and the company for whom I worked at that time had been engaged in a series of charters which were more of an endurance test than anything.

A daunting distance of about 10,000 miles had to be covered to a tight schedule. Starting at Bombay, across Arabia and Africa, to Lagos, in what was then British West Africa; a short rest, then returning all the way back to India. A long way for such a small aircraft, and we relied heavily on the automatic pilot to ease the strain. It was always a very black day to have to start out on one of these charters with an autopilot that the engineers had been unable to fix — this was to be another one of them. The incident had happened as we wearily flew the return trip. Fatigue had admittedly been somewhat self-inflicted, as we had all been up late the previous night.

Now I was alone in the cockpit, eyelids heavy, hand flying the aircraft eastwards from Kano. Behind me, I could just hear snores from the Captain, sleeping soundly atop a pile of suitcases in the forward baggage compartment. Opposite him, Singh, the radio operator, sat sprawled at the table by his set, head resting on his arms, also deeply in the embrace of Morpheus, the God of Sleep. As dawn started to break, both hands on the control wheel, I continued my desperate struggle to stay awake. The pale dawn sky above the desert near Lake Chad was suddenly shattered by the screaming dive of an aeroplane. As the speed of our diving Dakota increased, the propellers began to over-rev. The crescendo of rising noise from the two tortured engines, coupled with the increasing air noises of slipstream, jarred a crew member into wakefulness. Singh leapt into action from his radio compartment; he struggled forward to find out what was happening. There he found me slumped forward, chin on chest, sleeping soundly.

"Wake up you bastard," he shouted, hammering his fist on my back. With an electrified start, my hands shot forward to the control wheel. Gently, gently, I had to fight the urge to pull back too hard and maybe damage the Dakota's speed-tortured structure, but they had built these aircraft tough in Santa Monica. My left hand eased the power off the engines with the throttles — the aircraft steadied in its headlong dive, and levelled off. We had lost a lot of height. During the dive, the din and the suddenly increased air pressure on all our fare paying passengers' eardrums had awakened them all. For

a short while confusion reigned. Our air hostess came forward and anxiously enquired if everything was OK. Sheepishly I muttered an apology to Manohar Singh, and then glanced back at our Captain — he was now propped up and gazing down from roof level with jaundiced eye. Seeing all had apparently returned to normal, he was soon back to sleep again. I climbed the aeroplane back to our flight planned level, and the incident was not even mentioned again.

Minimum rest periods for weary aircrew were unknown in those post-war years. No one seemed to bother too much; to arrive at your destination in one piece was good enough.

A CURIOUS WAY TO TRAVEL TO WORK. MY FATHER, ONE TIME SHIP'S CAPTAIN, HARBOUR PILOT AND MANY YEARS LATER, PORT CONSERVATOR AWARDED THE M.B.E. ON RETIREMENT, RIDES A TROLLEY PROPELLED BY TWO BOATMEN CIRCA 1930/40. HE WAS A HORSE RACING MAN WHOSE LUCKY TREBLE WIN STARTED MY FLYING CAREER.

CHAPTER 2

It had all started for me in the sun-drenched city of Madras, set beside the sparkling waters of the Indian Ocean. A very long shot accumulator bet, placed by my father at the races, had come up and the rest followed. I suspect gambling must have run in the family. A world wandering grandfather played the stakes in the heyday of the Empire — he had made and lost two fortunes in South Africa and India during the twenties and thirties. He had even journeyed to far off China prospecting for business opportunities. And now my father, still immersed in the euphoria of his good win at the races, looked up from his evening newspaper, and said to me, "How would you like to learn to fly, young fella?"

It certainly took me by surprise — I had up until then assumed that I would be following in the old man's footsteps and going to sea as an apprentice deck officer, but this was something else. Time was certainly no problem; waiting for school leaving examination results, left me with plenty of that on my hands. The *Madras Mail* of that evening had carried a Government advertisement aimed at encouraging Indian Nationals to learn how to fly. The country's airlines needed Indian pilots, but there was nothing to prevent Europeans from taking advantage of the offer too. The flying was certainly good value, but my reaction was mixed.

The next day found an awkward youth, aged sixteen and a half years, in the office of the Chief Flying Instructor of the Madras Flying Club. My application to start flying was accepted, and the following week I was to begin in this strange new dimension. The much admired wooden aeroplane models that I had made over the years were one thing, but to actually fly a real one was causing me not a little doubt. As I stood at close quarters beside one of the club's beautiful little silver biplanes standing outside the hangar, I was filled with awe and admiration.

The characteristic smell of dope, oil, petrol and varnish, as I stuck my head into the open cockpit, would be something that would linger for all time. The unfamiliar controls and instruments within did, however, once again cause me to wonder how I was going to cope. These were the last twilight days of the Raj — British India was very shortly to be no more. Most of my fellow student pilots were Indian, but the Club was still presided over by a European, an ex-RNAS pilot

of World War I and a legendary character in Indian Aviation: Chief Flying Instructor, Harold Tyndale-Biscoe. Years before, in 1937, he had taken me up for my first flight in an old Leopard Moth. The joyride had been a birthday treat at the age of seven.

Being a fellow white certainly did not mean any preferential treatment, when flying training commenced. The big moment of the first solo came after eight hours and twenty minutes of dual instruction. This was about average, but old 'T.B.', as he was affectionately known, must have nursed a king sized question mark, for I was called in after my big moment of solo flight while he wrote a note to my father. He picked up a scrap of brown paper, that looked more like the toilet variety, and dated it 26 March 1947 — I still have it to this day — 'My Dear Whitlock, Your son went off solo this morning, just one circuit and landing. I'd describe him as a sort of sleep-flyer. He never seems to be fully awake, and if he wants to be an aviator he will have to get the sleep out of his system and become alert and aware. So I trust you can inculcate the necessary wakefulness. Yours sincerely, T.B.'

Even though the note generated a long lecture on returning home, the fascination of moving in this new element was taking hold. I now had a khaki flying helmet of which the local tailor had made an excellent job. War surplus goggles completed the kit. The warm climate of India permitted flying in short sleeved shirts in the open cockpits. Now becoming a more familiar sight, seated in the front cockpit, my instructor sported less orthodox headgear. His flying helmet could have come straight from the relief of Khartoum or the Zulu wars, but was more likely an ancient Indian polo topee. He was a past master in the art of flying and aerobatics, so I learned steadily as the lessons progressed — circuits and landings, as thousands of pilots before me — wheelers, three-pointers and recovery from a bounced landing — stalls and spinning, the earth revolving madly round, the nose pointing vertically downwards, and the bottomless feeling in the pit of the stomach.

All of this initial training, and my first solo flight, was done in a

FIRST FLIGHTS IN THE INDIAN SKIES AGE 16½ YEARS.

DH 82 Tiger Moth registered VT-ARQ, or just 'ARQ' to all of us at the Club.

Never in my wildest imagination could I have foreseen that this very aeroplane would still be flying over 43 years later. She was destined to crash and be rebuilt after a long interval, then be registered VT-DHB, lie in bits for years, until a Canadian buyer came along and took her home with him to become CF-EIP. The old Tiger had other owners, but finally finished up in Texas, repainted yellow with RAF markings, in immaculate condition and registered N6353.

I would never have dreamed that I would be invited over to Dallas by the present owner, Mr Henry 'Bud' Molloy, and fly the very same machine again after the passing of over four decades.

We became firm friends and one day when we had been flying circuits and landings together in the old Tiger at Lancaster, Texas, having just landed, he stopped the aircraft, climbed out and said "There you are, go do some flying."

It was a memorable occasion for me alone with my thoughts in the skies above Texas, and it was later published in *The Guinness Book of Records*, 'Aircraft Facts and Feats'.

"The longest period between 'solo' flights in the same aircraft is a most unusual category, but British Airways pilot Captain Arthur Whitlock makes this claim in relation to a de Havilland D.H.82 Tiger Moth with the constructors number 86069. On 26 March 1947, Arthur Whitlock made his first solo flight in this aircraft (then registered VT-ARQ) at the Madras Flying Club. Despite a busy life as a civil airline pilot he always retained an interest in the old 'Tiger', eventually tracing her (now registered N6353) to Dallas, Texas. There thanks to the kindness of its present owner Henry 'Bud' Molloy, he flew his first love again on 15 April 1991, just over 44 years after the original 5 minute solo. A flight on 4 October 1995 brings this time to $48^1/_2$ years."

Before graduating to cross-country flying, forced landings were next on the list. Here I came to discover my old veteran instructor's skill.

We had been flying over open countryside, gliding down with simulated engine failure to several large fields, sometimes touching the wheels on the ground, then with a roar of engine power, climbing back up again.

With T.B. in control, we then set off down the coast. We were flying over a seemingly endless sea of casuarina trees, when control was again handed back to me. Knowing that the crunch was about to come, I was searching frantically — there was not a scrap of space worth talking about in sight. At that very second, all went quiet as the throttle was chopped back from the front cockpit. The order, "Forced landing Whitlock," came through the Gosport Tubes to my ears. Sweating hand on the control column, with the engine popping as it idled, I glided down. Feverishly I searched about, but it was no good. Grabbing the speaking tube I blurted, "Th.. there's nothing available."

There followed an exasperated silence as we continued to lose precious height. Then a pointing finger stabbed out into the slip-stream from the front cockpit, "Oh! yes there is — I have control."

I watched in complete amazement as he headed down towards an absolutely diminutive patch of ground. A demonstration was in progress, and I watched in awe as he commenced with a few lazy turns working downwind. The chosen spot was becoming clearer now. This was madness. It was bounded on three sides by the tall swaying casuarinas. The remaining side, towards the corner, had a perilously narrow slot in it between the trees. The biplane continued to snake earthwards, then made a spectacular last minute sideslip to lose a bit of excess height. The wingtips literally whisked past the branches waiting to snatch us from the sky. A final succession of fish-tailing rapidly killed off the excess airspeed, and the next second there was

FORCED LANDING PRACTICE NEAR THE COAST OF MADRAS, SOUTH INDIA.

a drumming of fabric, rubber and steel; the wheels and tail-skid had made perfect contact with the ground. A short roll along the ground, and then the engine roared into life. A few bumps and we were into the air again, our wheels brushing over the tree-tops at the far end. The rest of the session, on that sunny Indian morning, was spent practising the exercise. I came back again often on my own to this spot among the casuarinas, and repeated that heart quickening challenge. Eventually I too got it to perfection.

THE DEMONSTRATION.

The learning process continued, and it soon became clear that aviation was not to be taken lightly. Flying Club aircraft were being crashed at regular intervals; some were fatal. The shock of realizing that a colleague was no more was sometimes difficult to accept. Low flying was the main cause, and Instructors took vigorous action to discourage it. At random, barographs were secretly put aboard aircraft and their telltale altitude traces examined later — to be caught

1
VT – AMC
COMPLETELY ABSORBED
IN THE PLEASURES OF
LOW FLYING ALONG THE
MAGNIFICENT STRETCHES
OF UNSPOILT BEACHES
OF SOUTH INDIA........

2
VT-AMC
....TWO FLYING CLUB BUDDIES
'BITE THE DUST'. LEARNING
THEIR LESSON THE HARD WAY,
FORTUNATELY NOT FATALLY...

3
IT WAS THE CLASSIC CASE OF NEITHER PILOT BEING SURE WHO WAS ACTUALLY DOING THE FLYING AS THEY WENT INTO THE GROUND.
4
WHEN HE CAME TO ... MY FRIEND EXAMINING THE REMAINS OF ALL HIS FRONT TEETH, TOP AND BOTTOM.

meant severe disciplining. Two friends, who crashed, fell into the classic trap; each thought the other was in control as the aircraft slammed violently into the ground — one related later how his admiration for the other's daring was suddenly shattered by the crash.

They were lucky to survive. One was trapped upside down by a petrol tank in the front cockpit, resulting in his face being disfigured for life. The other, when he came to, remembered wondering what his front teeth were doing lying around on the earth.

Far worse though was the fact that their flying training was stopped and their careers ended.

A FRIEND'S FIERY END AT CUDDAPAH.... HE HAD ROLLED IN THE GRASS TRYING TO EXTINGUISH THE FLAMES, THE ONLY TRANSPORT AVAILABLE WAS A BULLOCK CART.......

About this time, a very strange tragedy occurred which made an unforgettable impression on us all. A young club member was about to be married. As was the custom among Indians, he visited a Palmist;

it would be unthinkable to enter such an important stage in his life without having a horoscope cast. The holy man had a high reputation, and his utterances were always taken seriously. What he had to say to our friend, shook him to the core. "Exercise great care. You are approaching a time of great danger. You may die within two weeks. Therefore you must not expose yourself to any danger."

When told that his client was a trainee pilot, the Palmist was mortified and insisted that he did not go near an aeroplane for at least a month. As he seemed a bit concerned, we at the club advised him likewise.

About a week later, the evening newspaper reported the chilling news that there had been a fatal crash involving a Flying Club aircraft at a place called Cudapah. No other details were included in the news item. I did not for one minute think that it could have been our friend, but unbelievably it was. Next day at the airfield we learned the awful details. The club had been short of aircraft, and as a result there was a long wait for cross-country flights, so our colleague had decided to take his turn. He had considerable experience, having flown Spitfires in the Air Force. Was it the horoscope that had played on his mind? Was it a control cable which investigators suspected could have broken? Or was it just an inexplicable mystery of the Orient?

.... FOR HIS LONG AGONISING FUTILE JOURNEY TO A VILLAGE HOSPITAL, WHERE HE DIED LATER OF BURNS.

More shocks were in store, and this time right in front of the clubhouse. It was during the hot weather season, and I was doing my six month stint of training in the hangar. We were set to work doing all aspects of overhauling and rebuilding aircraft and engines during their checks. Hard at work one morning, the airfield crash siren suddenly shattered the oppressive heat. Running from the hangar, I was met by a sight that I would never forget. Vivid red flames almost completely engulfed a Tiger Moth, its nose buried vertically in the earth. A thick jet black column of smoke was rising hundreds of feet into the air, laced with vicious tongues of flame. Worst of all, the realization hit us that one of our friends was perishing in the holocaust.

We started running wildly towards the burning aeroplane; I suppose it was in the vain hope that we might be able to help. When I drew near, the heat was still intense but foam was beginning to blanket the inferno. As I gazed in shock at the pitiful remains, I realized I was getting my first lesson as to the dreadful consequences of a mistake. Our friend had not long gone solo. He had bounced on landing, pulled the stick back in panic, and at the same time opened

MY AB INITIO CROSS COUNTRY PASSENGER OF LONG AGO. A FUTURE JUMBO CAPTAIN WHO CAME CLOSE TO GIVING IT ALL UP AFTER THAT FLIGHT.

AN INTERESTING CROSS COUNTRY FLIGHT IN SOUTH INDIA.... THE VAST ANCIENT BATTLEMENTS OF GINGEE FORTRESS PERCHED ATOP A ROCKY ESCARPMENT WHERE TWO CENTURIES BEFORE..... INDIAN KINGS, THE FRENCH AND BRITISH HAD RULED IN TURN.....

the throttle to full power. Eye witnesses had seen the aeroplane shoot up nearly vertically. It had stalled and spun straight back into the ground.

The accident took some getting over, and we were each helped by being directed to make a short flight that day.

However, despite the many deterrents, the temptation of the marvellous exhilaration of the occasional indulgence in low flying could not be resisted. Whenever an opportunity presented itself, down would go the nose, the earth would drift closer, and the rest was sheer delight.

THE WONDERFUL EXHILARATION OF LOW FLYING.... 'BEATING UP' THE CRUISER H.M.S. 'DEVONSHIRE'... LEAVING MADRAS HARBOUR. A LIFELONG WEAKNESS FOR THE SHEER ENJOYMENT OF IT WAS ONLY CURED VERY SLOWLY OVER THE YEARS BY CONTROLS.

VELLORE, INDIA 1948.
A CURIOUS MULTITUDE APPEAR FROM NOWHERE, SURROUNDING THE LANDING FIELD TO WATCH A STRANGE FLYING MACHINE AND IT'S LONE WHITE PILOT REFUEL AND DEPART. FOR MANY OF THESE WATCHERS, THIS WAS THE FIRST CLOSE SIGHT OF AN AEROPLANE.

The vast country of India was so ideally suited where the sun shone most of the year, and the magnificent deserted beaches, stretching for hundreds of miles, were open invitations to descend for a closer look. Swaying coconut trees would float past, with brilliant white sand below being lapped by the sparkling sea.

At the minimum age of seventeen, I had gained my Private Pilot's Licence, but had to stretch time out until I was nineteen years old in order to qualify for a Commercial Pilot's Licence, which is necessary to obtain employment.

During those two youthful years time seemed to go slowly as the required two hundred flying hours were spun out.

Then suddenly came an unexpected setback. It happened without the slightest advance warning whatsoever. There was to be no more subsidy for non-Indian nationals — overnight flying fees for Europeans were up fivefold. The British were in the process of pulling out of India, and here was an early victim! The situation was grave. With about eighty hours still to be paid for, what was left of the 'race winnings' would not stretch to it. The reaction at home that evening was very cold. "I do not have that much money available,"

SHOUTING TO MY INSTRUCTOR THROUGH THE SPEAKING TUBE AND HANGING ON FOR DEAR LIFE, MORE OUT THAN IN THE AIRCRAFT, AFTER NOT TIGHTENING MY HARNESS SUFFICIENTLY BEFORE AEROBATIC PRACTICE.

said my father, adding cheerlessly, "I will have to borrow money, and that will mean you will have to accept responsibility for paying it all back."

A bleak thought, and I soon set about seeing how I could scrounge some extra flying hours. The Flying Club, knowing my plight, was helpful. They permitted me to do any joyrides that turned up occasionally at the club. It did not yield much flying and meant hanging round day after day.

A few more hours came, on two ferry flights. One of these turned out to be quite interesting as it was to be a first encounter with the gold smugglers of India.

Two of us from the Flying Club had made our way northwards, a slog of about a thousand miles by rail and bus. We arrived eventually at Panagarh in West Bengal. It had been a US Air Force base during World War II — the peeling walls still bore the marks, names and graffiti of long departed American personnel. A skeleton staff of Indians were now engaged in the unequal task of keeping the undergrowth at bay. The airfield was packed with hundreds of war surplus aircraft lined up row upon row. Countless chunky tailed, four-engined Liberator bombers and bulbous Curtis Commando transports shared space with smaller types.

We found our way to a hangar where our two aircraft were being prepared for flight. The Stinson Sentinel L5s were high wing liaison machines that had been in the thick of jungle fighting, and were still in camouflage paint. Their newly allocated registrations were painted over their still visible US Air Force symbols. We familiarized ourselves with the controls, started the engines when work had been completed, and prepared to do a short air test. I remember the curious experience of having to find my way to the runway through tall grass and weeds that stood well above the wings on either side of the taxi track. It would not have been a surprise if a fabled Bengal tiger had stepped out from those towering walls of grass. The aircraft flew well, their six cylinder engines purring smoothly.

Signing acceptance, we were soon refuelled and prepared to

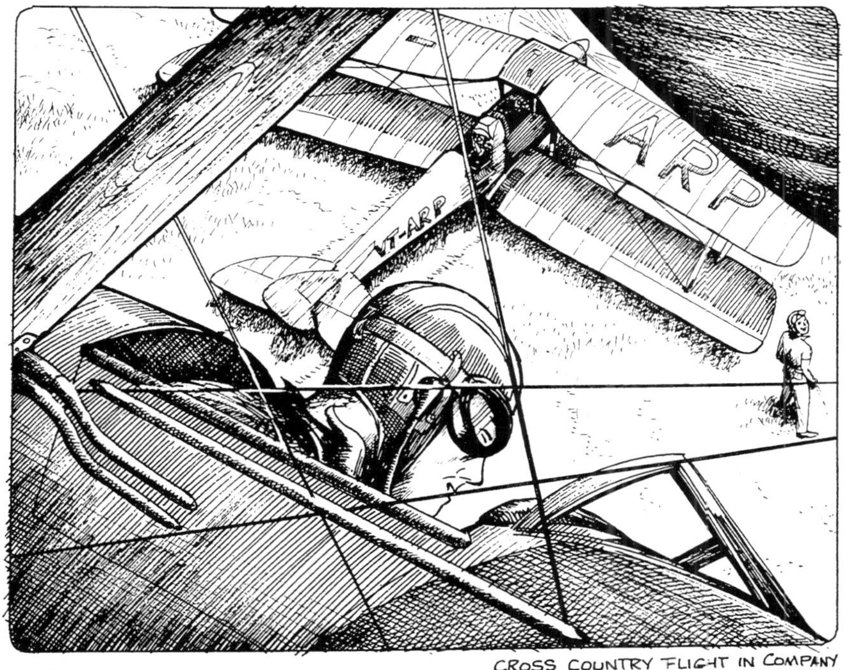

CROSS COUNTRY FLIGHT IN COMPANY AND A HIGHLY UNAUTHORISED VISIT TO THE PRIVY........

depart for Calcutta. In the air once again, before setting course, we let our waving ground engineers get a close up view of their handiwork. They had succeeded in getting at least two aeroplanes back into their natural element. As both of us passed low in formation, skimming over all those forlorn rows of grounded aircraft, I wondered how many of them would ever make it back into the wide blue

BUZZING PANAGAR, DEPARTING WITH A U.S. WAR SURPLUS SENTINEL L.5.

yonder.

Leaving Calcutta the next day, we were again in the air heading south-westwards — a flight of three and a half hours to Bhubaneshwar in Orissa. We flew down the coast in company, my colleague about half a mile ahead. The day was brilliant, with a dazzling heat haze. Gazing down at the endless white beach shimmering below, I suddenly caught sight of something glinting up ahead. Approaching closer, there were three aeroplanes parked on the sand below. Imagination? No, they were really there, miles from anywhere, one twin-engine and two single-engined aircraft. Circling above, I could distinctly see figures transferring packages between the aircraft. The activity continued as I orbited above in wide circles. My partner in the other L.5 was by now a mere speck in the distance. It was time that I was on my way. As I left I saw one of the mystery aircraft start its engine with a swirl of sand. It took off and headed in the opposite direction, to the north.

I never did catch up with my colleague. On landing, I joined him in the small control block. The aerodrome officer clearly did not believe my story. He had no information on any aircraft movements in his area. As a courtesy, however, he did telephone the Calcutta Area Controller, but it drew a blank. I got the distinct impression that I was under suspicion of imagining the whole episode. The matter remained unexplained.

More than a year was to pass before some light was to be thrown on the mystery. And that was when I, too, was part of a smuggling operation involving gold, the quantity so large that it caused a severe hiccup in gold prices at that time.

Going flat out, the Commercial Pilot's Licence was at last in my hand at the age of nineteen years. The triumph was extremely short-lived. Calls from my father for repayment of the debt were becoming positively clamorous. Solemn pledges as to sincere intentions on my part were just not enough. Employment had to be obtained, and quickly.

A FIRST ENCOUNTER
WITH A SMUGGLING
OPERATION, ON A FERRY
FLIGHT OVER ORISSA..

CHAPTER 3

The few flying jobs to be had, at that time, existed mainly in Calcutta. So it was to olde Calcutta that I journeyed, and by the time honoured way, by sea. Aboard a ship of the Asiatic Steam Navigation Company, signed on as supernumerary crew, I sailed northwards from Madras. The venerable old steamship chugged along across the blue waters of the Bay of Bengal. Some three days later it gradually changed to a muddy yellow — we had arrived off the notorious Hooghly Sandheads. A pilot came aboard, and we cautiously threaded our way up-river through the treacherously shifting shoals. The ship berthed not far from the huge span of the Howrah Bridge, and conveniently for me within long walking distance of the city.

Stepping briskly ashore early next morning, full of hope, the search for a job began. A month later, footsore and weary legged, I was still trying. The ship had long since sailed. I had found accommodation at the YMCA and later, the floor of a pilot friend's digs. Money had run out. My father had then sent me a final contribution (the equivalent of seven pounds) with a curt note, 'I can afford no more. If you are unable to find employment, then you will have to return here, to go back to England.' I conjured up pictures in my mind of 'square bashing' in the Air Force, if they would have me, and it spurred me on to greater efforts.

Every airline company in Calcutta had been on my visiting list. They were all, it seemed, thoroughly fed up with the sight of me. Doormen at two of the large scheduled airlines had even been instructed not to admit a certain troublesome white youth. However, perseverance was soon to be rewarded. The charter company, which I was headed for that morning, had their office in the once stately Grand Hotel. At least their air-conditioned office would be a welcome respite from the heat outside. Someone must have been in a good mood, for I found myself being admitted to the General Manager's office. Shifting from foot to foot on the plush carpet, I was getting the same old familiar negative. In desperation I tried to put my situation across. My commercial licence was virtually useless without a Dakota endorsement on it. This was the type of aircraft that all the airlines operated at that time. Scrounging old notes, I had sat and passed the Dakota Technical Examination. Now I needed to fly as extra crew, to do six landings, to get that magic passport to a possible job. On the opposite side of the room sat Kitty, the boss's girlfriend and secretary. She was a raven-haired beauty with a magnificent figure, who at the crucial moment turned out to be my salvation. The boss had hardly finished explaining how they would be losing out on payload with extra crew on board, when Kitty, elegant legs crossed, gently chided, "Oh! go on, Johnny, give the poor boy a chance." He mused awhile, and then relented. I was in.

They were as good as their word, and from that moment I was in a new world with superhuman aviators, who flew with ease mind-bogglingly complicated aeroplanes, not just one engine but two, wheels that retracted, hydraulic flaps that were lowered for landing, propellers whose pitch could be changed — and the list went on and on. I hung on to their every word when advice was handed out and wondered when I would ever master such an aeroplane. The six landings were eventually completed, with captains who were prepared to take a chance and talk a novice down where necessary while they followed through holding the controls as well, just in case. I soon had the precious DC 3 temporary endorsement stamped on my licence which should now make all the difference.

Two evenings later an ex Flying Club friend, who worked with Indamer Company, had a message for me — "Call again for an interview with the Chief Pilot." Luck was with me; they needed an extra co-pilot. I was hired, but on the strict understanding that it was temporary only. They never did terminate my employment while I flew in India, and what a wonderful company they turned out to be for which to work.

Thirty-four years later, passing through Calcutta as Captain of a Tristar, word got to me that Kitty was still there, running her own printing business. Although so many years had passed, I resolved to call at her office with some small gift to show my gratitude. From crew-cut youth of nineteen, to bald-headed gent on the wrong side of fifty was asking too much of recognition from memory when we met. There was a decidedly noticeable lump in the throat as I reminded Kitty of her kindness getting me started on my flying career long ago. Time had made its mark on us all, but as I handed her my gift, the hint of moistness in her eyes told me she was still the same big-hearted lady she had always been.

Enthusiasm for work in my new job knew no bounds. Frugal living soon had the debt to my father paid back. It was hard work by today's standards. The legal limit of 125 flying hours in 28 days was often

SHEER PERFECTION, IN THE FORM OF A 'SPITFIRE' FLOWN BY A FRIEND, BUZZES MY HUMBLE 'TIGER MOTH' AT ST. THOMAS'S MOUNT AERODROME, MADRAS. 1948.

TIMES YET TO COME; THE SLEEK LINES OF OUR AIRSPEED 'AMBASSADOR' (ALSO CALLED THE 'ELIZABETHAN') OVER THE COAL MINES OF NORTHUMBERLAND. 1959.

exceeded. A note from the Chief Pilot, which still resides to this day as a souvenir in my log-book, reads cryptically, 'Whitlock to log only first two trips: 7 hours 50 mins., not 10 hours 50 mins., to Bagdogra on 1 June 1951.' In this way the books were kept in order from time to time. Large overtime earnings compensated for lack of sleep at home. Slumber was done in turns during flights. Three days on,

followed by one day off, was the minimum work pattern, but that rest day was well and truly needed, after the daily rising at 01.30 in the dead of night and getting back home about 10 p.m. for a couple of

hours' sleep and a change of clothes.

The drive to Barrackpore Airfield was a protracted affair, a long drive over dusty Bengal roads after visiting every part of slumbering Calcutta, picking up bleary-eyed crew members. One and a half hours before dawn, our Dakota would lift into the blackness and head northwards, climbing away loaded with freight, ultraviolet lights glowing eerily in the cockpit. Now the next important decision had to be made — who would sleep first? Two foam rubber mattresses were standard equipment on board the Dakotas. They would be used alternately laid out on any convenient flat surface, either atop freight or in the tail area. To further enhance comfort, I carried an air pillow in my briefcase. It was a matter of pride to only part inflate it while on the ground — if it had been done correctly, the changing air pressure, during climbing, would do the rest — a perfect pillow on which to flake out when cruising height was reached.

Flying towards the Himalayas in darkness, just before dawn a curious sight often could be seen. As the sun rose, it would light up the lofty summits of Mount Everest and Kanchenjunga, which could sometimes be seen as little pink specks of light set brilliantly like jewels in the semi-darkness, while we were still over a hundred miles away.

On landing, with the first rays of dawn, mainly general cargo was unloaded. We would have a cup of tea while the hard worked Dakota was reloaded, crammed full of tea chests, so full that to reach the cockpit the crew had to crawl forwards on hands and knees along the narrow tunnel between the cabin roof and the chests. Three round trips and back home by 10 p.m., to start all over again in the small hours. Flying at this pace soon had experience piling up, but the result was weary crews.

Two events in those early days nearly brought a budding career to an abrupt end. Strangely enough, both were connected with airborne shut-eye. However, nowadays by law pilots must be given the opportunity to get enough rest.

Only a last minute programme change saved my life. With dismay we heard one day that one of the company Dakotas was missing. The night before I had been taken off that very flight — to even up flying hours, a Captain had been substituted to fly as co-pilot. The next day news came in, relayed from the wild mountainous country of Bhutan in the foothills of the Himalayas, that the wreckage had been located, and our worst fears were realized. There were no survivors.

A few days later my good friend, Leo (our Operations Manager), and a medic, succeeded in getting through jungle and across mountains to the crash site. It was wild country. His Bhutanese trackers eventually hacked their way through. In its last moments of flight, the Dakota had by some quirk of chance literally brushed its wingtips against the sides of a slot in the hills, as it flew on to slam into a vertical rockface. The remains were pitiful — the dial of the skipper's gold watch, a small section of charred vertebrae — but it was the half torso of a crew member, who had been sleeping in the tail section, that provided the clue. Analysis showed strong traces of carbon monoxide, and this could only have come from one source; the villain of the piece must almost certainly have been a crack in an exhaust pipe jacket, thus allowing the deadly gas into the aeroplane's heating system. The doomed aircraft had flown on and on, auto-pilot in control, towards the mightiest mountain ramparts in the world.

Again, much later, in Africa, fate lurked stealthily once more. Another mammoth flog across one of the most inhospitable and deserted regions of the world. Our take-off from the walled city of Kano, Nigeria, in West Africa, had been a struggle. We had a full load of passengers aboard, all twenty-one of them, and a lot of fuel. The wailing trumpet call of the Emir's man, sitting astride his camel at Kano Airport, still lingered — in those days the trumpet was blown for the arrival and departure of every aircraft. Dawn was just breaking as we climbed upwards, setting the Dakota's nose on course eastwards, our destination being El Geneina in Western Sudan. The Skipper, whose need seemed to be the greatest, had left me in control. He settled himself to sleep in the usual spot, atop the baggage in the forward hold. The first stint started uneventfully. The featureless terrain made map reading rather futile. Of other navigation aids, there were of course none in this wilderness. If we were drifting off track at all, then it would be corrected when we reached the landmark of Lake Chad ahead. About two and a half hours later, the huge water mass slowly came into view and it was not where it should have been — we were off course. Instead of passing along the lake's southern shore, we were well to the north.

With our position now pin-pointed, I made a large alteration of course for El Geneina. It was still over three hours away. There was movement behind me. It was a well chosen moment. Yawning and stretching, the Skipper climbed back into his seat

My turn off, at last. He was satisfied with our position, and noted our new course. Settling myself down on the mattress, I watched the radio operator, Manohar Singh, go forward and take my vacated seat in the cockpit. In his hand he held the special board that clipped on to the throttle pedestal. I knew that a game of poker was about to commence, with the auto-pilot doing the work. Drifting off to sleep, the cards were being dealt and the game was on.

Stirring from sleep nearly two hours later, the Dakota's engines were still droning away steadily, but there was another sound. It was the noise of charts and maps being spread around the confined cockpit. The smell of fear was in the air. Singh's tense hand was twirling the radio compass handle on the cockpit roof. He was looking up at the dial in desperation, trying to tune in a signal for a

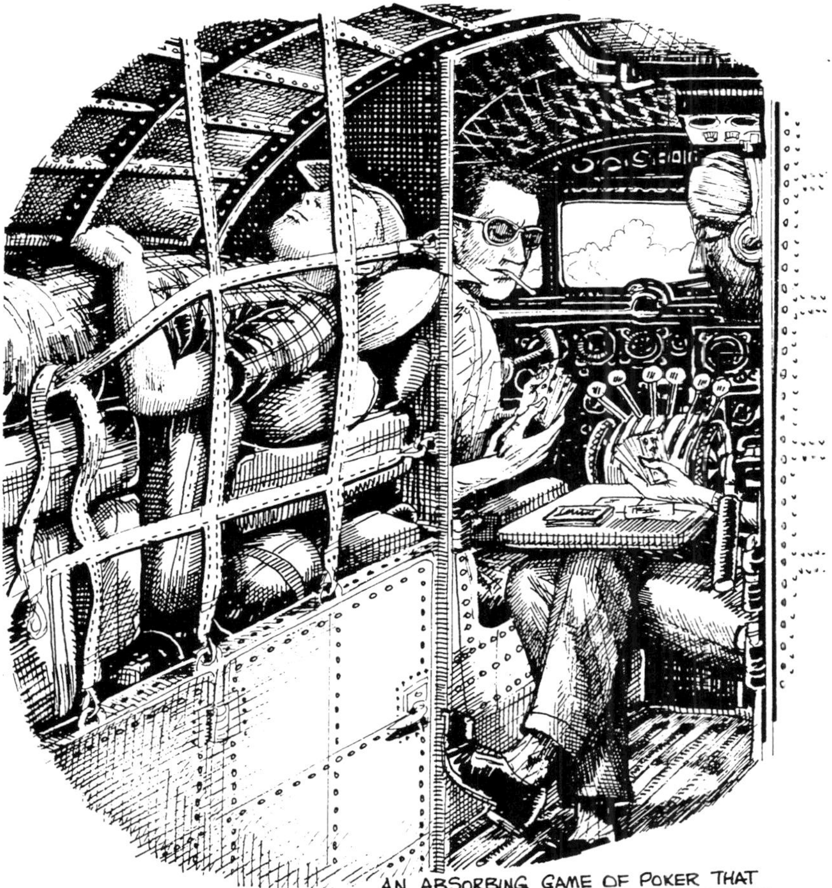

AN ABSORBING GAME OF POKER THAT NEARLY BROUGHT US DOWN IN THE DESERT.

bearing. Guessing at the trouble was unnecessary — we were lost.

Outside the heat haze was starting to rise and the glare was becoming fierce, as I climbed back into the co-pilot's seat. Clutching a map, the Skipper hissed, "Can't get El Geneina." So much for the game of poker, I thought. Even if head winds had held up our progress, we should be receiving the radio beacon by now. It was our only means of guidance — we carried no other navigational equipment. If we missed the place, we would be in real trouble.

Nervously the fuel contents selector was flicked from tank to tank

— it was not encouraging. The Skipper's hand moved to the propeller pitch levers and eased them slowly back. The engines lowered their note as the revolutions decreased. Next, he inched the fuel mixture control levers carefully towards the cut-off position, one at a time. As each engine in turn started to cough and splutter, the lever was moved again forward slightly — not a recognized procedure — it was a trick known by some to extend flight time. No doubt it would not be doing the engines much good, but it might just save us.

The maps were not much help. There were huge blank spaces, with such legends as 'area not surveyed, magnetic variation unknown, or rocky outcrop unconfirmed.' I had flown with Martin, the Skipper, many times before, but never had I seen him look so pale. Our predicament was getting worse. El Geneina was long overdue. Which way to turn? Left would take us into the sand wastes of the Sahara, right would take us into a desolation of scrub.

Just coming into view below us was a vague discolouration in the sand. The Skipper's finger pointed at a thinly dotted line on his map — a dried wadi running roughly east/west, but that was over a hundred miles from where we should have been. "We'll have to chance it," he blurted, "we'll turn on to a south-east heading — at least that way we'll be flying out of the desert."

Our hope now was to find El Fasher, deeper into the Sudan. Every now and then, one of us would check fuel remaining in the tanks. It was now getting very low.

It was about this time, as I peered ahead through the haze, that I thought I could see a vague shape far away. At first it seemed it was my imagination, as I squinted trying to pierce the glare and haze.

"Martin, I think I can see a mountain ahead and to starboard. If it is, it can only be Jebel Mara."

This isolated mountain was a landmark which I had seen many times before — it lay between El Geneina and El Fasher.

"If we alter course on that and you're wrong, we're sunk," said the Skipper. Nevertheless he decided to gamble again, and he turned the Dakota towards where El Fasher should be if our mountain was correct.

It was a good decision, for our radio compass needle, that had previously been going in circles round the dial, now started to point uncertainly ahead. El Fasher was two hundred miles beyond our original destination, and whether we could stretch our flight that far, was an entirely different question. We had drained two fuel tanks dry, and were now using the remaining two. The fuel gauge needles were nearly on the empty marks. The fuel cross feed cock had been opened. Now, when the tanks ran dry, both engines would stop together, but it might give us just that little bit longer.

Gradually the desert was giving way to semi-scrub, but there was a fair amount of flat area for a forced landing. The radio operator was talking to El Fasher, and it was now that the Skipper demonstrated his nerves of steel. With engines that could stop at any minute, he listened to the Sudanese Controller enquiring:

"You are flight planned overdue at Geneina — please explain."

I did notice Martin swallow hard as he picked up his hand microphone!

"We had sufficient fuel, so decided to overfly Geneina. No contact possible. Presume they have radio problems."

And he did not even bat an eyelid as he added, "We have encountered unexpectedly strong headwinds past Geneina, and are now a bit short of fuel."

That was some understatement!

We were now at the stage of frantically looking ahead for El Fasher. Fuel booster pumps were on to get every drop of petrol out of the near empty tanks. We were mentally flying from one good flat stretch of ground to the next. Our air hostess was busy at the back trying to keep the now restless passengers happy. At last a wonderful sight came into view. First vaguely, then more clearly defined, we saw El Fasher's cross runways. Throttling back, we descended earthwards. Not daring to waste time doing a circuit, we landed on the nearest runway ahead of us, regardless of wind direction. It surprised us all that the engines stayed running until we had taxied to the control tower.

Over a cool beer that evening, it was all anticlimax. Our engineer described how he had dipped the fuel tanks after the flight. It caused reflection on just how lucky we had been. The dipstick had revealed five US gallons of usable fuel in one tank, and seven in the other — enough for perhaps five or ten minutes flying at the most.

From my log-books, the date was October 1951, and we had been in the air 7 hours 45 minutes. At the time, I had not fully realized the dire position we might have been in; that was to come later, when I was to see how unmerciful the desert could be.

Drawing to the end of that first year at work, the accident rate was appalling. Dakotas were biting the dust with monotonous regularity — at least one a month, and most of them fatal; astonishingly high by today's standards, but they seemed to be accepted as inevitable at the time. What were the causes of all this aerial havoc?

CLOSE BY DUM DUM AIRPORT, CALCUTTA 1949. A FATAL NIGHT CRASH IN WHICH TWO FRIENDS PERISHED... ONE HAD FORGOTTEN TO PULL A SIMPLE KNOB ON THE PANEL TO UNCAGE THE HORIZON GYRO... LATER, WARNING FLAGS WERE FITTED.

Human error, the favourite scapegoat, was hardly on the cards when training; flying tests or periodic checks and recurrent training were non-existent at that time in India. Without regular compulsory practice, a lot of pilots got used to thinking that an engine failure on take-off just won't happen to me, or with luck, the monsoon will be kind this year. Airline companies had no call to spend revenue on training pilots when there were no regulations demanding it. It was a most enjoyable carefree existence, but people were being killed at an amazing rate.

One day, word got around that yet another scheduled airline passenger Dakota had been written off at Gauhati, a town on the Brahmaputra river in the Assam valley. We happened to be going there ourselves that afternoon, so no time was wasted after landing before walking over to have a look. A sorry sight indeed. It was not difficult to find by just following a swath of flattened young trees, which led to a first glimpse of the tail. The aircraft had wedged itself well and truly into the larger trees of the surrounding jungle. By some miracle the Dakota's nose had just missed a tree trunk, which had embedded in the wing root — a foot further over, and the occupants of the cockpit would have had a nasty time of it. But the unfortunate pilot's problems were by no means over. We were told later that, after everyone had extricated themselves, the unhappy group made their way back on foot. As they struggled through broken branches and undergrowth, the passengers' displeasure was focused on the Captain; he was rather short of stature, and it was claimed that his legs had not been long enough to reach the rudder pedals properly. He was harangued vociferously all the way to the airport building.

A SHORT LEGGED PILOT'S DILEMMA...LOSS OF RUDDER CONTROL AT GAUHATI - ASSAM - 1950

Well into my first few months of employment, it became necessary to present myself to the Medical Centre at Cawnpore — this was for flying licence renewal. Finances could now stretch to a discounted air ticket. So in due course I boarded the regular scheduled airline flight from Calcutta. After take-off, I was invited up front by the co-pilot, whom I knew. How the other half lived — these crew members wore smart uniforms! The Captain, a grizzled Australian veteran, greeted me affably. When he learned that I, too, flew Dakotas, he said over his shoulder, "Come and sit yourself down Snow."

Clambering out of his seat he added, "I'm going back to see what we have in the passenger cabin."

The fair-haired, instantly nicknamed 'Snow', happily climbed into the Captain's left hand seat — quite a privilege for one so inexperienced. What was to follow would have caused more than a few questions to be asked nowadays.

The Skipper had a brief chat over our shoulders before leaving the cockpit. We got on with flying the aircraft towards Cawnpore. Eventually the time came to commence descent, which was always done in good time and gradually for the sake of passengers ears.

THE CAPTAIN EMERGING THROUGH A WALL OF FLAME CARRYING THE CO-PILOT AND THE RADIO OPERATOR, ONE UNDER EACH ARM. HE WAS LETTING THEM PRACTISE A TAKE OFF TOGETHER WHEN THE R/O. LOST CONTROL! LUCKILY AN ALL CARGO FLIGHT......

BEFORE AND AFTER... A LANDING MISHAP AT BALURGHAT ASSAM..A CRITICALLY SHORT LANDING STRIP, OF APPROXIMATELY 700 YARDS OF WARTIME PERFORATED STEEL PLATE.... WITH WATERLOGGED RICE FIELDS AT EACH END.......

There was still no sign of the Skipper, so down we went.

As she got lower, our DC3 started to bump about a little as we entered the haze layer. At long last a smiling Aussie face peered over my shoulder, squinting into the glare ahead.

"Yer look like yer doin' oak-eye, Snow!" and adding, "yer mite as well carry on and have a go at the landing."

I could not believe my ears. Here was a Captain prepared to let an unknown nineteen-year-old have a go at landing his passenger aeroplane for him. Recovering from the shock, I hastily accepted his offer. The chance to do a landing from the Captain's seat was too good an opportunity to miss.

The dust haze was quite thick now, but with their map spread across my knees landmarks were slotting in well. Starting a turn, a voice close to my right ear, slightly tinged with anxiety, enquired, "Where is it, Snow? I can't see the airfield."

Not that I could either, but with the help of some imagination, a vague line could just be made out. Still descending, I turned again, and the runway now became clearer. The landing gear went down, and we continued with the checks. Happily my new found benefactor was not let down. The landing went well. Another load of fare paying customers had arrived back safely on terra firma, albeit unsuspecting of what had been going on up front.

Back in our bush flying world of charter work, the scene was often so different. In those times we could do more or less as we pleased, once away from Calcutta. To liven up a day's flying, most of the captains would regularly go down for some low flying. It was a habit that became difficult to break, and my experience of it was to be enhanced far beyond anything previously. The sheer enjoyment of doing part of a trip at 'deck level' was something few nowadays have a remote chance of experiencing.

This was a different league in which I found myself. These were expert practitioners. Favourite times for a 'beat up' were on the early morning and late afternoon trips. There was less turbulence and the air more settled. Flying along rivers always yielded a variety of interesting sights, and an abundance of animal life. It was wild and majestic country to see at close quarters. There were other sights to see as well. One morning I remember the Skipper, with whom I was flying at treetop height, suddenly letting out a whoop of glee — we had stumbled upon a group of village women taking their morning bath in the river. As they splashed around, some waving, some trying to cover their naked bodies, my friend was doing a vertical turn. Wing tip arcing just above the treetops, we came round for another review. We might have stayed circling all morning admiring some of the statuesque beauties if we hadn't had to be on our way to deliver our load.

By far the most fearless exponent of the art was 'Wally'. We were crewed together quite often, and his relaxed style was a pleasure. We were making a short hop one afternoon to a tea estate in upper

Assam to collect another load of tea chests. Flying along just above the treetops, the endless jungle stretching away into the distance was beginning to get monotonous. Suddenly, away over to one side, I spotted a moving plume of smoke — a train. It was too much of a temptation for Wally. He peeled off in spectacular style, and away he went in hot pursuit.

Minutes later our Dakota came up behind a long mixed passenger and goods train. As we passed over the middle carriages, the aircraft was so low that if the wheels had been down they would almost have been rolling along the carriage roofs. At that second, the Skipper's hand reached up to the engine magneto switches. To my amazement he switched the whole lot off. Not surprisingly, deprived of ignition, both engines started banging and spluttering fiercely. The engine makers, Pratt and Witney, never in their wildest possible aberrations ever meant anything like this to happen.

A LESSON FROM 'WILD WALLY' ON HOW TO KICK A DAKOTA SIDEWAYS THROUGH FACTORY CHIMNEY STACKS....

Without power, our Dakota was slowing rapidly as we approached the train driver's cab. We found ourselves looking down at the glow of the firebox, with the fireman stoking away. Whether they heard our banging engines above the clatter in the cab or saw the aeroplane's shadow first, but they both spun round together. For a split second almost frozen in time, two wide-eyed blackened faces looked up in eyeball popping astonishment, while two smiling faces looked down at them over the Dakota's blunt nose. She was by now rapidly running out of flying speed, so Wally calmly reached up and flicked on the magneto switches. The long suffering engines spluttered, crackled, and then roared back into life again. With the smell of coal smoke still lingering in our cockpit, we were once more on our way.

Belated repentance do I offer, on my Captain's behalf, for disturbing these two Bengal railmen at their work so long ago. Hero worship of the greatest exponent of the art of hair-raising flying came to an abrupt end during the monsoon of that year. Alas, Wally, his co-pilot and radio operator, fell victim to the monthly toll — they vanished without trace. It was thought that they had crashed into some remote mountain in heavy rain. Their disappearance was total — their remains and the smashed pieces of a Dakota with its cargo no doubt lie, to this day, somewhere in the remote jungles of Assam.

The sad event triggered off a widespread search. All aircraft operating in the upper Assam valley were requested to keep a look-out. For three days the rest of our company Dakotas were flown over a vast area. The three remaining aircraft each covered separate sectors of Assam on either side of the Brahmaputra river. Ranging as far as the Chinese border, we flew over thick jungle rainforests and threaded our way among the Himalayan ramparts, many steep slopes ravaged and desolated by massive landslides. Eyeballs ached

A FUTILE SEARCH FOR A LOST AIRCRAFT..........

with the strain of maintaining constant vigilance. Our friends' lives might hang in the balance if we passed them by. A swath cut through the dense foliage, a blackened patch, or the glint of metal wreckage; it could be any or all of these aspects for which we were looking in this wild inhospitable country. Wherever the monsoon clouds permitted, we searched at different levels. Over vast tracts of the country below us, there was no sign of human habitation — had man ever set foot in these remote parts?

On the third day of the search, I was flying with the Chief Pilot. Try as I could, by mid-afternoon, I was having great difficulty keeping my eyes open, when suddenly we came upon a sight that had us spellbound. Crossing over a ridge, a lake lay before us. It was like no other lake I had ever seen. The water was of the clearest sparkling turquoise, beautiful fir trees covered the craggy surrounds, and the translucent waters lapped against white pebbly shores. The weather had chosen this moment to clear, and brilliant sunshine highlighted a scene of complete perfection. Was it some Shangri-La?

The monsoon had been kinder to us than it had to Wally and his crew. The next day the search for VT-CHT, named 'Joe's Folly' after one of the directors, was called off. We would now have to pin our hopes on information filtering back through District Officers, tribesmen or villagers. Hopes rose, some days later, when reports came in of a sighting. A propeller and some wreckage had been found in a remote part, but they turned out to be old wartime remains. Time went on, and nothing was ever seen or heard of our colleagues again.

Flying during the monsoon period in North-Eastern India was a challenging time. Less venturesome pilots would take their annual leave. Using modern radar, the cumulo-nimbus thunderheads have been precisely measured; some reaching an awesome 65,000 feet have been recorded. From such monsters came frightening deluges. Cherrapunji, in the Khasi Hills of Assam, reputed to be the wettest place in the world, records an average annual fall of over 500 inches — compared with Manchester's modest 30 to 40 inches.

Because of the terrible violence of the storms, no one in his right mind would even consider flying through a large cumulo-nimbus. If it was impossible to get round, then under it would be, but often easier said than done because of the torrential rain. While one pilot flew quite low to keep contact with the ground, the other would map read, and this required the utmost concentration. It was a vital necessity to know what was going to loom up ahead. The usual tactics

THE DC3 STORM WINDOW IN USE AT "DECK LEVEL" DURING THE INDIAN MONSOON....

were to follow a river or a railway line, peering ahead through the storm window. The makers had got the design of this window just right, very near and almost in front of the pilot's face, the small panel could be moved across. With the sliding side window also open, the blinding rain, with which no windscreen wiper could cope, passed directly through and out. The suction of the side windows kept the water away from the two pairs of eyeballs that would be probing ahead. The map reader would have his finger moving along the map, noting time, heading and searching for clues outside, while shouting any necessary information to the other above the clatter of hail, rain and the engine noise.

There were other problems too. Here were two air cooled radial engines trying to run but being cooled more by solid water. The cylinder head temperatures would plunge right to the bottom of the scale, and the motors would start to splutter. This sometimes called for extraordinary measures, like lowering the wheels for extra drag, then increasing power just to keep the cylinders a little warmer.

These huge clouds of this equatorial zone, where the tropo-

sphere rises to its highest, often turn destructive killers with such a plentiful supply of moisture to fuel them. A former Flying Club friend died when his Dakota lost its wings. Perhaps even Wally and his crew met the same fate.

DURING THE MONSOON DELUGE.... A SLOWLY SHORTENING RUNWAY IN ASSAM, BEING EATEN INTO BY A FLOODED RIVER.........

Our popular Chief Pilot had a chance to demonstrate exceptional flying skills one day during the downpours. Arriving over a rain soaked jungle strip, he eyed the pools of standing water. Perhaps it might be prudent to circle and give the water time to drain away a bit, but there were storms all around. Queuing up to administer another drenching, he executed a perfect three point landing. Unfortunately there was a patch of water deeper than the rest, and it reached out to trip the landing Dakota. The tail rose skyward.

"Christ," he yelled, heaving hard back on the control wheel, but there was no response. The nose continued its downward plunge to meet the runway. With split second reaction, and against any normal flying instincts, he grabbed the throttles and slammed them fully open. The propellers were within inches of the runway when the

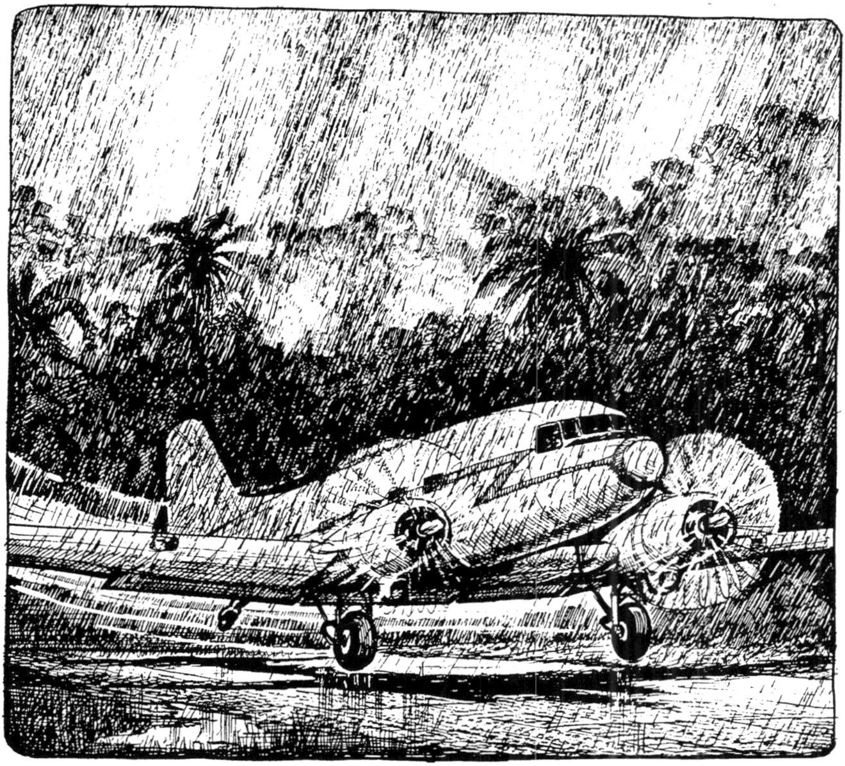

A BRILLIANT PIECE OF FLYING BY OUR CHIEF PILOT TO RECOUP BEING NOSED OVER ON A FLOODED RUNWAY..... INDIAN MONSOON, ASSAM. 1949.

elevators started to bite into the propwash. A sort of see-saw motion started, but at last the tail was got down as the aircraft ran into smaller puddles.

There was no shortage of characters flying out of Calcutta then. I consider it my good fortune to have seen some of them in action before settling down to the tamer scene later on.

DAKOTA STORM WINDOW IN USE AGAIN FOR ANOTHER PURPOSE........ A COLLEAGUE, VULTURE SHOOTING WITH HIS ·45 NEAR CALCUTTA, WHILE I FLY THE AIRCRAFT ON HIS INSTRUCTIONS, AS SLOW AS POSSIBLE AND TO THE DEAFENING ROAR OF THE REVOLVER......

Occasionally one stalwart Captain would bring along his revolver, which was a large .45 calibre weapon — very impressive looking too. He would produce it in flight,

"Right, Whit, we're going to do some vulture shooting today." This would be my cue to take the controls, smiling in anticipation of the sport to follow. The favourite time for our 'aerial shoot' would be on returning to Calcutta for breakfast. The vultures seemed to be more numerous in the sky along the River Hooghly; perhaps this was because that great muddy waterway carried with it all manner of debris, including even the occasional corpse. As we descended towards Barrackpore, the revolver would be loaded and the storm window opened. The game was on again. My instructions were simple — reduce speed and fly towards a circling vulture, so that it passed very near but down the left side of the aircraft. In the cockpit, the revolver's fire was deafening. Wearing radio headsets over the ears helped somewhat. The enormous birds would sometimes take violent evasive action, shedding feathers in their frantic attempts to distance themselves from this unusual disturbance. To my knowledge no hits were ever scored, but supreme sport it seemed at the time. I wondered why it had not caught on more generally in aviation.

Needless to say colliding with one of these great scavengers of India, the kitehawk or vulture, could spell disaster. A Flying Club friend had a lucky escape. A vulture had slammed into the nose of his Dakota. The whole aircraft shook. The noise was like a small bomb. A gaping hole was punched in the nose and forward bulkhead,

'CLOSE' FORMATION FLYING WITH PASSENGERS ABOARD......

which absorbed the main impact. The bird had by no means finished. It burst upon the rudder pedals and splayed upwards, like a body-line punch from a heavyweight. Dazed and winded, my friend looked down at what was his clean uniform — blood, entrails, muck and feathers covered him from head to foot. The malodorous stink caused the air hostess to retch, and she darted away for an air sickness bag. Although his fellow crew members treated him like a leper for the rest of the flight, he had been lucky. He could have had his head taken off, and he would not have been the first pilot to be killed by a bird strike.

In that decade, the city of Calcutta still retained its cosmopolitan atmosphere. The ambience of the British Raj at its height had long faded, but a few of the embers still lingered on. The rewards of hard work could still be enjoyed in style. Days off, however, were unfortunately too few to permit over-indulgence.

GIVEN TO SUPERSTITION AND WITCHCRAFT BORNEAN TROOPS RECOIL IN HORROR. THE AUTO PILOT, SET AT MAXIMUM SENSITIVITY JERKILY FLIES WITH A PAIR OF GLOVES WIRED TO THE WHEEL.... THE CREW, WHO HAVE WALKED TO THE TAIL ONE BY ONE, PLAY CARDS....

BUSH FLYING IN INDIA...... A TYPICAL MIXED BAG LOAD OF PASSENGERS AND CARGO...

A CLOSE VISIT TO MIGHTY KANCHENJUNGA, WITH MT. EVEREST BEYOND, BOTH SOARING TO OVER 28.000 FEET AND TOWERING HIGH ABOVE OUR PUNY DAKOTA AND OURSELVES STRUGGLING AT THE LIMIT OF OUR OXYGEN AT ABOUT 15.000 FEET.........

CHAPTER 4

Something entirely different was about to come upon my world of aviation. A charter flight to Hong Kong and the Philippines had come up on short notice. I was to go along as co-pilot. Exciting news, as this would be my first international flight.

Two days later our Dakota climbed into the sky above the lush vegetation, coconut palms and seething humanity around Calcutta's Dum Dum Airport. Course was set south eastwards towards Rangoon. The aircraft was loaded full of plimsoll shoes, an unlikely cargo indeed to be hauled all the way to Hong Kong. We flew down the Burmese coast, past Chittagong, Cox's Bazar and Akyab. The golden pagoda of Schwedagong, glinting in the early afternoon sunshine, guided us to Rangoon's Mingaladon Airport. Here we landed to refuel and have lunch. Later that day, in the last light from the setting sun, we glided down over the endless rice fields of the Siamese delta to land at Don Muang Airfield, Bangkok. The capital breathed even more magic than it does today, as the tourist invasion had hardly begun. The crew spent a wonderfully enjoyable night on the town. Some lovely Siamese ladies made our entertainment complete. Our guide that evening was an amiable American, who had met us at the airport to smooth our way through. His real purpose was to become clear to me much later.

Nursing king-sized hangovers, early next morning we departed for Tourane in what was then French Indo-China. The place was later to be in the thick of America's war in Vietnam, but in those times it swarmed with soldiers of the Foreign Legion, and on the airfield were rows of Gruman Bearcat Ground Attack Fighters of the French Air Force. A brief stop for refuelling, and we continued on to Hong Kong.

We approached the island, flying up the coast, at about 1,000 feet in ideal weather conditions. Below us, Chinese junks under full sail were plying busily about on a sparkling blue sea. It set the tone perfectly for a first visit to the oriental colony. Eventually the picturesque city of Hong Kong, with Kowloon on the mainland, came into view. The airfield was not a particularly easy one to approach then, being tucked over in a corner and hemmed in closely by hills that had claimed many an aircraft. Floating gracefully on the adjacent water, several flying boats lay at their moorings.

At the hotel that evening, there was a knock on my door. It was Manohar Singh, our bearded Sikh radio operator.

"We're meeting in the Skipper's room in ten minutes," he said, and laughingly added, "be prepared for a surprise."

When I entered, a whisky bottle was out and festivities seemed to be developing. As well as our four crew members, there were two others — an American and a Chinese — and introductions followed.

The American, a tall fair-haired Texan (who turned out to be the brother of a pilot I had flown with once in India), spoke first.

"Have you ever been in the yellow business, Whit?"

My blank expression, as I puzzled the question, prompted further explanation.

"We're figuring on shipping in a consignment of gold into India," adding with a grin, "through the back door of course."

He went on, "All you have to do is not tell a soul, and string along with us."

My share was to be 2,000 Rupees, plus spending money on this trip. It sounded like a marvellous adventure, and I accepted eagerly. Too eagerly perhaps, for if I had known the enormous quantity of gold involved I could have held out for a much higher share of the profits.

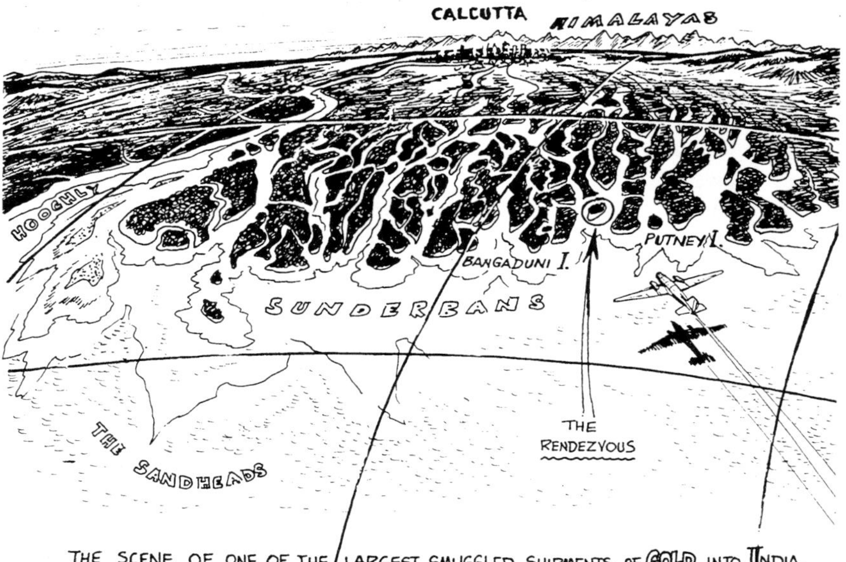

THE SCENE OF ONE OF THE LARGEST SMUGGLED SHIPMENTS OF GOLD INTO INDIA.

Full of enthusiasm, I was dispatched to fetch a topographical map of lower Bengal from my briefcase. Returning with the map, the plan was unfolded. Loaded with the gold, our objective would be to locate a small mangrove island in the great delta of the Ganges, south of Calcutta. In case we missed this rendezvous point, an alternative island was marked in. That old topographical map, with the original marks put on it in our Kowloon Hotel, is still in my possession today. We were now all in it together. Our Texan friend handed us a wad of dollars each, and suggested that we enjoy ourselves on the town that night, which we proceeded to do. Dinner was magnificent in a first class restaurant. It was followed up by a visit to a premier night-club. Here we lingered far too late for our health, getting back to our rooms in the early hours.

Next morning, nursing yet another heavy head, we set off across the China Sea bound for the Philippine Islands, our destination being Nickolls Field, Manila. Evidence of the late war with Japan still lay all about us. Around the harbour area, dozens of masts, funnels and superstructures of sunken ships grew at random from the water like some vast marine cemetery. The purpose of our visit was to pick up a return cargo for India. That was the official version. As half-expected, the consignment did not materialize. Signals were exchanged, lunch was taken, the aircraft refuelled, and we set off for a return to Hong Kong. Leaving the island of Luzon behind us, we recrossed the China Sea back to the Colony.

Yet another enjoyable night on the town followed, but while the crew relaxed amidst the bright lights of the city, others were busy elsewhere. Our American friend and a syndicate of Chinese had financed and acquired a huge quantity of gold bullion. In the dead of night it was ferried out to Kai-Tak Airfield. It was loaded aboard our parked Dakota by ground engineers employed by a US international airline. Being on night duty, their activities need not arouse suspicion.

Next morning we boarded our 'empty' aeroplane. Walking upwards towards the cockpit along the gradient of the cabin floor, we stopped at the forward baggage hold. Underneath an oily section of tarpaulin lay an open tea chest, which was about three-quarters full of slabs wrapped in greaseproof paper.

"You're looking at a fortune in gold bullion," said Martin to the three of us, "all of it real 24-carat stuff."

We gazed down at it in utter amazement. I doubted if I would ever in my life see such a concentration of wealth. Scaled up to present day standards, we were about to carry contraband gold to the value of sixteen million pounds.

Also loaded aboard was a large roll of stout khaki cloth and many hanks of thin rope — their purpose would become clear soon. Naturally the Skipper was anxious not to hang around unnecessarily. We would not welcome a pre-departure visit from Customs. Formalities had been completed so, without delay, we took off for a direct flight to Bangkok.

The weather continued settled and fine. Hainan Island was in sight as we took great care to remain to seaward. It was a strictly prohibited area, and it was at this point that troubles started. One of our engines started to falter and lose power, the engine note fluctuating and falling alarmingly as power surged. Our engineer needed no summoning, and in a trice his head popped into view between our shoulders — he sensed the trouble immediately.

"Fuel," he grunted, his hand going for the 'wobble' pump behind the pilot's seat.

The pump was used primarily to boost fuel pressure when starting the engines. In response to the engineer's steady strokes, the motor picked up and returned to normal. The culprit was a failing engine-driven fuel pump. There could be no hold-ups now, and the rest of the trip was spent with one crew member in turn pumping away steadily, being a job that soon made for aching forearms. Relief was, however, eventually at hand. Landing at Bangkok, another evening of delight lay ahead to refresh us, but this would follow much later for our engineer as first he had to get the cowlings off and the fuel pump changed.

In town that night with our group, it was a mix of business and pleasure. Our American agent was again in the chair. He had been at the airport, located a spare pump, and assisted our engineer. More gold had been put aboard our Dakota, and it now stood securely locked on the tarmac. Our Skipper, Martin, and Manohar Singh spent some time talking business with the American. The three of them had made a private arrangement, putting up their own cash for some of the extra gold that had been loaded earlier.

The evening was rounded off at a night-club, and much later I found myself invited home by an exquisitely beautiful Siamese lady. Her home was a taxi-ride away in the suburbs of Bangkok. I remember a very attractive verandahed bungalow, almost straight out of a

Conrad novel. A mosquito netted double bed completed the picture, and while I lay in a mellow void another young girl slipped gracefully under the net. She was barely matured, and could not have been more than thirteen years old.

"My younger sister would like to meet you also," I was told, and so she did. A while later her mother also entered the dimly lit room, and expressed a desire to join our *ménage à trois*. Here the line had to be drawn. A hasty retreat was beaten back to the hotel, with the thought of the big adventure that lay ahead making itself felt over the euphoria of the evening.

We were awakened, and up before dawn. As the first light of day brightened the sky, our Dakota's wheels left the ground, and we droned on course towards Rangoon. Once more we saw the great golden Schwedagong pagoda, and someone said, "Just look at all that gold sheeting! — that's what the Burmese spent most of their post-war Marshall Aid on instead of rebuilding factories."

True or not, the result looked spectacular. The Skipper added the final words, "Yes, let's make sure none of ours finishes up on their temple as well!"

Our time on the ground at Rangoon was to be nerve testing for Martin; we were ahead of schedule, and would have to delay awhile on the ground. Four o'clock was the prearranged rendezvous time at a small uninhabited mangrove island between the Raimangal and Hariabhanga Deltas, south-south-east of Calcutta. We killed time with a leisurely lunch, while our engineer had the cowlings off, feigning work on an imaginary engine snag. The time dragged painfully slowly, but fortunately Customs did not bother us. Our trail had been well covered.

At last, back on schedule, we were off and away from Rangoon. This sector was to be a busy one for us all. The gold would have to be wrapped in cloth and roped up, each bundle containing five bars and the bundles would then be tied together in clusters of five. As our Dakota droned along the jungle-clad Burma coast that afternoon, the three of us worked away seated on the cabin floor. It looked more like a combined tailoring and packaging business than an aeroplane in flight; scissors snipped away at cloth, rope whirled about, and gradually our assembly line of bundles grew. They were stacked near the large freight doors at the rear of the cabin. As we worked, I remember Singh laughingly chided us not to let him catch either of us pinching a bar.

In reality secreting a bar would have been a near impossibility. The weight of each ingot was surprisingly great for its size, and it took considerable effort to lift. It was a sobering thought though. On its own a single bar was worth a small fortune, and when resold on the Indian market the value would double. The reason for this was complex, and what better person to explain than my expert friend, Singh.

"No one trusts Indian paper money too much. Remember what happened about the 100 Rupee notes?" he asked as we worked away. I did indeed. Not many years before, the Government had suddenly declared all those notes invalid. Banks would change them, provided possession could be explained. Overnight there had been some very, very red faces and howls of anguish — black marketeers with illicit hoards, tax evaders, law breakers of all kinds, and the list went on. Singh elaborated more on the subject.

"Gold is much sought after in India because it is used as a

PACKING AND ROPING TOGETHER THE GOLD BARS BETWEEN RANGOON AND CALCUTTA.... READY FOR THE DROP ON THE DESERTED BEACH...........

yardstick of wealth. Women will wear gold bangles on their wrists rather than admire a slip of paper from the bank." He went on, "There is more gold hoarded and hidden away in India than you would ever dream possible. Look at it this way — we're just satisfying a market."

We had been beavering away so busily, that time had flown. When I rejoined the Skipper in the cockpit, we were already past Akyab. Martin was in a cheerful mood as I prepared my topographical maps of the Ganges Delta.

"We'll set course from a point on the Burmese coast to give us the shortest possible crossing of the sea — we've got to strike our island first time."

The tropical jungle-clad Burmese coast line continued to slip by our starboard wing, and eventually the town of Cox's Bazar came into view. Here we took our departure from the coast. We set a course that had been checked and rechecked, and great care was taken to maintain it accurately. When we located our island, we would be looking for a light aeroplane and two pilots on a beach. We now had a distance of about 180 miles to run across the waters of this corner of the Bay of Bengal.

The sea below us gradually changed colour to the muddy yellow-brown of the delta, and the first faint traces of the Sunderban Islands appeared through the hazy afternoon sunlight. There were no problems with radar identification in those days! — it did not exist! To give us time, our radio operator, Singh, had also sent out a fictitious position report to Calcutta Area Control, which put us 50 miles back from where we really were.

The part folded topographical map was spread out over my knees. I had a feeling of emptiness in the pit of my stomach — the navigation was my responsibility, and find our mangrove island I must. These maps were surprisingly accurate, for I would hold this very same one in my hand 33 years later, while flying at the undreamed of height of 35,000 feet in command of a wide bodied jet. I would ask the co-pilot to gently bank the 300 seat Tristar, as if in salute, while I looked down out of the side window and clearly identified our island looking just as we found it those many years before.

Then suddenly I was sure that this was our rendezvous island — it fitted in like a jigsaw puzzle. Putting the Dakota into a fairly tight turn, the Skipper began a circuit round the island. The other two had now joined us up front in the cockpit. Four pairs of eyes now scoured the mangrove and sand from the banking aeroplane. On our second time round none of us had seen any sign of the aeroplane, let alone the two pilots.

"You must have the wrong island, you bugger," Singh exclaimed into my ear.

"No I haven't — this is the one," I retorted, not shifting my scan. We were on our third circuit of the island's twisting shoreline (and someone had even mentioned the alternative rendezvous) when suddenly there was a shout. The engineer's finger stabbed past our heads, "There they are," he almost screamed.

Sure enough, before they disappeared under the banking wing tip, I caught a glimpse of two figures jumping about on the beach waving wildly. No wonder we had nearly missed them! Expecting a light aeroplane as large as life on the beach, our friends had done a good job hiding it. It was a Sentinel L-5 and only part of a wing protruded from under a tree. They had concealed it very well, almost too well in fact.

"OK chaps, you know what to do. Let's go!" called Martin above the noise of the engines.

We lowered a quarter flap, so that we could fly slower during the drop. I climbed from my seat, and went aft to join the others, while the aeroplane banked and pitched as Martin commenced his first run — it became a balancing act in the tail. I checked that the rear freight door was secure and opened the forward one against the slipstream. The radio operator and engineer prepared the first group of bundles to be kicked out. With the two seated on the floor, feet against the gold, and both my hands against the part opened door, we all looked forward tensely towards the cockpit. Concentration on all faces, we fixed eyes on the Skipper's raised right hand, holding a white handkerchief. Down it came, and out went the first load. I watched the bundles, roped to each other, tumble through the air and strike the sand, flashing by so close below us. It was brisk work, as the Dakota was banked steeply for the next run, so a fresh cluster of bundles was prepared. Six more times we repeated the performance, and all our load had been dropped.

I ran up to the cockpit to confirm all the gold gone, and then on impulse said to Martin, "How about one last run to let them have something to drink? We've got a lot of spare bottles of Coca-Cola back there." His thumbs up sent me scurrying back into the cabin.

About a dozen bottles tumbled beachwards on the next run, and it was to the credit of the manufacturers that most of them, we learned later, survived the drop.

The Skipper was to tell me a few days later, "I was asked to pass on to you that your thirst quenchers were the best thing we did that afternoon."

We had climbed steeply after the last drop, approached Calcutta's Dum-Dum Airport, and landed. The whole operation had gone without a hitch. Total secrecy was demanded. I remembered well the chill recollections of our American friend in Bangkok. He described in detail how a pilot had been found dead in Singapore, having been knifed because he had crossed the syndicate. The stakes were too enormous to be trifled with. During the time I was to remain in India, I did not breath a single word of our exploit to a soul.

My share, two thousand Rupees, was paid to me some while later. "Don't put any of it in your bank," I was told.

About a month later Manohar Singh discreetly mentioned to me, during the course of another flight in Assam, that both the American brothers from Texas had been told to leave India.

"Things are still very dangerous. They are trying to find out how the gold came in. There is such a lot being traded, and the market price is fluctuating. Keep your mouth shut tight if you are questioned."

Fortunately nothing like that did ever happen. It had been a marvellous adventure, and I had been only a very small cog. I did not dabble in the 'yellow business,' again. However, others did. A year later, in England, I was to hear that my old Skipper, Martin, had been caught bringing gold into Bombay. He had jumped bail and fled the country, forfeiting ten thousand Rupees.

For the next few months, until leaving India permanently, I was transferred to operate from Bombay. These Africa charters took us to places as interesting and varied as they could possibly be. The company Dakota and our load of twenty-one passengers had to make the long flight in easy stages. An average round trip to British West Africa and back took about eleven days.

Our first stop was usually Karachi and, when still miles away, the giant airship hangar stood out like a huge dark box in the distant arid landscape, long before any other building or details could be made out. It was an enormous structure over 200 feet high of steel and corrugated iron. In any wind it moaned, screeched and clattered as the ironwork flexed and loose sheets banged. The airship, for which it was built, never arrived. As is well known, it met its fiery end on rising ground near Beauvais during a night storm, having hardly started its long journey. The massive hangar at Karachi has long since vanished, victim of the scrap iron merchants.

Sharjah, at the entrance to the Persian Gulf, was normally the next stop-over. Oil rolled into the sand served as a runway, and the aircraft would be parked just below the walls of the fort. It was a picturesque spot, with thick ramparts and a fortified gateway supporting cannons. The heat of the place could be furnace-like but it did have, if one was lucky, the only air-conditioned rooms we could get on the route. The town was a collection of mud huts and small adobe houses, as was Dubai with its creek a few miles to the north. A mere 30 years on, they would be vast high rise cities, exuding wealth from their architecturally superb buildings and ultra modern airports.

Our passengers were Indian traders and shop assistants, and for them a visit to the duty free shops of Bahrain was a highlight of their journey. On this flight across the water to the island of Bahrain, I would scan the aquamarine sea during climb and descent. The translucent waters often yielded the spectacle of fantastic coral formations, and the occasional glimpse of large sharks gliding lazily about.

Our route would take us across the centre of the Arabian desert. This was sun-scorched country with sand and rock formations in many different hues and shapes. Hour upon hour of flying over glaring sands would eventually give way at last to the sparkling blue waters of the Red Sea. We would either come down at Jeddah or cross over to Port Sudan to refuel. Often very strong winds blow here because of the rising ground inland, superheated by the sun, and the adjoining relatively cooler sea. Today's modern jet pilot rarely gets as white knuckled as a struggling Dakota pilot trying to bring both main wheels on to the ground in the sometimes fierce cross winds and searing thermals, all this while doing a Fred Astaire on the rudder pedals to prevent a swing and get the tail down in a straight line. It was sometimes a short sharp shock that would set the pulse racing while the action lasted.

Once again we would rise into the air, and by the time we completed this next sector we would have been on the go a long time. A day's rest beside the waters of the Blue Nile at Khartoum was always welcome. A large river boat was permanently moored opposite the hotel under the big shady trees overhanging the Nile. It served as an annexe when the hotel was full, and that only happened when aeroplanes broke down.

It was here one afternoon that youthful impetuousness and my love of swimming took me into unimagined peril. Hot and sticky after our crew's arrival at the hotel and with the Nile flowing past just outside looking very inviting, I donned swimming trunks and made for the river.

Diving in, I struck out strongly for a temptingly picturesque sandbank opposite. Judging I was about half-way across, I stopped for a breather. Horrors! My sandbank was no longer in sight. I was being swept downstream at an alarming rate! With heart beginning to pound, I immediately turned round and started back from whence I had come. This took some while to accomplish, and I came ashore in an area of rushes and weeds which were the devil to get through, and this was then followed by a long and uncomfortable barefoot walk back along the sun-baked riverside road to the hotel.

The Sudanese hotel manager happened to be standing in the foyer as I entered after my hike back.

"You have been swimming the the river, Sir?" he said, with voice rising. My answer brought a look of horror.

"Crocodiles!" he choked out. "The Nile is full of crocodiles!"

He was now almost screaming. "The currents are deadly! There is bilharzia in the river! Give thanks you are still with us!"

I came to agree with him entirely when I had had time to reflect on my rashness and heard tales of the dangers to which I had foolishly exposed myself.

A day later we would be experiencing the fierce dry heat in the walled city of Kano, Nigeria, and the next the stifling humidity of Lagos, on a coast that was known as 'white man's grave'.

The Skipper was free to vary the route to his own convenience and refuelling requirements. On the way back we would often go via the beautiful highlands of Eritrea to the duty free port of Aden. The aircraft would depart noticeably heavier, with bargains not easily available in India.

This meant further variations in the route, and my first visit to Masirah Island was interesting. It was just a collection of buildings, sand and oil drums by the thousand, a staging post run by the Royal Air Force. A posting here was more like a sentence. Some of the men had not set eyes on a woman, let alone a white woman, for quite a while and when we landed any excuse would be used to meet our air hostess. I was shown the Mess hut ceiling on which were several ladies' footprints with messages and signatures alongside.

"They're not getting me inverted up there again — I've already left my mark," said Colleen, and I could understand the impact her shapely legs had made on these long suffering servicemen.

It was a pity the lads had not paid such detailed attention to our fuel supplies. As we left the low sand island behind, climbing on course towards Bombay, we were in for an almighty shock. It would be a long, over-water, flight across the Arabian Sea. The Skipper had just settled himself comfortably in his seat for a sleep, but had barely nodded off when he was rudely awakened. There was a series of loud bangs from our starboard engine, and Martin leapt clear above his seat with a startled shout. Oh! to have captured that moment on film, it would have been a world masterpiece of comedy. I could have laughed myself hoarse had it not been for what I saw just outside my side window. The engine seemed to be trying to shake itself clear of its mountings, the cowlings were flicking in circular arcs about the engine, and above all this was the terrible backfiring.

"Water in the bloody fuel," gaggled Martin, as he hastily throttled back the engine and snapped off the autopilot. "Tell Masirah we're coming back."

The aircraft was already in a descending turn as I gave the Skipper the course and made the call. The other motor was running none too smoothly either as we continued down. Passengers bravely peered through the cabin windows at the vibration-wracked cowlings, as we touched down again on the RAF's lonely island. More fuel was put aboard, and a thorough water check carried out using the under wing drains. A few sarcastic remarks to the refuellers, an engine run up on the tarmac, and we set off once more for our long over-water crossing. The flight back to India this time was quite uneventful.

A MOCK ATTACK BY TEMPEST FIGHTERS.... THE EXCERCISING OF KEEN JUDGEMENT APPRECIATED BY ALL PARTIES... NEVER A THOUGHT OF NEAR MISS REPORTS IN THOSE DAYS AND NO ONE EVER COMPLAINED......

We remained crewed together for a few more flights, the old 'yellow business' team: Martin, our Skipper, Manohar Singh, our stalwart Sikh radio operator, and myself. Perhaps it was because we got on fairly well together, in spite of being cooped up in such a small aeroplane for days on end on these extended flights. We were lucky, for clashes of personality, when it occurs among crews, has long been a recognized problem and even more so when two skippers had to be crewed together.

One of the worst cases, about which I heard, took place on just such an occasion, and I personally knew one of the captains. Singh related the serious incident which had occurred when he had been doing an African charter as radio operator with the pair. They had been at loggerheads for most of the trip. Hardly on speaking terms, they simmered on the verge of explosion as the flight dragged on. Deciding to visit the toilet, one of them rose from his seat to leave the cockpit. As he did so, he trod on the other's plastic computer-cum-circular slide rule, which had been placed on the floor. Why on the floor one might ask? The simple answer was that there was hardly any stowage space in the cramped Dakota cockpit. Unfortunately an offending foot came down in exactly the wrong place. There was a very noticeable cracking noise and this was followed by a bellow of uncontrolled rage.

The first hint, which Singh had of the trouble up front, was a loud shout, "You bastard, you bloody well did that purposely."

Tempers could no longer be controlled, and fists immediately started to fly. The two figures began lunging round the confined cockpit. In the course of the violent struggle, bodies were slamming

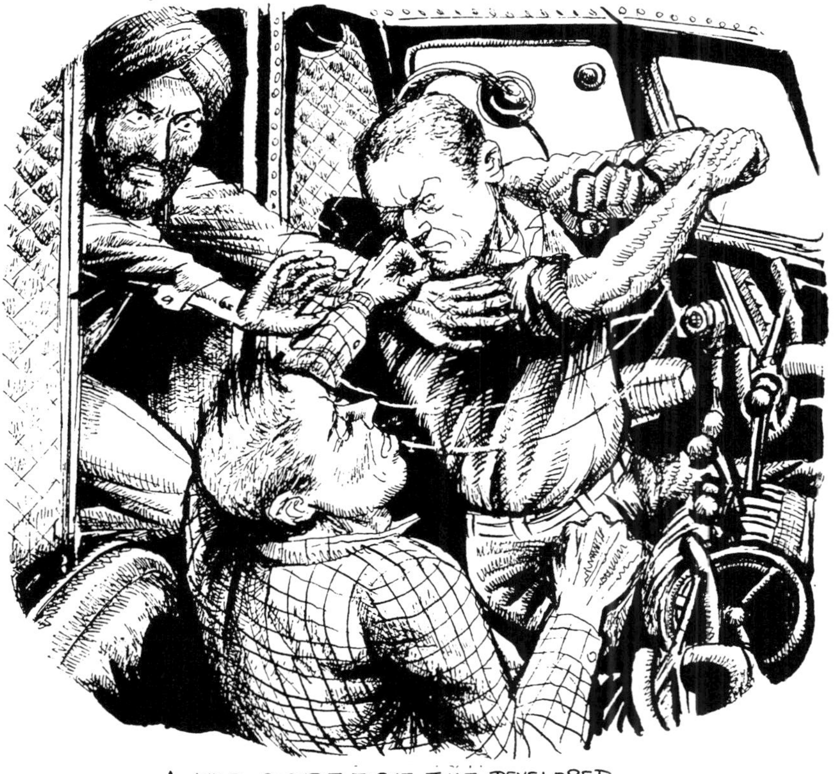

A WILD COCKPIT FIGHT THAT DEVELOPED WITH UNSUSPECTING PASSENGERS ABOARD...

against the throttle pedestal between them. On this, the cluster of levers, which controlled the angle of the propeller blades and the power of the engines, were getting treatment they had never had in the air before. As the levers were shoved and pushed, the aeroplane's two motors were going wild. Above the noise, the passengers clutched at their seat arms as the aircraft skidded and yawed about alarmingly. My friend, Singh, lurched forward, steadying himself with any convenient handhold. It was time to intervene before events got any worse and the Dakota went completely out of control.

As Singh got to the cockpit screamed curses, thudding blows and flailing arms made it seem an impossible task to separate the combatants. One of the pilots' heads had just banged viciously against the windscreen, and several hard blows struck the unfortunate radio operator as he waded in. He did not seem to make much headway. In desperation, at the top of his voice, he screamed that he would put in a written report to the Director General of Civil Aviation on return to India. This appeared to sober up the two of them, and the fighting ceased.

Still cursing, the two Captains sat back down again in their seats. The passengers meanwhile had quite clearly heard all the shouts and commotion. Urgent questions were being asked. The air hostess, half guessing, came forward carefully closing the cockpit door after her. She gasped in amazement at what she saw. Still muttering, the two crouched in their seats, bruised, swollen faced and bleeding, on the verge of exploding again. Singh took the air hostess aside, and they had a brief consultation. The subject, needless to say, was excuses. In this, Singh's imagination was as good as ever and obviously quick with it too, for she was on her way aft immediately to reassure her charges. Tongue in cheek, she related how the aeroplane had developed a sudden hydraulic leak. The pilots had been shouting to each other as they had struggled with the difficult emergency repair. Everything was now OK and there was no need for further concern. Singh had obviously had a severe shock, for even relating the incident to me long after it happened, he seemed to become very agitated.

It would be unthinkable that a full blooded brawl of that sort could happen nowadays, but in the aviation of that day it did occur. I cannot criticize, for flying in Europe three years later, I was to become involved in a similar argument that stopped only just a whisker from blows.

Unrestricted by any form of control, we continued at times to fly with the situation verging on getting out of hand. On one occasion, having arrived in Khartoum late the previous evening, we were due to make a start for Kano in the early hours of the following morning. That evening after supper, Martin, our Skipper, asked us if we would like to visit the G.B. Club. He suggested we could vacate our rooms and leave straight from the club for the airfield at about 2 a.m. The hotel was apparently short of rooms and had, no doubt, made our wily Captain a proposition to his advantage on the bill. We fell in with his plan quite happily. The G.B. Club was always a lively place, with the European girls of the cabaret a welcome contrast to the dusty surroundings of Khartoum. Martin had said to me:

"It's your sector in the morning, Whit, so I hope you will be staying reasonably sober!"

As events were to turn out, I sure was glad I did.

A good evening's entertainment was had by all, particularly the Skipper. He seemed to be sinking a fair old quantity, but none of us realized just how much. When departure time came he could barely walk to our transport. Loyalty demanded that we would have to look after him and do our best. At that time Khartoum Airport was closed for major reconstruction and Wadi Seidna, a wartime strip some distance from the city, was in use. Arrangements there favoured us when we arrived at the airfield.

Singh kept Martin out of sight, so that I could complete the flight planning, paperwork and other formalities.

While trying to keep as low a profile as possible, we set out to spirit our jovial Captain across the tarmac to our waiting Dakota. He now began singing quite lustily while supported upright by the radio operator and myself. In the middle of rendering that old RAF favourite, "We are leaving Khartoum, by the light of the moon ..." we wobbled past a four-engined Skymaster parked next to our Dakota. Here we halted.

"I say we take this one instead tonight," Martin slurred, pointing shakily at what was considered the ultimate transport aeroplane of that time! Not such a good idea, thought his two supporters. After a good deal of persuasive talk, we managed to steer Martin away from that plan and eventually to the door of our Dakota.

Using maximum tact and persuasion, we succeeded in conducting our inebriated commander to the cockpit and settled him in the co-pilot's seat. With luck he would soon be asleep. Alas, this was not to be, or not just yet anyway.

The passengers were boarded, undercarriage pins and control locks were stowed, the checks completed, and I prepared to start the engines. Inside the cabin, aglow with lights, our air hostess was busy attending to her passengers and checking seat belts fastened. Then the lights went out. Total blackness embraced us all. The reason for this was not difficult to see — Martin's hand still rested on the battery master switch, which he had just flipped off. In the dim glow I could see a mischievous grin on the Skipper's glassy-eyed face as he tried a stage whisper, which unfortunately came out with sufficient volume to be heard in the tail section, "Now's your chance, Whit, go back and ravish the hostess!"

It was back to square one on my engine start. The radio operator

OUR BLIND DRUNK CAPTAIN BEING LED DISCREETLY TO THE AIRCRAFT AT KHARTOOM

came to my rescue, and between us we managed to talk our bibulous Captain into quietening down. The battery was restored, and after a few more minor interruptions both engines were started.

I taxied the aircraft out, keeping a wary eye on the occupant of the right hand seat. All was OK as I completed the engine run up, obtained take off clearance from the Control Tower, and lined up on the runway. The throttles were opened wide, and our Dakota roared away into the night down the desert runway.

As we gathered speed, easing right forward on the control wheel, I lifted the tail, enabling the wing landing lights to shine out ahead of us. In horror, I suddenly heard Martin's slurred call, "Gear up?"

He had already reached down with his left hand and pulled up the undercarriage safety latch on the floor. I instantly let go of the throttles and, with my right hand now free, just had time to deflect his arm as it moved backwards to the now unprotected gear lever. Just one slight upward movement of the handle and our speeding aeroplane would sink on to its belly on the runway, with almost certain catastrophic results. Martin's hand was still intent on locking on to the lever. For seconds it was a duel of the arms, with me at a definite disadvantage, as I kept half an eye ahead. To my shouts of, "No Martin, not yet! No!" I eased the Dakota into the air.

Twenty-one unsuspecting passengers became airborne, never knowing how close they had come to perhaps a blazing inferno. As we climbed up higher, safely on our way with the Skipper now sleeping peacefully, I reflected on how thin the dividing line could be.

The desert stars slowly gave way to the dawn of another day as we flew westwards across the empty wastes of the Sudan to El Geneina.

Still with the same crew, another unpleasant experience was to be my lot — this time as a victim of a practical joke. We were flying empty after a charter, returning to Bombay's Santa Cruz Airport. I advised the Skipper that I was going back to visit the toilet, and climbed out of my seat. Meanwhile Singh, the radio operator, who was up front at the time, said to Martin that he wouldn't mind practising some flying. Naturally a member of the same poker school would never be refused such a request. With some general sarcastic comments, Singh climbed into my seat. Before leaving to walk to the toilet aft, I chided my friend as he gripped the control wheel, "Don't forget to put on some nose down-trim, Singhy, as I go back!"

He knew exactly what I meant, for my weight shift aft would cause the nose to rise. As I left, I reached down and gave the elevator trim wheel a small tweak forward.

"There you are!" I said.

Ambling through the empty cabin down the centre aisle, I had just reached the last row of empty seats, little suspecting the diabolical plot being hatched up front. My knees started to bend and my body was getting very much heavier. Spinning round and using the seats for support with my hands, a glance forward at the cockpit immediately gave me the answer. Two smiling faces peered rearwards. The next second my feet left the floor as the control column was pushed forward. Martin was giving Singh some flying all right. A lesson on how to have sport with his co-pilot. I landed upright after this brief few seconds of weightlessness, but my legs buckled under me. 'I must grab hold of a seat leg and lock on to it,' the message had flashed through my mind; however ... too late. I was weightless once again, but this time horizontally, floating upwards nearly to the cabin roof. When I came down again after this excursion, it was with a bone-jarring crash on my back. I experienced a severe jolt of excruciating pain.

'My God!' I thought, 'my back's gone.'

The two in the cockpit had seen what had happened, and fortunately they immediately let up. The pain was terrible. Barely able to raise my head to look forward, I could see two beaming faces up front admiring their handiwork; but the smiles froze and their expressions quickly changed when they realized that something was badly wrong. Singh came hurrying aft to where I was lying.

"You OK?" he enquired.

My groans, interspersed with curses, were sufficient answer. He assisted me into one of the seats, where I sat for some time gradually

1951 – A PRACTICAL JOKE THAT NEARLY WENT SOUR.. INDUCED WEIGHTLESSNESS IN THE TAIL OF A DAKOTA.

trying to progressively restore some movement. When I was able finally to toil back up front, they were suitably apologetic. For fear of provoking the wrath of the youth, the two refrained from saying what they might have said:

"If you can't take a joke, you shouldn't have joined!"

We were, after all, good mates, who had shared many a laugh, drink, good time, hard slog and adventure together.

It was now early in the year 1952, and my father was due to retire from India. Not yet twenty-two years of age, I decided that this would be as good a time as any to take passage for England to try my fortune in aviation in that fair land.

ROPE STARTING A DAKOTA, WHEN ALL ELSE HAD FAILED WITH THE NORMAL AND STANDBY STARTING SYSTEMS.

I was sadly destined never to see my good friends, Martin and Manohar Singh, again. Six months later, poor Singh was to meet that fearful lingering death of thirst and exposure in the Nubian Desert. Martin was killed some years later, also in the Sudan, in an air accident at Khartoum.

In England, I was to see in a London newspaper dated 20 September 1952 a small item briefly stated: 'MISSING HAJ PLANE, NO PILGRIMS ABOARD. The Indamer Dakota aircraft, chartered by Aden Airways, now three days overdue, was still missing today. About 15 search planes were out from Port Sudan in search of the missing aircraft.'

The Dakota was eventually found, but too late to save the crew. An Indian pilot friend, who was in London, related to me what had happened. The ill-fated Dakota had taken off from Aden at night. They were flying empty to Jiddah to pick up Muslim pilgrims. It was thought that perhaps they had tuned their radio compass to the wrong ground station. Had they been aware that there had been a

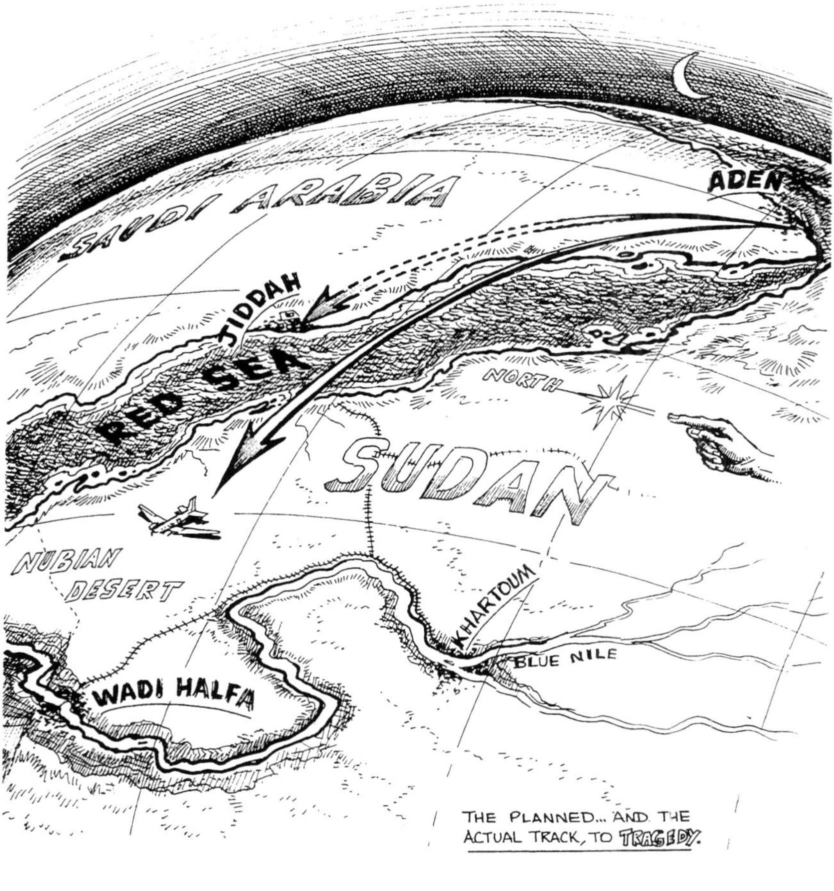

THE PLANNED... AND THE ACTUAL TRACK, TO TRAGEDY.

recent change of frequencies? Had they, some time during the night, altered course for the more powerful radio beacon at Wadi Halfa? A change of only about twenty degrees and from that moment onwards, unbeknown to them, they would have commenced being stalked closely by fate. In the pitch blackness below them, they would have had no idea they were flying diagonally across the Red Sea. The unfortunate three would now even be flying over the wrong continent, having crossed from Arabia into Africa.

The Dakota had overrun its flight time and they were totally lost, but the radio beacon, to which they were tuned, was still luring them onwards. Singh would have been sending out frantic radio messages.

Whether they were received or not by some distant ground station, nothing could be done unless they could locate where they were. Their situation would now be desperate. While they still had a little fuel left, Captain Shine made his fateful decision to force land the Dakota.

In the darkness, he made an excellent job of putting the aircraft down in the desert. His luck, however, did not hold out during the final bouncing impact. As the aeroplane slithered over the uneven ground on its belly, a rock smashed up through the floor of the cockpit breaking the Captain's ankle.

When dawn broke they took stock of their situation. The coolness of the night was rapidly disappearing as the sun rose. There was very little water aboard. Singh and the co-pilot made the Captain as comfortable as possible. They would have debated whether to try walking from the crashed aircraft, and they no doubt would have been aware of the grave dangers of attempting this. Very few aviators, who had been forced down in the desert, had succeeded in walking out. The advice had always been the same — stick with your aircraft and await help.

Thinking they had come to earth in Arabia, they must have reasoned that if they walked westwards then they must eventually strike the sea. Singh and the co-pilot decided they would try it, and set forth to take their chance of finding help. The aerial search for the missing aircraft was initiated without delay, but the hunt was concentrated on the Arabian side of the Red Sea. Days later, the pair were found by a Sudanese camel driver. Fate had indeed been unmercifully cruel. Their footsteps had taken them parallel and not far from the Atbara to Wadi Halfa railway line. Only a slight deviation might have stopped them from staggering unknowingly deeper into the Nubian Desert.

The camel driver had chanced upon them too late. They were found collapsed in the sand. Their raging thirst had forced them to the last stages of delirium. In their tortured madness, they had ripped most of their clothes away in a futile effort to keep cool; their tongues were swollen and protruding from their mouths; their skin was burnt a horrible hue by the sun, and the heat had caused their eyeballs to burst from their sockets. Marks on the two crew members' bodies indicated there was a strong possibility that at some time previously an argument had led to blows, which will forever remain a mystery but most likely it was a dispute over the direction they were taking.

The location of the accident had been established too late to save my friend, Singh, and his colleague, and still a long long chain from the camel driver back to civilization. The news eventually filtered through, and the search area was switched. In a relatively short time the wrecked Dakota was located, but alas too much precious time initially had been lost as they were too late to save the Captain.

The three unfortunate victims of the merciless desert were buried at Wadi Halfa, beside the Nile. The tragedy and suffering of the crew lies completely masked, and recorded only briefly in Indian aircraft registration lists: Dakota VT-CGB. Owner, Indamer Co. Ltd., Bombay. Write-off in forced landing 10 miles east of Station Six on Wadi Halfa to Atbara railway. Registration cancelled 27 February 1953.

RAF search aircraft from Khormaksar, Aden, recorded the crash site lying in latitude 20 degrees 45 minutes north and longitude 32 degrees 33 minutes east amid rock outcrops and sand.

It served as a sad reminder of how unforgiving aviation could be. Did they do right to try defying the desert? It could be argued that the aircraft might never have been found if they had not, which after all was thought to have crashed on another continent.

The famous French aviator, Antione de St Exupery, survived a similar situation. Sheltering under the wing of his aircraft, he happened to notice at dawn dew formed on the undersurfaces which, mopped up, proved a very brackish drink, but it helped his survival. Others walked across the desert by night, sitting still and remaining covered by day until the fierce heat had passed.

Poor Singh's fatal exploit was not completely in vain, for there is one at least who would never again fly across a desert without careful preparation. About 4 years later, now in command of a lumbering twin-engined Vickers Viking, I was to fly into this region once more. We had landed at Benina, a coastal airfield on the edge of the Libyan desert. Here we would refuel, and set off for the long 5 hour haul slap across the Sahara to Wadi Halfa. Our air hostess, a somewhat frosty veteran, had nodded rather off-handedly when I had said to her, on stepping off the aircraft, "Don't forget, Marjorie, would you please have all the water containers filled right up."

On climbing back aboard prior to departure, a surreptitious tap of the finger on a galley water urn as I passed produced a distinctly hollow sounding clunk. The tank had not been touched, and was less than half full. On enquiring the reason for this, I was told that the water had been checked and there was sufficient for the trip. So the flight was delayed while all the water containers were filled to the brim. I found myself not the most popular person aboard, in fact the young lady was downright hostile and regretfully did not speak to me much for the rest of the trip.

However, that evening over a cool beer at our night stop hotel in Wadi Halfa, the subject of the water had again come up. When I recounted the misadventure of the three aviators at rest in the cemetery just down the road, all was forgiven, and I remember the co-pilot even chipping in with a laugh, "So that's why so many drift sight observations are requested by the Commander! — why he checks my navigation and the compass course so often on these desert flights."

SOME AVIATION TYPES.

CHAPTER 5

It was goodbye to India, as the P & O liner *Himalaya*, with myself aboard, sailed past the 'Gateway of India' arch, leaving Bombay behind. The holiday atmosphere aboard ship during the voyage soon came to an end. The cold and gloom of Tilbury docks, and the thought that I must find a job before my savings vanished put a slight damper on my arrival in England. Traveller's cheques to the grand total of £235 stood between myself and insolvency, which would not be too long making itself felt if I was unsuccessful in finding work.

Before I could get a flying job, my Indian Commercial Pilot's Licence had to be converted to a British one. So it was back to school, intensive study, examinations and tests, and all the while watching funds dwindle.

Down to my last few pounds and with winter approaching, I was employed on probation by British Overseas Airways Corporation, although there was not going to be any pilot's seat for me then nor in the foreseeable future.

The Corporation recently had lost, very unfortunately, one of their four-engined Handley Page Hermes, which had been on a night flight between Tripoli in Libya, and Kano in Nigeria. Hundreds of miles off course due to a gross navigational error, it had come down in the desert. To reduce the possibility of it happening again, more crews would become qualified navigators. All new co-pilot entrants would in future first serve as navigators for several years before moving into the co-pilot's seat. It was not a prospect to be relished, but the wolf had to be kept from the door and the starting pay of £500 per annum would certainly help.

The selection and interview process had been extensive, but I did eventually get through to a final interview with the Chairman himself. Sir Victor Tait was an absolutely charming old gentleman and, seated in a solitary chair on a plush carpet facing him at his enormous desk, I nervously responded to a few opening pleasantries. Glancing up from my file, he looked at me intently. "I say, Whitlock, your father wasn't out in Mesopotamia, was he? I seem to remember a Wing Commander Whitlock, Royal Flying Corps, out there."

I confess that I secretly did wish the old man had been a Wing Commander in Mesopotamia — it might have clinched the interview! "No, Sir, he was in the ranks — a mechanic, Sir." I left the interview a short while later, and was quite surprised some days afterwards to hear that I was in. Once again I found myself seated in a classroom.

Existing in an Earls Court bed-sitter, barely large enough to accommodate a bed and a small cupboard, was cramped enough. Add to this a gas fire that swallowed money at an alarming rate and was capable of producing splitting headaches within minutes, completed the miserable picture. Bitter winds, snow and slush, were a contrast to the sunshine, warmth and flying life of India.

The examinations for the Flight Navigator's Licence were recognized as the toughest in Civil Aviation. Normally a full year's work, but we had to complete it in less than six months. Course notes piled up and the work was intense.

I had another project on the go too, which was to obtain an Instrument Rating. It had now been eight months since I had sat in an aeroplane, and to make matters worse I had done hardly any instrument flying before. These were not happy times at all.

Valuable cash had to be laid out for a crash course on the link trainer — that marvellous instrument of torture, box-like, with little stubby wings and tail, in which a pilot sits cut off from the world, while it hisses and moves, and he can sweat buckets while he tries to make a moving pen on a chart go the way he wants it to go. Two attempts at taking the flying test at Stanstead in a small twin-engined Consul, belonging to the Ministry of Civil Aviation, ended in failure. But at a test fee of £5 a time, it was invaluable practice. Depressing rail journeys across the snow-clad countryside to have a go at the Instrument Rating, shivering with cold most of the time, was a low point of my life. Perseverance, however, finally paid off with success. There would be no more early morning transits through bleak, sooty, Fenchurch Street Station!

After a trudge through the snow on a Monday morning two weeks later, the twelve in the class were in for a nasty shock. The corporation had decided to give us what they called 'a progress check', starting that very morning. The papers were dished out — I felt choked — it was the sort of stuff of which bad nightmares are made. In the past I had always been able to work towards any examinations, now there was nothing for it but to leap in with both feet. It was all over by Friday when the results came out. Three of us had failed by a ridiculously small margin. A brief interview and that chapter ended.

I departed with not a scrap of rancour. It was almost with relief the very next day, clutching my Flying Licence with the newly acquired Instrument Rating, that I walked straight into another job. What a tonic! — to be flying again at last. As an added bonus the last two months of classroom work would prove invaluable, when it came to studying to get my passport to promotion as Captain with the examinations for the Airline Transport Pilot's Licence.

As events turned out in the years to come, I had made a very lucky choice. The charter company, which I had just joined, had their head office in fashionable Mayfair. The inscription on the brass plate of the respectable business premises, B.K.S. Aerocharter Ltd., Old Burlington Street, London W.1., contrasted dramatically to the scene on the pavement immediately outside the front door. Here were some of the most elegantly beautiful women I had set eyes on; finely dressed ladies, plying the oldest profession in the world, promenaded by, umbrellas swinging, and the occasional poodle on a leash. This area, just off Bond Street, was the territory of the highest class pick-ups in London.

Once past temptation and inside the office on my second visit, I was issued with a predecessor's second-hand uniform. It was a big moment. The fit was within reason and, after a few alterations, proud admiration followed standing before a mirror wearing my first flying uniform.

My new company was not one to let its pilots remain idle. I was to report to the Overcliffe Hotel, Southend, to leave the next morning for an extended stay in Berlin. This was the aftermath of the 'Berlin Airlift' in the reverse direction — the evacuation of thousands of refugees who were flooding into the city while they could. The 'Berlin Wall' was yet to be built.

The next day, bright and early on a crisp spring morning, I was once again sitting in a real aeroplane ready to depart from Southend's grass field. The Skipper climbed into the left hand seat of the Dakota, and settled down. Before starting the engines, he turned and said to me in a gruff Yorkshire accent, "Do you know how to retract the wheels after take-off?"

With pride grievously hurt, I managed to refrain from reacting as I might have liked to; instead I gazed bleakly at him in silence, and replied, "Yes, I think I will be able to manage that."

We were soon on our way to Hamburg and then Berlin's Templehof Airport.

A new era had dawned for me — I was flying in new skies, but as I was soon to find out, very different ones. Gone forever were those happy-go-lucky bush flying days. These chaps were obviously not going to let me pull them down to my standards; I was going to be yanked, somewhat unwillingly, up to theirs, and I could not have picked a better bunch to do the job.

The reasons for all this concern over standards were quite simple. The rapidly varying weather conditions of Europe demanded it. Fog, ice, low cloud, sudden changes in weather and the sheer density of air traffic, being but a few of the reasons. What is more, to make sure these standards were maintained, there were people about who were paid to see that they were. As the years went on, this control was to become even tighter. While flying in India no yearly checks were necessary; now it was to be a once yearly Instrument Rating test. I might have had a nervous breakdown if I had known, over 30 years on, that no fewer than six tests per year would be required, plus of course a medical check every six months.

So the remoulding process got under way. I was lucky enough to find myself crewed with a Skipper who, although a hard taskmaster, turned out to be the best. Our paths were to part, but we were to remain firm friends.

"Not much flying for you, lad, until you can first navigate," he said, adding as an afterthought, "properly."

There was plenty of scope for this. Our charter operations covered a lot of ground for a Dakota, ranging from the Far East to Africa and all points in between. Summer-time was fully occupied flying British holidaymakers to resorts; the company being the first in the inclusive tour market with a flight to Corsica and Majorca. Winter-time we would range far and wide on charters — Ministry equipment to Singapore, a load of seamen home from Ceylon, dynamite to Kuwait for the oil wells, bombs to Malta during the Suez crisis, trooping to the canal zone, ship's spare parts to South Africa, and the list could go on and on.

My mentor would make frequent checks of my navigation log in flight. A finger would jab at it, "What sort of abomination do you call this? When did you take your last drift sight? I want to see it entered in the log, and at least one every 15 minutes!"

On longer sectors, and particularly over water, a two or three position line radio fix was required to be taken, worked up and plotted on the chart every 40 minutes. My protests once, at not having a chart table only my lap to do all this work on in the cramped cockpit, were brushed aside brusquely. Thoughts of rebellion were fortunately kept sublimated because 'Supremo', as he became known, did his stint too once I had shown willing. To give him his due, he did indeed practise as he preached.

The day finally came when my work must have been considered to have reached the necessary standard. He vacated the Captain's left hand seat, and we proceeded to exchange duties. This practice has, of course, long since been prohibited, but in those times it was normal for the handling pilot to fly from the left hand seat. 'Supremo' then proceeded to demonstrate how a co-pilot's navigational duties really should be executed.

A Dakota, flying at about 150 m.p.h., offered plenty of time to permit the lengthiest of calculations. The man produced a log which, at the end of our flight across the Mediterranean to Malta, was worthy of framing. On it there was all that had been demanded of me, and much more. There was a 'point of no return' and 'critical points' for airfields on each side of our track in Italy, Sicily and Sardinia. If we had lost an engine at any time, we would have known exactly where to go. It was a yardstick to work towards, and it would stand me in good stead in the future to help out of more than one tricky situation.

Just like getting blood out of the proverbial stone were any attempts to get my Captain to recount his wartime experiences,especially as I had a fair idea that his war had been no run of the mill story. Perhaps it was his modesty, but perseverance that was to span 35 years enabled me to extract answers to most of my enquiries and piece together his story.

At the ridiculously young age of twenty, he had been in charge of a crew of six and flying in command of a four-engined Lancaster bomber. Johnny and his team had so far managed to cheat the statistics, the aerial carnage raged at its worst, as the seven of them with their lethal loads of fuel, ammunition and high explosives jinked and weaved their way across the German skies. They had become expert practioners in the art of staying out of the sights of German night fighters by never remaining in straight and level flight for more than a few seconds. It must have been a sheer hell of air-sickness for those crewmen, sitting in the confines of the bomber, to have to endure hour upon hour of this violent twisting and turning in the dead of night. However it had got them safely through so far; so far that is, until the A.O.C. Bomber Command, decreed that in the future, continuous evasive action would cease and steady formation flights would be maintained over enemy territory.

On their very next raid, acting on these unwelcome new orders, they were shot down.

A brief burst of tracer shells from a German night fighter, a sudden inferno of fire as their wing lit up and blazed like a torch, a hastily shouted order, "Bale out!" on the intercom and it was every man for himself. Their young Skipper was the last to leave, dropping through the nose floor hatch. As he drifted down through the night skies of Germany lit by distant fires and flares, with flak bursts and gunfire receding above him and his blazing aircraft drifting earthwards, he had at least the satisfaction of knowing that all his boys had made it. Six parachutes floating downwards below him, but only two of them, however, were to survive the war; the other five, most probably fell victims to the vengeance of civilians, who rarely spared so-called 'British terror-flyers' who fell into their hands.

Johnny came down in open country, but there was no sign of any of his crew. He therefore decided to start working his way southwards across Europe without delay, pinning his hope on his RAF uniform being much the same colour as the Wehrmacht's. On day two his luck ran out, when he was surrounded by German farm workers, as he crept along a hedgerow trying to get at some apples to satisfy his maddening pangs of hunger.

The next few years spent in a POW camp were not entirely wasted — he completely mastered the German language and this came in most handy long after the war when I found myself in need of my Captain's help as an interpreter while based in Berlin chatting up the German girls!

Bombadier/Gunner, 'Brad', the other survivor, did not however fare very well during his captivity. He suffered severe frost-bite and the loss of some of his toes, which permanently affected his mobility. Successful escape, foremost in most prisoners' minds, soon presented opportunities in a Germany now very much on the receiving end, with conditions becoming increasingly disorganized.

Seizing his chance, Johnny made his escape, and in the process inadvertently fell headlong into a cesspit. However this setback did not deter him, and as he worked his way towards the advancing allied lines, he fell into the company of an American Colonel trying to rejoin his compatriots.

The pair were lying low in a wood, with the sound of fighting very near at hand, when a German heavy machine-gun crew dashed up and set up their gun within spitting distance of where the two lay pressed rigidly to the ground hardly daring to breath. After firing briefly, the German infantrymen decided to pull back and disappeared as quickly as they had come.

The vanguard of the advancing Allied column soon came into view in the valley below the wood where the two watchers lay hidden. The Colonel suddenly whooped with joy, "It's our boys down there!" he shouted recognizing the US markings, while Johnny tried to restrain him. Their contact would have to be done cautiously, lest a trigger-happy bullet ended all their efforts at this eleventh hour. After some nail biting exchanges, contact was made and at last they were among friends. A celebration was called for and a bottle of brandy was produced.

The normal pint drinking Johnny had not been anywhere near even a drop of alcohol for years (sugarbeet and turnips rooted out of fields had been his only recent food) — the celebratory libation proved disastrous. After only one glass he was flat on his back, hopelessly drunk and frothing at the mouth too as the brandy reacted with the sugarbeet. At this point, events started to go very wrong with the entry of several burly US Military Police. To them, the figure lying speechless and frothing at the mouth, dressed in a mucky blue uniform, could only be German — they knew all their tricks. Without further ado, the MP drew his pistol, pointed it at his intended victim's head and was about to fire, when a desperate shout was raised. "Hey, no! This guy's a Limey flyer!"

Looking upwards from floor level, down the barrel of the gun, in an alcoholic daze, still frothing and completely at peace with the world, Johnny was only vaguely aware of the discussion taking place above him on which his life hung. Fortunately for my old friend, a stay of execution was granted and he was eventually shipped back home to England. By all accounts of the witnesses present on that day with the Americans, it was the nearest he had come to death during his war.

Although for me as a co-pilot time had to be served patiently, whatever the sentence. Some serve more and some less, all a necessary part of learning the trade. Although I did not know it then, I was to be a co-pilot for a further two years, but there was plenty of variety.

Still crewed with 'Supremo', we were returning empty one day to Southend. Our Dakota was cruising along at 8,000 feet in clear blue skies above the Zuider Zee. At the time, I was sitting alone in the cockpit, and looking up from the instrument panel a sudden flashing movement of metal caught my eye. It had been an aircraft diving past us very closely, and now out of sight under the nose. I called back to the Skipper, who was standing just inside the passenger cabin. He came forward and we looked around.

"Must have been an Air Force jet practising aerobatics."

He had hardly got the words out when we both saw it. High in the sky, some distance ahead of us, an object could be seen suspended in the air. At first we thought it was a balloon, but it soon proved otherwise. As we closed rapidly, a figure suspended below a parachute and waving frantically drifted past us. The Skipper had lost no time; he already had our aeroplane in a spiralling turn downwards, while I called up Amsterdam Control.

Following our descending parachutist down, it now dawned on us how close we had come to being struck by his abandoned aircraft moments before. Down we went in wide circles, sometimes coming quite close to the waving pilot. By the time we had got down to near sea level, our exact position had been passed to the Dutch Controllers by radio. The pilot landed with a splash in the Zuider Zee, inflated his dinghy and struggled into it.

Meanwhile we had spotted a ferry steamer some distance away. 'Supremo' called out, "Now's our chance to use that Very pistol — get to it lads."

The radio operator and myself between us loaded the gun and slotted it into the special fitting for it in the roof. A word from the Skipper, the trigger pulled, a deafening bang, and our first flare arched into the sky.

We continued to encircle the drifting pilot. Seeing the pyrotechnics, the ferry boat Captain got the idea and altered course. They eventually came alongside the dinghy, and the pilot was soon clambering aboard. He waved enthusiastically as we made a final low pass over the steamer before continuing on our way to Southend. What a relief it was to be flying in a straight line again; the tight spiral down so many thousands of feet had made me begin to feel decidedly queasy.

An official letter of thanks came in a fortnight later from the Netherlands Air Force. The stricken aircraft, which had come near to downing us as well on its way down, turned out to be an F-84G Thunderjet. Incidents of this sort, in later years, became virtually inconceivable with the extensive use of radar.

There were many of our passengers in the early fifties who had to endure quite gruelling experiences before getting back on to terra firma, and much of it could have been avoided by the use of the radar network of today.

The Côte d'Azur was nearly at its best one day as our Dakota climbed into the sky for the trip back to England. Broken cloud, but still plenty of sun, and the high mountains of the Alpine chain to the north-west of Nice were clearly in view. It was the classic trap, and the Skipper fell right into it.

"Looks clear enough, we'll cut the corner — save a lot of time." Indeed it did look good enough to get through as our old aeroplane scrambled for altitude. There was layered cloud to the north and the mountain tops ahead were all in sight, but the weather front mentioned by the Met. man at Nice was closer than he reckoned and moving fast.

At first wisps of cloud licked past our machine, then they became more persistent.

"We'll try and climb above it," said the Skipper.

He knew only too well that approval to take this direct route was conditional on being able to keep the mountains in sight all the time. As we climbed, we expected to break out of the tops of the cloud at any moment, but it did not happen. The Dakota, being non-pressurized, was not permitted to carry passengers above 10,000 feet because of diminishing oxygen in the air. We were now approaching that limit; ice was beginning to form on the wings and fly off the propellers, banging against the sides of the passenger cabin as it did so.

It was decision time, and a difficult choice at that. If we turned back, we would have to land to refuel, then go all round the mountain barrier and through the Rhône Valley. The company would not have been very pleased with the delay and extra expense. The Skipper said, "We'll climb above 10,000 feet — it should only be for a short while. No danger to other aircraft as we're well clear of the airways."

The seat belt signs were already on because of the bumpy conditions in which we had been flying. The steward was asked to remain seated, and then up we climbed. We both knew that we would have to go up now to 16,000 feet at least. There was grave danger lurking somewhere over to our right. The cloud shrouded granite ramparts of Mount Blanc and its lofty neighbours. We staggered up and up through weather that seemed to be getting thicker by the minute.

We had often in the past flown at 14,000 feet, when carrying freight, to get above weather. Here we were now, in our poor old Dakota, mushing along at 16,500 feet and, because of the limited radio coverage in those times, had lost contact with ground control.

It came upon us at first with deadly stealth, neither of us the slightest bit aware that our brains were being starved of life-giving oxygen, the onset of lethal hypoxia. A feeling of false well-being was upon us and nothing mattered very much at all.

It was at this time that another small passenger caught my eye and became the very centre of my attention — a fly. The little winged insect was taking passage aboard our aeroplane from France to England, but at that moment was in very poor shape indeed. Spread-eagled on its back, with all legs pointed upwards in an undignified manner, he reposed on a bed of cotton wool about a foot in front of my face. The cotton wool, commandeered from the aircraft's first aid kit, was regularly wedged into the lower frame of the sliding window to prevent the pilots' trousers from being soaked by rain-water.

At that very moment one of the fly's legs was observed to twitch, ever so slightly. The Captain's attention was now also drawn to this mid-air drama.

TRYING TO REVIVE A DOWNED FLY. THE STRANGE EFFECTS ON BEHAVIOUR CAUSED BY LACK OF OXYGEN AT 16,000 FT. OVER THE ALPS.

"He's obviously short of air," he said. "Try blowing on him." What an excellent idea, I thought, so hastily, rolling up the flight plan to form a tube, I made an immediate start to attempt to resuscitate our tiny stowaway. Blowing through the tube, I proceeded to unwittingly squander further precious oxygen.

Now, our total attention was riveted on the experiment. Such were the strange effects of hypoxia that the fate of our struggling Dakota and all aboard seemed to be of little consequence.

The blowing continued and then, at last, success. There was another twitch of the fly's legs. Greatly encouraged by this, efforts were redoubled, cheered along by the Captain. With each successive lungful of life-giving air, the fly's condition improved in leaps and bounds. All his legs were now pumping away vigorously. Before long he was on his feet and tottering unsteadily about on the carpet of cotton wool. This was our moment of supreme triumph — it was like being given the powers of resurrection out of the blue. A great smile spread across the Captain's face, and he beamed with delight as he congratulated me on my success.

I was becoming vaguely aware of a dizzy feeling after all my efforts at blowing, and at that moment the steward's face appeared at my shoulder. He did not look in good shape at all as he mumbled something unintelligible, his eyeballs seeming to roll, and he then promptly sank slowly down onto the floor between us. Without leaving my seat, I leaned down and shook him. Dazed, he squinted upwards with a bemused expression on his face. I told him to sit down on the small jump seat behind the Captain.

While the unfortunate steward was struggling to his feet, the Skipper had been watching.

"Christ," he said. "We've got to get down."

Somehow the spectacle must have triggered off realization of our situation. His hand dragged the throttles back, and we started down.

"We must be over the highest peaks by now."

As the power came off, the labouring engines seemed to heave a sigh of relief, and our ears began popping as the Dakota descended through the thick cloud.

As senses started to return to normal at the lower levels, finding out where we were became more and more important. Our best guess was that we were somewhere between Dijon and Lyon, but our radio compass was still not much help because of static. Meanwhile, I had at last established contact on the radio, the bad weather continuing to cause constant crackling in the headsets. We were through the worst though.

The 'Fasten Seat Belt' sign was switched off, and passengers were once again free to wander aft to the toilet if they so wished, a journey their legs would almost certainly not have coped with earlier without buckling. We were lucky none of the passengers suffered any ill-effects from their high altitude flight, and that none of them had been any the wiser. The fly had somehow slipped unnoticed from the scene, and passed into the realms of the past.

The episode went down to experience, and I made a serious note to avoid falling into such a trap when I moved into the Captain's seat myself some day.

It happened to be the company's policy, during those years in the early fifties, to keep the same crew flying together; not too good for crews who did not get on very well, but in any case it became a matter of learning how to live with each other's whims, habits and faults. This, of course, is the very reason why permanent crewing in airlines today is no longer done.

Our radio operator was a bluff, stocky and often jovial fellow. Nicknamed 'Gentleman Jack' because of his very proper articulate manner of speech, he was at times given to somewhat eccentric behaviour. It had also not gone unnoticed in the past that he sometimes showed signs of extreme agitation at the prospect of adverse weather.

This time we had been chartered to carry a full load of explosives in our Dakota from Paris to the Persian Gulf. We had all had an absolutely marvellous night on the town and, as a result, were rather subdued as we climbed aboard our aircraft early next morning. The loaded Dakota was standing in lonely isolation on Le Bourget Airfield, parked miles away from anything just in case. There was much light-hearted banter on such topics as wills, next of kin, and so on. 'Gentleman Jack' was in good form as he fussed over checking the security of the cases of detonators stowed in the toilet. Our French Agent emphasized several times that provided the explosives and the detonators were kept well apart, "zen zaire ees no problem, Messieurs."

All being in order, we departed and by the next day had progressed as far as Cyprus to night stop. It was here that a strange incident was to occur to upset our routine and give us some concern. Next morning, the three of us, 'Supremo', 'Gentleman Jack' and myself, were in the Meteorological Office to check the route weather. We would be flying over the Eastern Mediterranean and then across the desert to Kuwait. The Met. man was full of forebodings, "Heavy sandstorms have been affecting the Gulf area. There is a strong possibility that your destination, Kuwait, will be out in rising sand when you arrive."

These words seemed to have a pole-axing effect on our radio operator. He had been standing near by listening, and it now became obvious that something was very much amiss. Beads of perspiration were appearing on his brow, and he was shaking slightly as though he had suddenly developed a high fever. 'Gentleman Jack' continued to shuffle from one foot to the other in apparent discomfort. We hastily signed for the weather report folder, and left the office to spare any further embarrassment, our Skipper enquiring solicitously if he was feeling ill.

When inside the aircraft, all we could hear were vague muttering sounds from the agitated and shaking figure. At last he blurted out, "I ... I don't like the idea of flying into sandstorms — I'm not happy about that forecast. Why don't we delay?"

'Supremo' tried to reassure him, "We've got five hours ahead of us and anything can happen with the weather during that time." He added, "If you can keep us up to date on the weather in the area, there are plenty of places to which we can divert. I can assure you if Kuwait is still out in sandstorms, we won't go anywhere near it."

This seemed to calm 'Gentleman Jack' a bit and we eventually departed, still feeling a little uneasy ourselves.

Later that day we started our descent after our long flight over the desert, and landed our load of explosives without much difficulty in hazy conditions. Dust hanging in the air was the only leftover of the blinding sandstorms which had long passed on their way. Our radio operator was extremely relieved, and that evening, during our night stop, the full story unfolded over cool beers in the Bar.

'Gentleman Jack' had been one of eight in a twin-engined Blenheim bomber, and was hitching a ride as passenger to an aerodrome near Alexandria in Egypt during World War II. A very bad sandstorm was blowing at the time of landing, and he sat cramped in the bomber's fuselage near the main spar of the wing. They all watched as the pilot made two unsuccessful attempts to land in the blinding sand and dust. At this stage, one of the other passengers, who was a higher ranking pilot, came forward. By mutual agreement he took over to make another attempt himself.

With the new man at the controls, down they came again into the swirling sand. The pilot, probing almost blindly in the gloom, came lower and lower. Suddenly there was a wrenching crash; the bomber's wing had struck a parked aircraft on the ground and they cartwheeled over. Inside they were all hurled around in confusion until, finally, they came to rest. Stunned, he was aware of smoke, flames and daylight, which was a break in the fuselage, and he hastily scrambled out through it.

OUR RADIO OPERATOR, OFTEN GIVEN TO ATTACKS OF THE JITTERS.... UNDERSTANDABLY PERHAPS: BEING THE SOLE SURVIVOR OF A CRASH IN AN EGYPTIAN SANDSTORM DURING WORLD WAR II.

Instinctively 'Gentleman Jack' stumbled away from the burning wreckage as the heat was becoming intense. From the wreckage he heard screams and shouts for help. He turned in his tracks to return and try to help. At that precise second the whole aircraft suddenly exploded right before him. The blast knocked him flat on his back. As he lay stunned looking skywards, he remembered seeing a huge section of metal floating downwards like a falling leaf out of the dust above him. It came down as if in slow motion, and he waited helplessly to be swatted just like a fly. However, he was again in luck — with a loud clang, the metal section slammed into the ground only inches away. He was the sole survivor.

We ordered more beer on it, and I was to notice in the future how much more understanding we both became about our colleague's sometimes strange behaviour.

During March 1954 we were to find ourselves right on hand in far off Singapore, where a milestone was reached in British aviation. Enough was about to be called on the mammoth duty periods pilots had very frequently been doing until then. The broken pieces of an airliner lying in the middle of Singapore's airfield was the spark that started it all off.

Our journey outwards had been a long flog by today's standards: 'two hops to Down Under' and 'Singapore direct' were as yet only a dream. The best our Dakota could manage was twelve 'hops' and that spread over no less than six days. In excellent spirits at the prospect of two days off before our return flight, we booked into an hotel. This was situated very close beside Kalang, which was then Singapore's civil airfield.

It had been only a few days before that a four-engined Constellation had struck the sea wall, and many passengers had tragically been killed. The crew had been so fatigued after an excessively long duty period that they had misjudged their height while landing.

The sun had not yet set by the time I walked into the bar on the top floor, but the other two had beaten me to it. The view of this exotic oriental city from the roof bar was splendid, until my gaze fell upon the stark sight in the middle of the airfield. The main body of the once elegant aircraft lay twisted and broken, and fire had ravaged the remains. Some of the crew had managed to scramble clear of the nose section and other parts.

The three of us tried to find something more cheerful to talk about, as the first cool beer of the evening slipped down. Further along the bar sat a group who, to the discerning eye, looked remarkably like aircrew, but on closer scrutiny it was immediately apparent that here was something just not right. They all had the look of condemned men about them, or perhaps ones who were trying desperately to drown some great burden in drink. It did not take long to uncover the mystery. This was the crew who had flown the 'Connie' into the ground and miraculously survived, so the barman very discreetly informed us. How cruel must fate be, I thought, to prolong their mental torture in this way. Who had so thoughtlessly put them in this hotel, almost on top of their burnt out aeroplane? They were now in the process of attending the investigation into the accident.

A pilot friend, who had survived a serious air accident, was to tell me many years later, "There must be only one thing worse than being killed in a crash and that is surviving to face the inquisition thereafter. Cross-examined as you are carried away on a stretcher, grilled in hospital, and tied up in knots in the witness box by well briefed barristers. Chairborne 'experts' who will tell how you did it all wrong. Vilified and asked how you could have been so unbelievably stupid. Confidence battered and your livelihood threatened."

He had not had a very happy time, and, back in Singapore in 1954, someone up here at the hotel bar was going through most of this for sure.

Legislation to ensure adequate rest periods for aircrew was soon to follow after this accident, but not quite in time though to have any effect on our impending flog back to Europe.

Landings at Penang, Rangoon, Calcutta and Madras, got us as far as Colombo in two days, where a large number of seamen awaited transport to Hamburg. Because of the heavy load, our 'hops' between refuelling would be even shorter and more frequent.

Never before had I been in a Dakota that had to make a fuelling stop between Karachi and Sharjah, but on this occasion we did — such was the combined weight of our burly sailors and their mountain of baggage. This coast is an inhospitable place. Early travellers, in the hot season, observed the heat was so great that flies fell dead on the wing. Jiwani, in Baluchistan, was roughly half-way and ideally suited for our purpose of refuelling. We had a job finding the place, and had to circle several times while we tried to make up our minds where to land. A small area of tarmac was our only clue, and we landed on the most likely stretch of hard earth. It was a rugged, rock strewn landscape, and the armed Baluchi tribesmen, who helped us refuel from 40 gallon drums, were a wild looking bunch.

On the Tristar, I was to fly along this coastline quite often, and it was usually at breakfast time. It was a scene of grandeur and fantastic colour from 30,000 feet. The aeroplane's first class menu was like eating in a five star restaurant with a 300 mile panoramic view; haddock and toast while looking down at enormous ravines and precipitous cliffs, sweeping down to an azure sea, were an excellent aid to digestion. Jiwani happened to be coming up ahead of us, when the co-pilot said to me, "How did the old timers manage for landing

grounds along this wild stretch of coast?"

Eating his meal, he must have been equally lost in thought admiring the scene, and his question could not have been better timed.

"There's a string of landing grounds along this coast," I replied, "Jiwani up ahead. I've been in there myself."

He looked at me in disbelief. On the shelf beside me was my log-book, which I picked up and opened to the back page. There, listed by the year, were the airfields I had visited during my flying career. It was an interesting reminder for me too. Strangely, it had been 30 years almost to the day since 'Supremo', 'Gentleman Jack' and myself had dropped in. I might have thought it, but I certainly did not say that our visit had been before my colleague had been born.

Back in England during the mid-fifties, there had been no means of knowing it then but my days as a co-pilot were about to draw to a close. Before that was to happen, however, a valuable lesson was to be driven home on the importance of considering the feelings of fellow crew members.

We were flying a series of night newspaper flights with a two-man crew. My Captain was a new recruit to the company, and there had been some mutterings already. It was winter and we had been having a harsh time; bitter, snow-laden east winds had been sweeping Europe for weeks. It was in these conditions that I turned up for work at Southend aerodrome in the pitch black of the early hours of the morning.

It was my first meeting with my Captain. He was a big burly man with a beard, and seemed to be given to issuing commands in a loud voice even over trivial items that were done routinely. I was also soon to find out that there would be absolutely no question of the co-pilot sharing any of the flying. However, it would have to be made the best of so I got on with my duties.

Loaded with the morning newspapers, mainly for the forces in Germany, we set off in the Dakota, crossing the North Sea and Holland, to land at Hannover at first light and, after a quick cup of tea, would be on our way again with a load to Dusseldorf. Then the final weary stage with the remaining copies for Frankfurt, where we had a brief afternoon rest in airport bunks, very rarely without plenty of disturbance. As the winter night came round, we would be in the air once more with the morning edition of the *Stars and Stripes* — half the load for Paris, and the rest for the US Forces in England.

I had done the circuit many times before, but never with such an unpleasant fellow. He had been at it steadily since leaving Southend, teaching me the true meaning of the word 'bombastic'. Quietly simmering, events were to come to a head on the way to Paris. As we ploughed through the clouds in icy blackness, I had donned my raincoat because of the cold. Still shivering, I reached behind my seat to check if the cockpit heat controls were on. These were a row of plunger rods which required very careful adjustment as they controlled air flow over the engine exhaust pipes and various ducts. Very surprisingly the heat was found to be off. No wonder the cockpit had become so cold. I commenced adjusting the heat, and gradually the cockpit started to warm up a bit.

After a while, I noticed the Captain reach across to the plungers. It was quite normal for both pilots to adjust the heat until a mutually acceptable temperature was reached, and I assumed this was the case until an icy draught began to build up on my feet near the rudder pedals. 'He's overdone it a bit,' I thought, as after an interval of suffering I reached back for the levers again. Strange — they were all fully off.

This whole sequence was repeated through several times. During the Arctic spells, I was beginning to build up a resentment at the way I was being treated.

Finally, the crunch came. The Captain's burly arm came across and slammed all the levers off. In stentorian tones he snarled, "The heat's going 'OFF' Whitlock — the way I want it."

I had never before snapped like I did on that night. It was a case of 'beware of the wrath of a patient man'. In a rage, half out of my seat, I shouted with fury through clenched teeth, "Oh no it's bloody well not, you bastard. It's going back on."

I had already crashed all the valves back on again. Now at full stretch, my left forearm wedged under his bearded chin as my hand fastened on the left hand sliding window handle.

"If you want some ventilation, you can bloody well open your side window," I bellowed.

The Captain had recoiled; he seemed to be trying to distance himself from my clenched fist, a fraction of an inch from his face. His head could move no further backwards; it was as if pinned against the side window. His co-pilot's unexpected outburst had clearly shaken our hefty friend, and in the manner of most bullies he rapidly climbed down.

DRIVEN TO THE LIMIT OF PATIENCE, BY AN OVERBEARING CAPTAIN......

"Calm down, Whitlock, calm down," was all he could manage.

I withdrew to my corner, and pointedly readjusted the temperature back to a comfortable level. Still glowering, my hand fairly and squarely blocking access to the levers, my friend was left in no doubt as to my intentions if any further action was attempted.

Once more back on the ground at Le Bourget, all was anticlimax. Stalking away from the aircraft to collect a weather report and put in a flight plan for the last sector back to Southend, a voice trailed after me across the tarmac. It was the Skipper. His manner of speech was very different now; gone was the imperious haughtiness as he explained to me how he preferred cold conditions. I was still bristling with indignation at the way I had been treated and I took the opportunity, standing on the tarmac, to tell him how I felt in no uncertain terms.

Looking back at that mid-air incident, there was really no winner or loser. Valuable lessons must have been learnt by both parties. I did fly with my friend again, and he was the essence of consideration. It was rumoured that I was one of the few co-pilots he permitted to fly. For my part, never would I, on becoming a Captain myself, ever treat a crew member with such inconsideration. Many a fiery tempered co-pilot or flight engineer was to fly with me, but over more than forty years of aviation I cannot ever remember a voice being raised.

It had once been said to me by way of a warning that one cannot expect too many chances after making mistakes in flying. In those times, much more than now, there were very many more traps for the unwary to fall into. It was for this reason that it was always handy to have someone working in the company, a rebel, who would 'draw the fire' away from the rest; the theory being management would be so busily engaged dealing with the problem pilot that life remained much easier for the rest.

I happened to be crewed with one such Skipper on a bitter winter's night out of Frankfurt. Flurries of snow were falling as we commenced start up, and the engines burst into life in turn, but all was not well as checks revealed one of the engine-driven electrical generators was not working. We both realized that the company would certainly expect us to go on just the remaining generator, even though it would be doing twice its normal work and might well fail itself as a result. We also knew that to be caught without electrical power, particularly on a night like this, would have dire consequences. Our load had to get through, and most of the other Captains would have chanced it. Things were going to be different this time.

"Bugger it," said the Skipper, "we don't get any thanks for sticking our necks out like this."

The engines chuffed and clanked to a halt as the Skipper yanked back the mixture control levers in the cockpit.

"I could do with a steak and a few pints of good German beer. We'll go in the morning."

As we climbed out of our seats to pack up for the night, I thought I knew what the Skipper meant by a few pints, knowing his unquenchable thirst. We made the most of our night stop, and the next day we finally got back to base.

Trouble was brewing. The US Forces had not had their morning papers to browse over at breakfast time. The newspaper contract was in danger of being lost. The Skipper was on the carpet in the Chief Pilot's office, and the Managing Director was on the telephone from London. Why had he not pressed on? The interview continued — it was touch and go, but happily a stay of execution was granted. It looked like he would be with us for a while yet, keeping management on their toes.

By way of a little disciplining though he would do a check flight, acting as co-pilot with the Chief Pilot. Events did not go at all well on this flight, that is not well for the Chief Pilot. They had been taking off from Calvi in Corsica. It was a picturesque strip, bordered on three sides by the pine clad mountain ramparts of the island of Napoleon's birth. Take-offs were always towards the sea, beside which towered the high walled 'Citadel' where Nelson had lost an eye. The fragrant pine scented air contrasted to the sometimes treacherously violent winds that swept down from very adjacent mountains. It was just such a gust that caught the Dakota as it roared down the earth strip, after the Chief Pilot had lifted the tail at the start of his take-off run. In cross wind gusts, this was usually the most vulnerable time for an aircraft with a tail wheel.

The Dakota started a vicious swing to the left, heading towards scrub and rocky ground. The Chief Pilot let out a yell of surprise and desperately kicked on full right rudder, but he was too late. The speeding aeroplane headed for certain disaster until, that is, the co-pilot took a hand in the take off. He had a lot to lose on this flight if anything went wrong, but as a Captain himself he had vastly more Dakota experience than his Chief. He slammed shut the right hand engine throttle under the Chief Pilot's hand; the aircraft steadied and then headed back through the scrub towards the strip. At precisely the right moment he opened up the starboard engine to full power again, and after a series of lesser swerves the pair of them got the Dakota into the air.

The Chief Pilot was shaken to the core, and as he climbed away, ashen faced, his trembling hands fumbled for his cigarettes. His co-pilot, our Captain under a cloud, waited in silence for further trouble but none came, just the cockpit gradually filling with smoke as the unfortunate Chief Pilot tried to collect himself after the near disastrous take-off. Nothing further was said, and on return to base co-pilot rapidly reverted to Captain again.

Alas, this was sadly not to be for long; the end came during one of these same series of Inclusive Tours that the company had pioneered to Corsica and Palma de Majorca. As the sun sank below the mountains along the island's north-western coast, our Captain and his crew got to the hotel, looking forward to the very popular once a week night stop ahead of them. The Palma of those times was very different to the highrise skyline of today; the town exuded the atmosphere and charm of old time Spain. Our old friend, the 'Skipper of the Thirst', was soon ensconced in a favourite haunt, and much later was seen arm in arm with a vivacious dark-haired señorita escorting her home.

However, completely unbeknownst to any of the crew, some other person of note was also in Palma. The Managing Director and his family were enjoying a short holiday and, moreover, were planning to return on the flight next day.

Morning came, and the bleary-eyed crew were up at crack of dawn. Trouble was brewing; there was no sign of the Skipper at breakfast, and neither was he in his room. A frantic round of enquiries proved fruitless, and further delaying tactics became impossible when, to the crew's surprise, the Managing Director telephoned from the aerodrome. Furious at the delay, he ordered the rest to leave for Son Bonnet Airfield immediately. He was a fully qualified pilot, and would fly the aircraft back personally. The luckless Skipper did turn up at the last minute by taxi, but too late. Our hero was relieved of his command on the spot, and had to ride back in disgrace as a passenger. Many a lesser mortal might have recoiled into the depths of remorse, but not him. He accepted his later demotion to co-pilot quite philosophically.

"I told her to call me at six o'clock," he recounted, "and she did too, but I just turned over, grabbed a handful of tit, and went back to sleep again. Next thing I knew, it was nearly take-off time!"

Life as co-pilot went on at an easy tempo and this carefree state, free from responsibilities, might have been allowed to continue indefinitely had it not been for my father. While residing in the family home at Ealing, I could not escape his constant badgering to obtain a higher flying licence. He realized, perhaps better than I did at the time, without a Senior Commercial or the higher Airline Transport Pilot's Licence that promotion to Captain was not possible.

Luck was with me here again, because in those years our flying was very seasonal. Winter allowed plenty of time for study, and with my recent Navigation Course still fresh in the mind I started on a Correspondence Course. It all paid off, and by the following spring I had a Senior Commercial Pilot's Licence in my pocket.

'HOLDING HER DOWN' TO HAVE SPORT WITH FISHERMAN RONALDSWAY. ISLE OF MAN. PERHAPS THE PASSENGERS SHOULD HAVE BEEN TOLD..." A SHORT DELAY TO YOUR TAKE OFF LADIES AND GENTLEMEN, UNTIL THE FISHING BOAT WE HAVE SPOTTED IN THE HARBOUR, IS IN LINE.....

CHAPTER 6

Not a moment too soon, for summer was soon on its way, and as the skies became busier there was the usual pre-summer rush to recruit more pilots. The company found themselves short of Captains, and my chance had arrived much sooner than expected. At the tender age of twenty-four, I was rushed through a brief command check and, scarcely able to believe it, found myself promoted to Junior Captain on a Dakota, albeit under probation only. Other co-pilots, some older and more experienced but without the necessary licence, took it in good part.

It was a big moment and the first few trips were flown with perhaps conscientious overkill, but the new role soon started to become more familiar, that is until a new realization was to dawn. I was to find that, at least once or twice a year, I would be in for a sharp shock. A situation would develop, usually totally unexpected, that would be frightening enough to make the pounding of the heart be felt in the throat and a bottomless feeling in the pit of the stomach. Such occurrences are practically non-existent today because of advances in aviation and vastly improved ground aids.

However, all this was yet to come, when one misty night, flying from the North of England with a full load of autumn holidaymakers for Jersey, we were confronted with one of those sudden Channel Island fogs. As we neared the island, the fog was getting thicker by the minute, but there was nothing to stop us having a go as these were the days long before compulsory landing limits. They were to come many years later after the bitter experiences of countless landing accidents.

Instrument Landing Systems, or ILS for short, had only recently been introduced and we all found it a great advance on some of the older landing aids. It was already dark when we started down through the murk following the invisible radio beam. Mindful of the menacing church steeple sticking up not far from the runway, we came down to about 200 feet to see only a tantalizing glow of lights. It looked hopeful enough to justify another try, but during the time we had spent getting into position again the conditions must have worsened, because this time just below 150 feet we were forced to climb away with that elusive glow of lights just below us. The tower spoke to us on the radio and told us that the visibility was patchy, which proved to be the carrot that tempted us to try yet again. The co-pilot had been busy cross-checking our remaining fuel, and up until then we knew we had enough to get back safely across the Channel to Bournemouth, where the weather was good. It was also just acceptable at the nearby island of Guernsey.

As we climbed away into the pitch blackness, a feeling of loneliness and fear started to creep in; I was getting my first lesson in the sometimes treacherous and rapidly changing Channel Islands weather. We would try just once more, and then go to Guernsey without delay. Round we went in the fog, and my hands, now clammy with sweat, gripped the control wheel as I concentrated on flying the two cross needles of the ILS bringing our Dakota droning earthwards down through the murk. The altimeter needle crept lower and lower; it now hovered just below 100 feet, and still there was only a vague blur of the lights below us. With the throttles opened wide, our Dakota clawed for altitude, and we lost no time turning on to a course for the adjacent island of Guernsey. Before long, we were in radio contact with them once again. It came like an axe blow as the tower began giving us their latest weather conditions, which had worsened considerably; our comparatively safe bolt-hole was receding rapidly. It did not bear dwelling on; chilling fear had to be fought back all the while. If we did not get down through the blackness of night, the fog and the mist, on to this island surrounded by the inhospitable sea, we would be in dire straits.

Guernsey's aerodrome in those days was a grass field, so I determined that we should line up as best we could and then just put the aircraft down straight ahead if at all possible. Hands still clammy with perspiration, but fear temporarily forgotten, I concentrated on flying the approach. There was no ILS to make landing easier here. We were doing what was called a QDM let down which was much less precise, and involved the co-pilot making brief radio transmissions, with the ground station sending back bearings to steer. It was an antiquated system, but with a little bit of rule bending, out of necessity, it got us down all right that night. A few lights loomed out of the murk, and drifted past below under the nose as we started to break through the low overcast. In the blackness, pushing the Dakota down through the mist and drizzle, our landing lights picked out blurred shapes and vaguely the kerosene lamps marking the touchdown strip on the grass came into view. The aircraft was pushed firmly down on to the grass and the brakes put on as much as I dared without tipping the old aeroplane on its nose. The field was none too long; we slithered and bumped across the wet grass, and finally came to a standstill with the trees at the far end illuminated by our lights. Terra firma once again, and what a relief it was; countless pilots have no

A CARTOON BY THE AUTHOR PUBLISHED IN AN AVIATION JOURNAL IN THE SEVENTIES.

doubt had similar experiences, but for me it was an early introduction to the traps that lay around.

No harm had been done, and I had been let off the hook at the last minute. The full meaning of that aviation saying was becoming clearer: 'The safest pilot is one who has experienced considerable fear, and will go to almost any lengths to avoid experiencing it again.'

The Company had acquired two new additions to its aircraft fleet, which were castoffs from the State airline, British European Airways. Their performance was considered far too high for just anyone to be trusted with; it was a sort of Senior pilot snobbishness. Our new 'hot ships' were the barrel-shaped Vickers 'Vikings' and they did fly a mere 20 knots faster than our old Dakotas, but had many extra vices.

The plan was that, while continuing to fly as Captain on the DC3, I would also spend some time as co-pilot on the new arrival. So in addition to more winter licence study, some of us were sent off to Bristol for an Engine Course, which was followed by some do-it-yourself preparation for the Technical Examination on the aircraft. A few times round the circuit at Southend Airfield to do the necessary day and night landings, and 'Viking' was duly stamped on my newly acquired Airline Transport Pilot's Licence.

That winter was spent doing some very pleasant sub-charter flights to East Africa. In the vicinity of Juba, where we stopped to refuel on the way, vast herds of elephants could be seen, and giraffes roamed over wide areas — our passengers appreciated going down to view the game whenever possible.

One of these off season flights took us on another visit to the Persian Gulf. Flying the Viking with a very experienced Captain, we had flogged all the way across Turkey. This mountainous land was certainly not a pleasant place to cross in mid-winter, because unable to fly above the weather, we were always at the mercy of ice and clouds when they blocked our path. An engine failure would have meant almost certain disaster.

Years later a four-engined Tudor aircraft crashed in this region, and one of the crew was a friend of mine. The wreckage was located later and when mountain rescue teams had reached it, they found that two of the crew had miraculously survived. It was reported that the two had staggered down the mountainside only to be eaten by wild animals, probably bears.

However, we had eventually cleared the mountains, and the weather improved immensely as we came south over the plains of

LOW OVER THE EAST AFRICAN GAME RESERVES WITH 30 APPRECIATIVE PASSENGERS....

Mesopotamia. We finally landed at Baghdad in the late afternoon, wearily refuelled, and prepared for the last relatively short hop to Basrah. It was then my turn to fly, and the Captain moved over to the co-pilot's right hand seat. From here he would be taking a turn at doing the navigation and also catching up with his accounts.

We all had an interest here, for we were expecting a little divvy from the profits of a modest currency fiddle. In Greece the previous day, we had bought up some Turkish money virtually at half-price, which had been used to pay the hotel bills at Ankara and of course the bills would be claimed at the official rate. Complacency had obviously set in, for as we climbed out of Baghdad, the Skipper glanced down at the navigation log on his lap and set the first course on the main magnetic compass, which was 240 degrees. I duly turned the Viking on to this heading. He was absorbed in his paper work, and I was wearily thinking of that welcome bath followed by a nice cool beer at Basrah.

The aircraft had just reached cruising altitude, so I levelled her off, trimmed the elevators, and engaged the automatic pilot. A glance at Baghdad's radio beacon showed it still pointing dead astern, indicating that we had not drifted off track.

It had been a long day's work, and squinting at the instrument panel, the setting sun and the heat was adding to my discomfort. The sun was shining straight into my eyes from ahead through the front windscreen. As the Skipper beavered away at his accounts, I continued to sit uncomfortably in the dazzling sunshine. It was damned annoying to have it shining right into my eyes, and my mind kept coming back to it. Why was it shining into my eyes? Suddenly it dawned; unless the earth had gone haywire over the last half-hour, we were heading in entirely the wrong direction. We were roughly ninety degrees off course and heading into the most desolate tracts of the Arabian Desert. By quick reckoning, we were well over 50 miles into it already.

The Skipper's normally ruddy face paled as I hastily spoke to him. Grabbing for the navigation log buried below his accounts, the error leapt at him. The distance to the Baghdad boundary was 240 nautical miles, and in the other column the course was 135 degrees. He had inadvertently set the wrong figure on the compass ring. I had already started the aircraft into a sweeping turn towards the east. There was a flurry of pencils, dividers and unfolded charts in the Viking's cockpit, and the hastily plotted course was reset on the compass as we took up a direct heading for Basrah.

There was some explaining to do, but the few passengers, who had asked about the extended flight time were quite satisfied when it was explained that we had been rerouted. The problem would never have arisen if the ground stations had been equipped with radar as they have been in recent times. The implications of our mistake were too worrying to dwell upon, and the consequences, if we had continued off course, could have been dreadful as we had been heading straight into one of the most barren wastes of the Arabian Desert, the An Nafud. The Captain looked very embarrassed for a while, and I had been mightily glad that I had discovered the mistake before him. It was never reported nor did it come to light through the crew.

However, it was not long before I found myself on a final check ride out of Southend with the Chief Pilot. On this flight an event occurred that was to be for me the beginning of a disenchantment with the unlovely Viking.

It was a beautiful morning as we flew smoothly southwards in clear blue skies near Bordeaux. I was seated in the Captain's seat

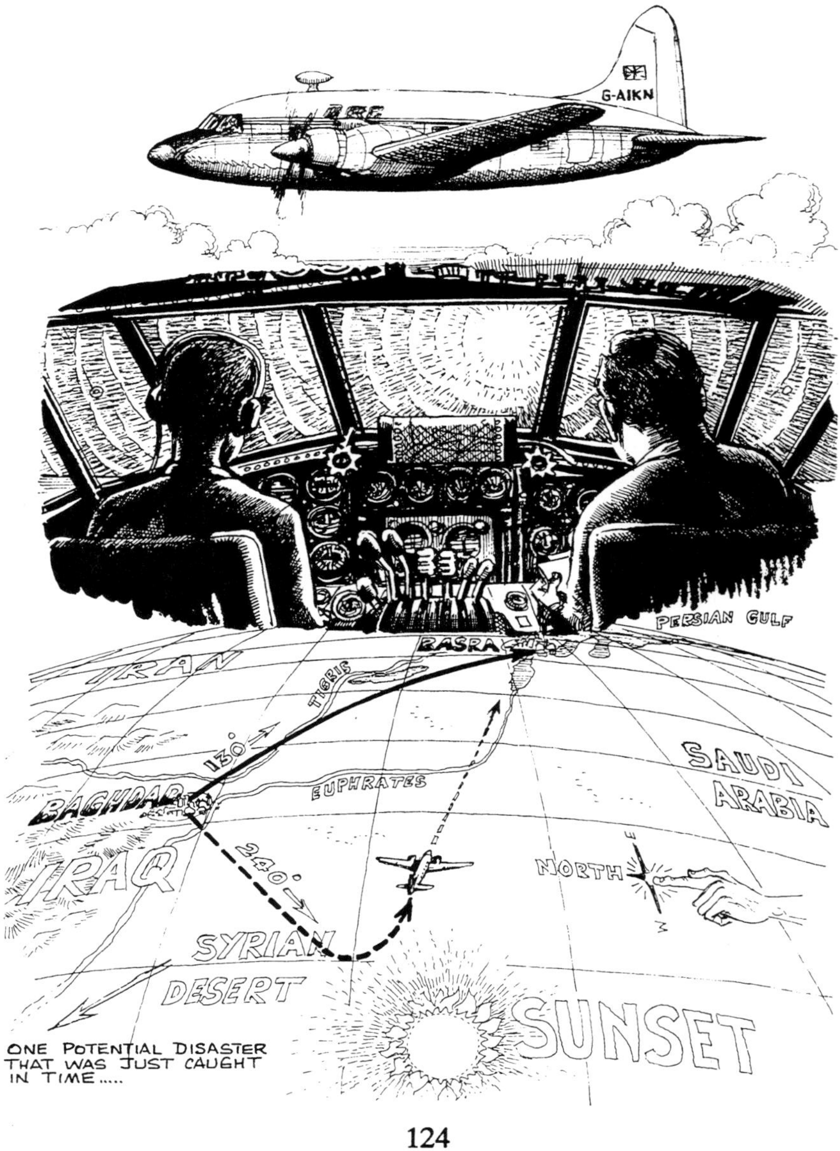

working hard at trying to put across a favourable impression. The Chief Pilot reclined, chain-smoking, on the other side of the cockpit, with ash spattered as always down the front of his uniform. Suddenly, without the slightest warning, there was an almighty bang that made me and no doubt everyone else aboard nearly jump out of our skins. The whole airframe shuddered and seemed to snap downwards.

"Christ! What was that?" was the shrill shout.

We must have hit something in mid-air was the first thought that flashed across my stunned consciousness. Disconnecting the automatic pilot, I put the aircraft into a turn to the left, advising the Chief Pilot what I was doing, and craned my neck to look rearwards out of the side window. I fully expected to see the wreckage of another aeroplane or a glider perhaps falling earthwards. I could see nothing but blue skies and the green patchwork countryside of France below.

Having got the aircraft back on course, my imagination was working overtime and I suggested to the Chief Pilot that perhaps it could have been one of the belly luggage doors that had come adrift, flown off and hit the tail plane. He readily approved of my suggestion to go back into the passenger cabin, and make an inspection through the rear windows.

Buttoning up my jacket and putting on as nonchalant an air as possible, I wandered back down the cabin. Every single pair of eyes were riveted on me with expressions ranging from blank amazement to open-mouthed bewilderment. As I stepped up and over the main wing spar that ran across the cabin, I spoke to passengers sitting near by saying that everything was all right and that we were checking. Smiling reassuringly as I ambled aft, I reached the rear row of seats. Leaning over towards the window, a passenger reached up and clutched desperately at my arm with both hands. Shakily he blurted out, "What was that? What was that terrible bang? We all felt it!"

There was a chorus of approval from adjacent passengers.

"Nothing to worry about ladies and gentlemen," I heard myself uttering the classic aviation excuse. Stretching across and squinting rearwards through the window, showed almost the full front section of the tailplane. There was not a sign of anything unusual.

On the ground at Bordeaux to refuel, we were out of the cockpit the minute the engines were shut down. We found absolutely nothing, not the slightest dent, nor a wrinkle in the aircraft's metal skin, nor anything out of place. The suspicion began to form that perhaps it might be some internal problem, but what it was we would only be

WING SPAR BOLT FAILURE OVER FRANCE..... 1957.

guessing at. The Chief Pilot did not even discuss any possibility of grounding the aircraft; we climbed back aboard and started out for the next sector to Oporto in Portugal. We would report the incident on return to base that evening.

It was night-time by the time we had a chance to talk to our Engineers at Southend. They would have another good look round, but ground the aeroplane?

"That's a laugh," one of the lads quipped, "how do you think we would manage over the weekend? The old kite's got a full load of passengers to shift to Palma on Saturday, and the same again on Sunday."

The engineer-in-charge did add though, "The aircraft's in the hangar on Monday for a check and we'll take a closer look at her then."

They were true to their word, and the company were exceedingly fortunate at that time in having a very conscientious inspector working in the Engineering Section. He read the report, and reasoned that a bang of such magnitude in flight could only have been caused by some failure in part of the wing itself.

Painstakingly they removed panels, crawled and squeezed into the dark recesses with torches and mirrors. After hours of work, their efforts were eventually crowned with success and our Viking's dark secret was revealed. Many lives had been hanging on a thread over the weekend; a broken wing spar bolt had been the culprit. The weakened wing, hanging on the remaining bolts, could have gone at any moment. It was a system that was a relic of the biplane era, and it was a happy day when manufacturers moved away from the habit of concentrating the strain of wing attachment on massive bolts.

Our 36 unsuspecting passengers and crew had really 'cheated death again', and, more amazingly over the next two days, 180 passengers, travelling over 4,000 miles, had done alarmingly the same.

Nearly thirty years later, driving in the sunny Transvaal of South Africa, along a road leading out of Johannesburg, a wonderful sight met my eyes. There, perched atop a building, was one of our 'hot ships' of 1956. The place was Vic's Viking Garage, and to pass by without a stop would have been unthinkable. When I related that I had once flown these aircraft, I was cordially invited to climb aloft and inspect the old machine more closely.

Alone with my thoughts while seated in the cockpit, I reflected on the aeroplane's virtues, which were few, and her vices, which regrettably were many. I thought of all those trips across the desert nervously watching the oil temperature gauges and wondering when one or both of the engines would 'gulp', losing all the crankcase oil in an instant. This was a serious flaw in the design of the Hercules engine, and several modifications were tried to prevent it happening. The only really effective measure was to warn crews to keep a close watch on oil temperature and keep them down using the cooling shutters. The aeroplanes had done most of their flying in Europe, but in hotter conditions, above a certain temperature, the oil would start to froth and within seconds all the oil would be sucked out through the crankcase breather pipe, leaving the engine to seize solid. This of course left the pilot with the strong possibility that the other overworked one would soon go the same way.

I remembered how, in the desert heat of Wadi Halfa, we had always, immediately after starting engines, rushed out for an early take-off, so that the temperatures would stay as low as possible. On one occasion as the oil temperatures had risen towards the danger point, we had risked stopping the engine to allow the oil to cool, and then done the same with the other in turn. Almost as a normal procedure, passengers seated near the wing would be treated to the spectacle of a large four bladed propeller at a standstill outside their window, while their air hostess explained, "Oh! that's just the Captain trying to cool down the oil a bit."

I thought of the aeroplane's miserable wing de-icer system known as TKS. Here alcohol was supposed to be pumped out, from porous strips along the wing's edge, by the pilot before he went into ice-for-

THE TEAM SPIRIT OF DECADES PAST THAT RARELY EXISTS TODAY...... CAPTAIN, CO-PILOT AND RADIO OPERATOR HELP OUR ENGINEER CHANGE A SET OF SPARK PLUGS WHILE DELAYED AT A DESERT AIRFIELD.......

ming clouds. The system just did not work, largely because of dead insects clogging the strips. How often we had staggered round the winter skies of Europe loaded down dangerously by ice.

Vic's Viking was well and truly bolted down on the roof. Just as well, because an empty Viking was one that would tip up over on to its nose at the drop of a hat. To taxi an empty Viking about an airfield was unthinkable without at least half a dozen hefty engineers standing in the tail section.

What a performance it had been flying a Viking, and as I climbed out of its barrel-shaped fuselage I felt how lucky I had been, during my time flying them, not to have bent one.

LANDING THROUGH THE 'SLOT' AT BERLIN TEMPELHOF
THE GRAVEYARD IS SAID TO BE THE LAST RESTING
PLACE OF THE GREAT MANNFRED VON RICHTOFEN...THE
RED BARON.

During the mid-late fifties, still flying the Dakota, I was lucky to get several interesting trips which made a welcome change from the routine schedules around northern climes. It was the sort of flying that the pilot of nowadays has very little chance of experiencing; for example, remote spots in Africa that modern jets bypass in huge leaps. There was the chance to see some very unusual sights at low level when flying freight instead of passengers, something now ruled out by modern flight recorders, the 'spies in the sky'.

Carrying a very heavy load aboard our Dakota to West Africa, we were obliged to follow the immense bulge of Africa in a series of small hops. Low flying to our heart's content, we raced along a coast that varied from spectacular cliffs to beautiful sandy white beaches. When desired, we would climb up a few thousand feet to get above the haze layer for a break or to have lunch and just follow the coast.

One of our refuelling stops was made at Sidi Ifni in Spanish Morocco. Fortress-like, it was perched atop a precipitous cliff, where the airstrip also was located. There were extensive barrack buildings all about, which were plain evidence of the hard wars that had been fought in the past against desert tribes. These forts served a vital need keeping Foreign Legionnaires alive.

That evening at Villa Cisneros, as we stopped for the night at another fort a few hundred miles further south along the coast, I was told by the Commandant that only about fifteen years previously the garrison had been wiped out. Fierce, heavily-armed nomads had

swept up the narrow strip of sand on horseback, done their killing, sacked the place, and then melted back into the desert again.

Late autumn of that same year, 1956, we were once again flying south, this time right across the centre of the Sahara bound for Cape Town, carrying an urgently needed turbine part for a ship that had broken down at the Cape. It was not a very heavy load, so we were able to carry more fuel and fly across some of the vast sand wastes of the Sahara. On this route, which we had done several times before to and from West Africa, it always gave cause for concern to locate Aoulef Oasis right in the middle of the desert. Aoulef was just a small collection of huts, mud structures and palm trees completely surrounded by endless sands. The oasis could not be seen until virtually overhead, and we relied on a radio beacon to home-in over the last 30 odd miles, but to strike that radiating circle, after a flight of well over four hours, was not taken lightly. The drift sight on the co-pilot's side was in almost constant use, with the course being adjusted accordingly. It was often very difficult, because of the featureless sand, to find an object below on which to line up the sight's grid lines. It was just not done to land at Aoulef Oasis without fresh vegetables and fruit, which were always accepted with enraptured gratitude by the French personnel.

This was an area that had seen triumph and tragedy in aviation, and the French knew it better than anyone else. Although we were not aware of it at the time, our track used to take us very close to a grisly relic of the past, but we never saw it. For 29 long years, perfectly preserved in the desert, lay the wreckage of a small biplane with the mummified remains of its pilot, Bill Lancaster, still lying beside it. A French Desert Patrol found the wreck about six years after our last visit.

Continuing on our way to the Cape, it was a trip of contrasts, from a night stop spent at Niamey beside the River Niger to the steaming jungles of the Congo next day. In the cool of the early morning, as we drove from our hotel to the aerodrome beside the lazy flowing Niger, downstream from ancient Timbuktu, the crew gaped spellbound at the statuesque native beauties bathing naked in the warming sun.

Coming in to land at Douala in the Cameroons next morning, we had a great laugh with three fun-loving locals. As we motored down for a landing, we noticed below the nose three figures making their way along a path across the cleared ground at the end of the runway. They were looking up at us, teeth gleaming in broad smiles, and giving

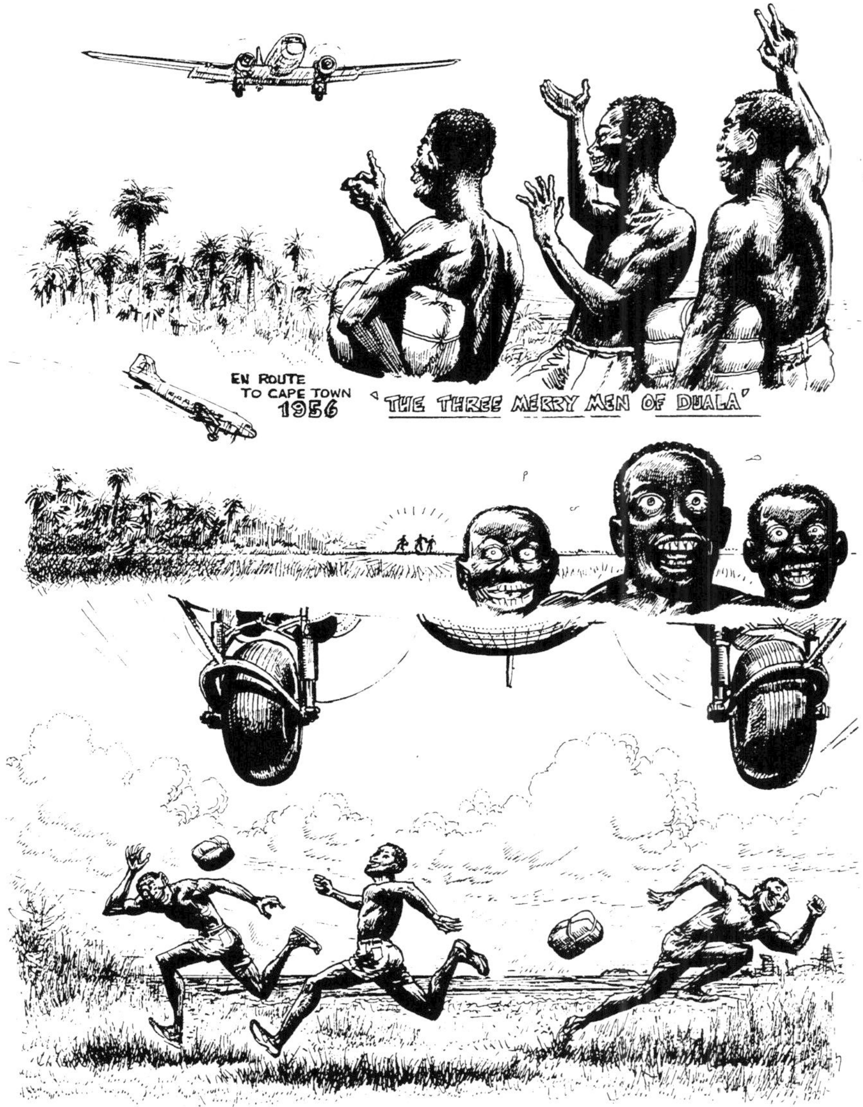

us what looked like 'V' signs. On an impulse, I nosed the Dakota over in a short steep dive at them; their expressions froze, and as they passed very close disappearing under the aircraft we had time for a brief glimpse of pumping arms and legs as the trio took off in a cloud of dust. Our extra speed carried us along level, skimming the grass until we reached the runway for our landing.

Later while refuelling, we noticed the three again waving from across a nearby fence. Uh-huh! trouble, we thought, but not a bit of it. The three were beaming all over, so we strolled across to have a chat. In between cackling laughter, the three were trying to get across to us that they would like the exciting game continued. They had clearly enjoyed the impromptu chase immensely. We parted great friends, after assuring them that we would be on the look-out for them, and hoped to meet them again.

We climbed above an endless carpet of giant tree-tops of the equatorial rain forests. The co-pilot had been this way before. "Parasolier trees," he said. "They grow to an average height of over 200 feet."

I was still looking down and marvelling at their lofty grandeur when one of our engines began banging and surging, and we had to return to Douala sooner than we expected. We nursed the old Dakota back, with the coughing engine throttled back, and landed, but this time there was no larking about. As suspected, it was the usual water in the fuel, and we were soon on our way again to Leopoldville in the Congo.

The next day we were once again making progress southwards towards Elizabethville, still flying over the unending rain forests, and gradually climbing as we approached the rising escarpment of Southern Africa. It was this that caused us a minor problem with our ground engineer, who had a beard and a shock of unruly hair a bit like Rasputin. His job was to take care of any mechanical problems that might arise, to check and refuel the aircraft while on the ground, and to make the odd cup of coffee or tea for the rest of the crew in flight. He could often be very cranky and the rest of us, knowing him well, made due allowance for bad tempered outbursts. As the day wore on and because of the higher ground below us, I had gradually climbed the Dakota up to 13,500 feet to escape the turbulence of the haze layer. As we cruised along, a sudden outburst in my ear took me completely by surprise.

"Look here, Whitlock," he almost shouted, "if you buggers think I'm going to run around at this altitude serving you guys soup and sandwiches, you're mistaken."

"Take it easy," I replied, "if you're feeling rough, sit yourself down. We'll be descending any minute now in any case." By way of trying to pacify his rage, I added, "OK — next sector we'll stay lower down." Muttering, our friend returned to the cabin. The co-pilot and I had a laugh about it, and between ourselves we came up with an idea.

On the ground we made a great fuss over our engineer, apologizing for having caused him discomfort, and shortly afterwards in the early afternoon were climbing on course towards Livingstone. Making sure we were not observed, the two of us started to wind back each of our altimeters, using the sub-scale setting knob as we climbed. Having wound off three thousand feet, we levelled off at 14,000 ft. in nice smooth air above the heat turbulence and, hearing the engine note change, it was not long before our colleague showed up in the cockpit. Well aware that we were under close scrutiny, the co-pilot and myself both pointed magnanimously at our two instruments.

"There you are! Look 11,000 feet. Feeling OK now?"

Smiling, he left, and later sandwiches were served with more than the usual goodwill and many more cups of tea as well!

Later, flying in beautifully clear weather, we spotted a wisp of what looked like white smoke rising on the horizon. It was dead ahead of us, and we suddenly realized that it was the plume of spray of Victoria Falls, known as 'The Smoke that Thunders', still nearly 50 miles away. By arrangement with Air Traffic Control we circled low round the enormous, spectacular waterfall before we landed. We spent that night at the famous hotel right beside the falls, with the sound of thundering water to sooth away tiredness.

Next day we were again in the air at high altitude, heading for the newly built Jan Smuts Airport at Johannesburg, and then on to Cape Town, with our engineer scampering about in the thin air, keeping us all well supplied with refreshments, while the co-pilot and myself busily twiddled with altimeters when not under observation. It had been an amusing practical joke, but it nearly all turned to worms next night at Cape Town.

Over a few beers, the cat could no longer be kept in the bag, and the full story of the doctored altimeters was out. It was touch and go for a moment as to whether our engineer's temper would not burst upon us.

"I'm going to be looking very closely at those altimeters for the rest of this trip. Any more tricks, and it's tea over your bloody heads," he erupted, but a few beers later he was back to his old self.

Cape Town was a very different city to what it is today. There was not a high rise building in sight, only Dutch gabled buildings with plenty of old world wrought iron and everything around exuded a captivating charm.

Back in Europe, events were in turmoil. Only a few days before leaving on this flight, I had completed several flights to Malta with full loads of bombs, probably destined for Egypt during the Suez conflict. The Hungarian crisis had reached a climax, and this was the direct reason for a delegation calling at our hotel. A group of South African students and volunteers had heard that our Dakota was returning empty to Europe. They wished to make their way to Hungary to help in the uprising. I gave them a hasty quote, and sent a cable to our Head Office in London. The price was good, but when it came to putting up the money they backed down. Just as well perhaps, for as events turned out their trip might have been a one-way journey.

Sadly we said goodbye to 'the fairest Cape', and started our return to the British winter loaded down with our own purchases of fresh fruit and other goodies. The first day's flight, under perfect cobalt blue skies that are rarely seen in Europe, took us down the sandy wastes of South Africa's 'Diamond Coast'. More than one pair of eyes gazed down desirously from our Dakota thinking of king sized gems lying around just for the picking up on those strictly guarded beaches. We landed at dusty Windhoek in the burning midday sun, then on to verdant Luanda in Angola for the night. During the next two days we stopped at Doula, Gao, El Golea and Barcelona. The flight had taken us 10 days and the flying time had been 78 hours 25 minutes. At the time, it would have been sheer fiction to suggest that, less than 20 years later, an aeroplane called a 'Jumbo' would do the trip direct with hundreds of passengers in about 11 hours.

It was not much appreciated at the time, but the company started to move towards scheduled flights within the UK and to Europe. Regrettably the charter flights to exotic far away destinations, such as the Far East, India, the Middle East and Africa, were gradually tailed off and finally ceased. I greatly missed those trips abroad while shuttling back and forth between, say, Newcastle and London day after day, but it paid off handsomely for us all in the long term. While charter firms folded up in droves, we survived — just.

I often marvelled at the spirit of those early scheduled passengers in the fifties; they stoically sometimes sat through incidents and experiences that today's customers just would not put up with. One of the company's Directors had been an airline pilot in the past and, liking to keep his hand in trim, he would often turn up without any warning to announce that he would be flying the aircraft. He was very much out of practice, and all Captains knew they had to be on their toes.

My turn came sooner than expected. Transferring myself to the co-pilot's seat, I watched in fascination as the boss climbed aboard, strapped himself in, and then pulled on his legendry pair of fancy yellow knitted gloves. Having done most of the spadework, I completed the job by starting the engines and away we went. It was a normal flight, and the weather at our destination, Leeds, was moderate with the surface wind a bit blustery and slightly across the runway. Those yellow gloves would have no difficulty coping with the landing, I thought, and indeed he got the aeroplane down on the short westerly runway reasonably well. The main wheels were hardly down though, with the tail still high and rolling up the pronounced uphill slope, when a gust caught us. The Dakota swerved to the right, straight towards a very adjacent hangar. It all happened so quickly that the Managing Director barely had time to shout "Fucking hell!" This exactly echoed my own feelings, but something more than his profanity was necessary.

I had been in this situation before, giving co-pilots landings, and instant action was called for. The starboard wheel was already off the runway when I kicked full corrective rudder on viciously with my left

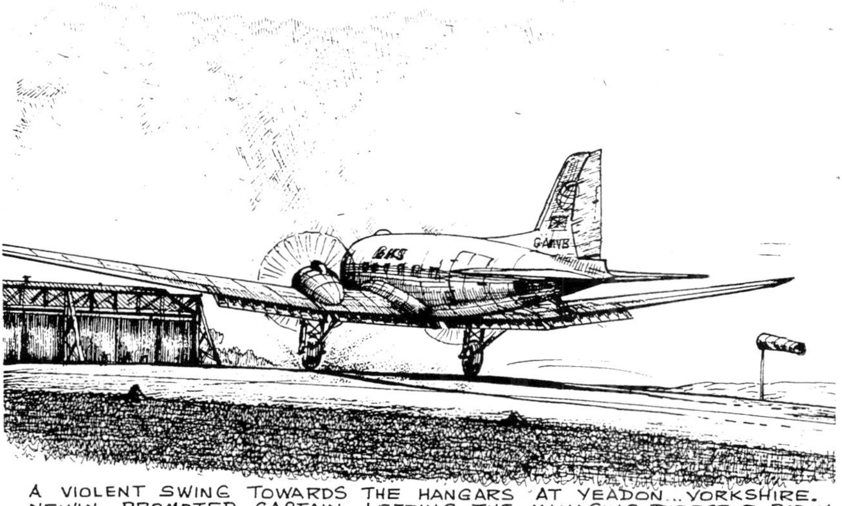

A VIOLENT SWING TOWARDS THE HANGARS AT YEADON... YORKSHIRE. NEWLY PROMOTED CAPTAIN, LETTING THE MANAGING DIRECTOR, BADLY OUT OF PRACTICE, KEEP HIS HAND IN AT LANDING... PASSENGERS ABOARD.

foot, and at the same time practically flattened the top of the rudder pedal down to the floorboards applying full left wheel brake. There was a screech of tortured rubber from the port tyre, which was fortunately still on the runway, and it held us. The oncoming hangars, which had been filling the front windscreen, moved as if in slow motion back over to the side of us where they should have been. With my pulse still racing, we taxied in and shut down the engines.

The passengers disembarked and as they filed past under the wing, fortunately on the Managing Director's side, not a few looked up scowling and muttering at our shaken leader sitting red necked up in the cockpit.

Someone said to me later, "Good thing for management to frighten themselves out of their wits occasionally flying aeroplanes, then when pilots' pay talks come round — Ha!"

It had begun to dawn upon me that a prime requirement of being a successful Captain was not only a need to stay out of trouble in an aircraft, but also the necessity of tact and consideration towards others. Being young and newly promoted, a certain element of overconfidence had perhaps started to creep in, but fortunately for all the hammering out process carried on apace. The levelling came among other happenings in the form of Murphy's famous law: 'What can go wrong, will go wrong'.

An example of this happened one day trying to land at Leeds' Yeadon Airfield in fog, which was too thick to hope to get through using the scant let down aids, so I decided to try an approach following the railway line from Harrogate, being quite acceptable in those days before landing limits. On this day a dense layer of cloud stretched over the area with Yeadon, because of its higher elevation, stuck up in the murk. Therefore we had let down through the cloud above nearby RAF Dishforth, flown underneath the cloud towards Harrogate, and then followed the railway line to Yeadon. The line went into a tunnel just near the airfield, and we knew that maintaining a heading from here would bring us over the strip.

Sure enough it worked out fine except the runway went past under the nose at an impossible angle only about fifty feet below us, but I just could not see enough to permit a tight banked circuit back on to the runway. "Overshoot," I shouted, opening up the throttles, and we climbed back up into the gloom heading back for Dishforth.

I had another card up my sleeve though, and that was opening the storm window, which would be like walking in front of a car to guide it in very thick fog, always improving vision just that little bit. The crew agreed that it might be worth one more try, and the stewardess was told to explain what was happening to our thirty-odd plucky passengers in the cabin; it being, of course, before the days of the cabin address system direct from the cockpit.

The whole exercise was repeated over again but this time, as we started to run into the fog while rushing along the railway line, I loosened the screw knobs of the clear vision storm window and shot the window across in its guides. What happened next, I would not wish to ever experience again. The metal trough, in which the window ran, had been used as an ashtray by someone previously, and as the incoming air whirled through the cockpit I caught the lot straight in my face.

Slap into my eyes and mouth came a mass of stinking ash and soggy cigarette butts, and being a non-smoker it was all the more

A NON-SMOKER GETS A FACEFUL OF CIGARETTE ENDS AND ASH, AFTER OPENING THE STORM WINDOW WHILE CIRCLING LOW OVER FOG SHROUDED YEADON AIRFIELD, YORKSHIRE.

obnoxious. I spat out a mass of the foul tasting mess, cursing vehemently, while trying to concentrate on following the railway line. The stewardess, who had been standing just behind us, handed me a tea towel she happened to be holding. Above the air noise, I shouted "Thanks" and hastily wiped my face, not daring to take my eyes off the fog-shrouded railway line racing by below for a second. I had very nearly vomited and been on the point of giving up, but that helping hand just gave me heart to continue.

With the window open I could see just that little bit better now, which made all the difference as we once again came over the airfield. I threw the aircraft immediately into a steep turn, the wing tip arcing round pointing at the ground, while the wheels and flaps were lowered in quick succession. With thumping heart I scanned the murk, and the runway came round beautifully right on to our flight path. At the last minute the wings were levelled, and seconds later we were successfully down. I remember the stewardess later passing on the congratulations of some of the regulars, such was the different world we flew in at that time.

Without any doubt some of my worst moments, during landings in those early days as a Captain, came whilst letting co-pilots fly. Many a Captain, whom I had flown with while I was a co-pilot myself,

A JOVIAL FISHERMAN OFF THE SUNDERLAND COAST... 1956.

had gone out of their way to pass on their experience and knowledge, and had stuck their necks out on countless occasions where others had simply refused to let the beginner touch the controls. They were not paid to teach people to fly was their excuse, but more likely just plain selfishness, and I had long determined never to follow that path.

On today's modern jets there is very little chance of getting into serious difficulties after a badly judged landing, and in addition extensive simulator training for new pilots lets them make most of their mistakes safely on the ground. It was a very different kettle of fish flying older piston engined aircraft, particularly those having a tail wheel.

Returning to Newcastle from Jersey in the Dakota with 32 holidaymakers aboard, the co-pilot was doing the landing. He had not flown with me before, but so far seemed to be managing quite satisfactorily, in spite of reports I had heard that he was not totally reliable. As was still the general practice at that time, he was flying the aircraft from the left hand seat and I was seated on the co-pilot's side. The problems started as he commenced his approach to land with the speed being noticeably lower than usual.

"Speed's a bit low," I called, and in response it crept up only a fraction. Now lined up on final approach with the landing gear down and the flaps going down progressively, I again prompted him to keep up his speed, but this time my demand was a bit more strident. His speed remained within the necessary limit, but still very much on the low side. At this point I began to think of taking over control; however, I decided against it. The man was very experienced, and I would discuss it with him when we got on the ground.

We were now approaching the runway with full flap down, and the speed was still very much on the low side. We would no doubt arrive like a sack of potatoes, and I would most certainly have strong words with him later. He continued down on to the runway, but I had reckoned without old Murphy. My crass colleague was just that split second too late with his final check back on the control column before the wheels contacted the ground. The aircraft bounced into the air as only a Dakota can, and we went straight up skywards. It had been done by countless pilots before but not many times, I fear, by someone with an apparent death wish like the one now sitting in my seat. In horror I felt him pull back on the control column still further without the slightest effort to increase power on the engines. Here we hung about fifty feet above the runway with the aeroplane on the very point of stalling. At any mini-second a wing would flick down and the Dakota spin in to destruction.

It really is true that one's past can flash before one, because it happened to me that day, but I did not have time to dwell on it.

"I have control," I yelled, knocking his hand off the throttles and, in the same motion, opening them up fully as quickly as I dared. My right hand had locked on to the control column, and I held it rock steady not daring to move it even a fraction forward. The engines fortunately picked up evenly and were soon roaring at full power. The air was blue with profanities as I cursed the co-pilot. Meanwhile we staggered level down the whole length of the runway, gradually building up speed as I ordered the wheels retracted and the flaps brought up in stages. While I flew the aircraft round the circuit preparatory to relanding, I asked the co-pilot in as calm a voice as I could manage, "At what bloody speed do you normally cross the fence on short finals?"

He looked at me, swallowing hard, as he replied, "75 knots."

I thought for a minute — why, that's right enough. Then it suddenly dawned. The two air speed indicators were calibrated differently with the co-pilot's in 'knots' for navigational purposes and the Captain's indicator, on which he had been flying, in 'miles per hour'. All was revealed!.— he had been aiming for the various approach and landing speeds in 'knots' and flying them on an 'MPH' instrument, but in the process had nearly killed us all. How he had overlooked this, I do not know, but it explained why he had been flying at speeds approximately 15% slower than required.

At this stage I thought it important that his confidence be restored, so I gave him a hurried briefing and handed back control to him to complete the landing. This time he managed much better, and to his credit he later bought me a double whisky saying, in the course of conversation that he had admired the way I had plucked the aeroplane out of the sky. This was all very well but, regrettably, he was the only co-pilot in my entire flying career that I was obliged to put in an adverse report on, and this was because the Operations Manager had been on the spot observing the incident from the control tower.

By coincidence the same co-pilot was again with me on a near disastrous winter's night incident at Orly Airport, Paris, but this time he was not involved at all. It had been a filthy black night with snow and low cloud as I made an approach to land. Flying down the ILS, we came out of the cloud at about 200 feet, our landing lights illuminating snowflakes rushing past. I had to do a last minute turn, very near the ground, to get on to the runway, and as I flared we ran into a heavier flurry of snow which reduced forward visibility to practically nothing. The windscreen wipers, going at full speed, made very little difference and, as it was too late to think of going round, we just ploughed on through the blanket of snow. The runway lights were just a glow, and the Dakota was sliding about in the snow as I kicked at the rudders trying to keep her straight. We did run over two or three lights, but we were on the ground safely and soon slowed down in the snow.

Greatly relieved, we taxied over to the tarmac and were soon walking away from the aircraft in gloves, hats and overcoats, thinking about the warm hotel awaiting us in Paris. We had been inside the Air France Operations Building for only a few minutes when suddenly there was a dull rumble. The floor shook and every window in the prefabricated building rattled. Our eyes were drawn to the window, where outside a fierce orange glow lit up the low cloud and falling snow. The very next instant there were two more muffled explosions, and there was no doubt in our minds over what had just happened. Everyone in that room realized in horror that an aircraft had just crashed, and a large one.

Sirens were wailing, and as I gazed at the distant holocaust the thought remained overpoweringly in my mind, as I am sure it was in everyone else's witnessing that sight, that no human being could possibly escape from such a dreadful inferno alive.

It was some time before the flames started to diminish; the snow continued to fall, and we delayed our departure for the hotel wishing to find out what had happened. The atmosphere in the Operations Room was electric, personnel were talking tensely in lowered voices in French, and the two of us were getting the occasional translation. The aircraft, which had just gone in, was apparently a Constellation. Awhile later, there was a further buzzing of voices and then the room went suddenly quiet. I edged over to enquire in a whisper from a Frenchman standing near by.

"Zay are coming, Captain, zay are coming," he whispered back tersely, and a few minutes later a strange and bedraggled column of figures shuffled into the room. Incredible! — we could not believe our eyes. These were the survivors, but how anyone could have got out of that inferno was beyond belief. All of them were wearing uniforms

SURVIVORS OF AN AIR CRASH IN A SNOWSTORM, AT ORLY AIRPORT... PARIS.

which were in tatters; some were bruised and cut, but generally looking battered and begrimed. A low gasp went up and this turned to a chorus of muffled cheering that rippled round the room. It was a most moving scene — the joy of seeing fellow human beings returning as it were from death's door. Smiling faces were all about, backs were being slapped and hands shaken. It had been a crew training flight so there had been no passengers aboard, which was most fortunate.

Gradually more information came in — the aircraft had been a Lockheed L-1649 'Starliner', the ultimate development of the famous Constellation. It looked like they had done a small turn near the ground, just as we had, but the huge wing of the Starliner had touched the ground and the aircraft had cartwheeled over. The long graceful fuselage had broken into three sections, which had been very lucky for the crew because they had been in the nose and had been able to scramble clear of the flames.

A flying licence has always been an essential part of employment as aircrew, a small enough collection of bits of paper but sometimes masking a history of its owner's sacrifices and difficulties obtaining it. To operate with a lapsed licence for even five minutes was a serious offence — it could mean the aircraft's insurance being invalidated. To fly with no licence at all in an airline, even in not so modern times, would be a near impossibility. To get away with it, without one for several years, requires sheer genius.

This is exactly what happened in the case of a certain radio operator, who shall be nameless, employed by the firm for a good many years. He was a likeable extrovert character, with a deep voiced impeccable manner of speech and the bearing of a gentleman to the core. He had been trained in radio in the services, and it had been made known that he had once been Lawrence's personal wireless operator, referring of course to Lawrence of Arabia.

The company had advertised for radio operators and the Chief Pilot had interviewed him, but when asked to produce his licence for the records there had been some stalling. The licence was up at the Ministry being renewed; in fact such was our man's bearing that the Chief Pilot retired from the interview with a strong sense of guilt at being churlish enough to have even asked to see Lawrence's Personal Wireless Operator's certificate.

And so it came about that I found myself, some months later with our recruit, landing at Lisbon on our way to West Africa. It was the custom in the mid-fifties for all aircrew transitting through Portugal to produce their licences before being permitted to continue, and here was where our problems started. Our radio operator did not have his licence with him; it was again with the Ministry being renewed! Permission to depart was denied and, as Captain, I was requested to return to the Control Office. A heated discussion developed as I vigorously defended my colleague. Couldn't they understand that the licence was being renewed, and being a hot-headed 25-year-old at the time I was becoming increasingly incensed with Britain's oldest allies, little realizing that I was playing the devil's advocate well and truly. We were finally released after I had signed a statement personally guaranteeing that the licence was valid and temporarily in the possession of our authorities. Later over a beer further down the route, our friend complimented me on my fiery defence of his case and we all laughed when he said, "By jove, Arthur, it looked like fisticuffs for a minute; your face turned so white with rage that they relented straight away."

The Ministry sleuths got him in the end, for he left the company but not before keeping many of us on our toes. My turn came during a night stop at Nice. It was about 2 o'clock in the morning when the telephone at my bedside jangled, and on the other end was the co-pilot phoning from the reception desk. He was having big problems with 'Lawrence's Personal Wireless Operator' and would I please come down to the desk. Hastily, pulling on some clothes and taking in a deep breath, I set off, wondering what it was going to be about.

The scene that greeted me was straight out of a comic opera; our radio operator had the French night porter by his coat lapels with both hands, while the co-pilot was trying to reason with his colleague, who was paying not the slightest attention, when I came upon the scene.

"Break it up," I said. "What the hell is going on? Let the guy go."

"What!" he exclaimed. "Release this bastard? Not bloody likely! When I was a prisoner of war, he was the Commandant of Stalag Luft 5."

The hotel manager was on his way; perhaps this had some influence on our friend, for we were able to prise his hands free of the night porter's collar.

"I am French, you understand, *Française*! I have never even been to Germany!" he protested indignantly.

The radio operator thrust himself forward again and shouted stridently, "Don't lie, Commandant! *Achtung*!"

But the well-known ruse had no effect whatsoever and the agitated night porter made not even the slightest attempt to jump to attention.

The manager and some other hotel staff arrived on the scene, and there was a great babble of voices, all trying to get in at once as both parties put their cases at the same time. The unfortunate porter was being denounced as 'Gestapo', and our man had been positively identified as 'ze mad drunken *Anglaise*'. I heard mention of summoning the police; the whole situation appeared to be getting out of control and it was time to take positive action. I spoke sharply to our man, telling him that if he did not let up immediately I would have to report the incident back at base.

"If you make it an order, Captain, I shall withdraw to bed."

AQUILA AIRWAYS
AN ERA SOON TO PASS.... AN AQUILA AIRWAYS 'SOLENT' FLYING BOAT, TAKING A SHORT CUT ACROSS THE FRENCH ALPS TO GENOA, OBLIGINGLY COMES IN CLOSE AS SHE GOES FAST.. SUMMER 1957.
AJW

Perhaps it was a move to save face — it would be worth a try.

"All right," I said, "retire to bed at once! That's an order." With a brief acknowledgement, to my surprise, he departed up the stairs. I made an apology to the hotel staff for the disturbance, but there always remained a small doubt in my mind.

In fact 'Lawrence's Personal W.O.' had been interned for a short while towards the end of the war, and he forever afterwards insisted that he had not been mistaken. Licensed or not, we had never had reason to complain about his efficiency while operating our aircraft's radio equipment, whereas with some of our other radio men, once aboard, anything could happen.

One old veteran radio operator was roused from his bed and taken from his hotel room at Bordeaux in the dead of night, ending up in a police cell, where he remained for over a month until his case came up. He fell victim to the practice in France of the hotel collecting all passports from guests, which were then checked by the police during the night. The aircraft was stuck in Bordeaux until a new R/O was flown out by special aircraft. The company were not at all pleased about the two day delay, and no one got to the bottom of why the arrest was made, beyond that the alleged miscreant had been the owner of a motor craft which had blown up in a great ball of fire off the Côte d'Azur many years previously.

Another R/O would spend hours during a flight chatting up the girls. How did he manage so much spare time away from his radio set was the question often asked. The answer came one day when he was caught out. We had put it down to conscientious enthusiasm how he had always insisted on accompanying the Captain and co-pilot on their pre-flight visit to the Meteorological Office, and keenly studied the weather maps. He was aboard a Dakota heading southwards, again to Bordeaux, in settled weather. A regular flow of weather reports were handed forward to the Captain from the R/O. All was well; weather at their destination was reported fair, that is until they came within range to talk to Bordeaux on R/T. A big shock awaited.

"Monsieur, are you coming to Bordeaux? But ze wezzair is below limits — we av thick fog. Ze airport has been closed all morning."

There had been a very red necked radio operator, and a very angry Captain on that trip.

Because of the seasonal nature of our flying during the years of the later mid-fifties, I began to think of trying to develop a sideline to keep busy during the slack periods of winter. It seemed natural therefore to go for something that I had been keen on since school days — drawing, and in particular drawing the comic strips.

Next to flying, and if there had been a decent living in it, strip drawing would have been my choice. So in London, spare time was spent wearing out shoe leather trudging from publisher to publisher trying to sell my work. This was not the United States, and jobs in this line were scarce and poorly paid. A small commission was eventually landed just off Fleet Street, but there was no further work available when it was completed.

However, I was given the address of someone else to try, and I soon found myself climbing six sets of rickety wooden steps to an attic office of a building scheduled for demolition in upper Gower Street. Here ruled Mr M. Anglo, 'Mick' as he became known, an amiable straight talking character who employed me on part-time contract work for more than three years. It was during the latter part of this period that conflicts arose between my flying duties and publishing deadlines. However, the start had been very slow; he had told me that he did not really need any new comic strip artists working for him, and almost reluctantly gave me only five pages to do on trial.

Clutching the script, I rushed home, got started, and soon had the set completed. It was for two weekly publications, *Marvelman* and *Young Marvelman*. The first set handed in came in for a lot of flak, but I got a half-hearted repeat order, and by the third set of pages I was making up the story as well. All this for the rock bottom rate of £2.10s per page!

With all the regular practice my work was improving, and before many months had elapsed I was told to step up deliveries. This was where my problems started to arise, for the summer season was again upon us and there was now just not the time available to meet deadlines. The solution came to me in a flash of inspiration — combine flying and drawing!

The Dakota proved to be a marvellously suitable studio, provided the weather was right, and with a co-operative co-pilot I could often complete five pages of Marvelman over a weekend's flying. This would involve setting out a page averaging six or seven frames each, pencilling in the script and pictures, and finally inking them in. In those early days of the package holiday, flying was done at a more leisurely pace; a passenger, for example, would spend about five hours in the air travelling from the south of England to, say, Corsica chugging along at a sedate 150 m.p.h.

COMIC STRIP CARTOONING.... A PROFITABLE SIDELINE CARRIED ON IN FLIGHT... THE ONLY WAY SOMETIMES, THAT DEADLINES COULD BE MET WITH THE EDITOR.... NO VISITORS WERE ALLOWED UP!

Once airborne, with the co-pilot looking after the aircraft, the drawing board would be got out, ink pot wedged beside the throttle pedestal, and work would commence. On one occasion a co-pilot, returning to his seat after a walk through the cabin, said to me, "There are a couple of kids back there reading, wait for it, yes, *Marvelman*! I didn't mention that the Captain was busy up front drawing 'em!"

Many of my colleagues in the company appeared as characters in the stories; the Airport Commandant of a certain Yorkshire Airport proudly carried around for years his own personal copy in which he

appeared as the Demon Controller. If ideas tended to be short, then I would work in my own experiences like, for example, the Hong Kong gold smuggling operation of earlier years, but on this occasion the villains came up against Marvelman and were foiled.

More than 25 years later, while browsing through a London bookshop, there on one of the shelves was Mick Anglo once again in print. He was now a successful author with several publications to his credit and, although I had lost touch with him many years before when *Marvelman* ceased being published, I hastily picked up one of the series. I found in "Nostalgia, Spotlight on the Fifties," quite a few pages devoted to the *Marvelman* comic production.

On reading further I was interested to see my name mentioned on a couple of the pages. Mick described how John Whitlock, a self-taught artist and a busy charter pilot whose passion was comic strip drawing, often used to sketch while his aeroplane was on automatic pilot. He went on to relate how I had posted to him a large packet of *Marvelman* drawings from Singapore, where a charter flight had taken me. Mick continued in a complimentary vein, talking about my drawing style compared with his other artists; he also wrote about my boldly drawn authentic aircraft introduced into the *Marvelman* series.

The three years spent working for Mick, apart from being very interesting and providing a useful income supplement, also gave me invaluable experience. Most of my contributions, bound into a thick tome, show a dramatic improvement from the first early pages to the latter ones in the volume. Publication eventually ceased because of increased pressure from foreign imports, and the original comics are now highly prized collector's items. So the era of the 'Marvelman Flying Studio' sadly came to an end and perhaps just as well, for with the coming of more complex aeroplanes there was not the time available for diversionary activities while flying.

My first summer season in command on the Dakota was spent based in Newcastle-upon-Tyne, working at an unbelievably high intensity and at the same time being in excruciating pain due to an abscessed tooth which went undiagnosed by a northern dentist. During the months of July, August and September, I had only about a dozen days off. There was always an excuse of one sort or another — the telephone would ring, "Operations here, Arthur — would you mind working on your day off?" Or maybe, "Will you help us out by doing an extra flight?" And so it went on. It was good to get over that slogging first summer, and a more proficient dentist soon sorted out my tooth trouble.

On the Dakota we usually carried 32 passengers, with only one stewardess to look after them and the crew. As can be imagined, in the air she was a very busy person indeed; she would have to serve coffee and biscuits, perhaps a meal, then follow this up with a bar service, and in between all this the work would be duplicated looking after the crew, to say nothing of the considerable aircraft duties too.

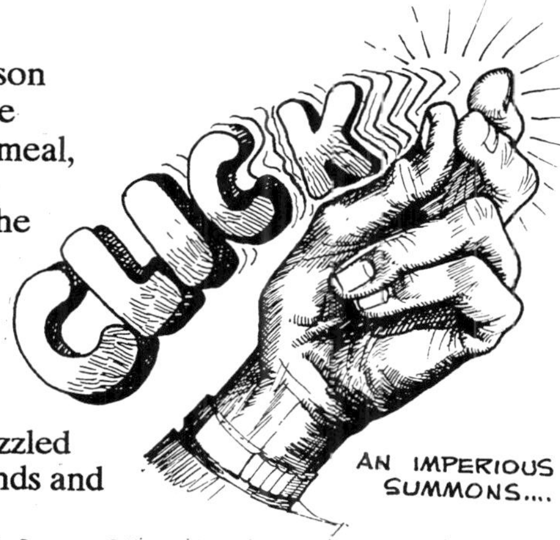

AN IMPERIOUS SUMMONS....

One day I happened to visit the passenger cabin, and was puzzled to see our stewardess on her hands and knees in the aisle imitating a dog. I could hear her going "Woof, woof," and calling, "Rover! Here Rover!" under the seats among the passenger's legs. When she saw me she nonchalantly got up, giving one particular passenger an icy look while saying something to him which I did not catch, and carried on with her duties. There was one very red-necked traveller, and the passengers sitting in the adjacent seats seemed to be highly amused, so when I had worked my way aft I asked to be let in on the joke. Our

.... AND THE FACETIOUS RESPONSE.

stewardess's feathers were still slightly ruffled as she replied, "We've got another one of the clicking fingers brigade on board over there. Who do they think they are calling for service like that?"

I laughed as she related how she had said to the offensive passenger, "Sorry, Sir, I haven't been able to find that dog for whom you were clicking your fingers."

Round about this time, quite an exodus of pilots occurred leaving the company to join other firms flying larger four-engined aircraft. At the beginning of that summer, therefore, Captains were urgently required. The policy had been to try to promote co-pilots from within the firm before recruiting Captains from outside. We had a co-pilot in the firm who had seen war service and had risen to a high officer's rank before being shot down over occupied France in a Halifax. He had spent the rest of the war in Colditz. Perhaps this had affected him because he tended towards fairly heavy drinking, which made him very highly strung and shaky while flying. This got progressively worse as the years went by, but as the Chief Pilot was pushed for Captains at that time, he decided to give him a chance.

There was much muttering among co-pilots who had to fly with him and all sorts of strange stories started to get around. The season had not progressed far when the half-expected incident did indeed happen. One Dakota, with a full load of passengers on the way to Jersey, was flying over Wiltshire when one of the engines started to vibrate very badly, and it got steadily worse.

It would have to be shut down before it shook itself clear off the wing. The co-pilot's story was that it was difficult to judge if the engine was shaking as much as the Captain's hands, as he agonized on what action to take next. Reluctantly he closed the throttle and mixture control on the shaking engine, and as it ran down order and smoothness started to return to the aeroplane. It now remained to feather the engine to tidy up, but unfortunately the trembling hand reached up and pressed the wrong feathering button. Pandemonium reigned as he had feathered the wrong engine. Everything began to go quiet as their Dakota slowed and started downwards with both engines dead.

The co-pilot realized immediately what had gone wrong, and took the initiative as the aircraft glided down earthwards. He went about trying to restart the good engine, which involved pulling back the propeller pitch lever, the throttle and then the fuel mixture control. Operating the feathering button again controlled an electric

DRAMA OVER WILTSHIRE... A PILOT WHO SHUT DOWN THE WRONG ENGINE.

pump which, through hydraulic pressure, forced the three stationary propeller blades to twist and once again form an angle to the air-stream. Meanwhile in the cabin, passengers had been subjected to a period of semi-weightlessness with a decidedly sinking feeling in the pits of their stomachs. It was with great relief indeed that they heard the engine roar back to life again, and between the two of them they nursed the Dakota back to base.

The Captain with the shaking hands reverted to co-pilot again, but even in that capacity continued to be a source of potential disaster; in later years several pilots, including myself, had narrow escapes involving him before he finally had to retire from aviation medically unfit through a nervous breakdown and alcoholism.

I had been tempted to find pastures new, flying larger aircraft, and with this in mind took two weeks' leave. A friend had arranged for me to do a freelance trip as navigator on a four-engined Avro York, and if I liked the set up I would change company. Because I was being paid cash for the flight, I had nothing to lose. The trip was an Air Ministry charter carrying freight from Lyneham in Wiltshire to RAF Changi in Singapore.

On a wintry January morning in 1957 the old York lumbered

into the air with the unforgettably smooth drone of four Rolls-Royce Merlin engines at take-off power. It was impressive enough, but it did not take me long to realize that the big machine had definitely seen better days. Flying towards Brindisi late that afternoon I got an early demonstration of the aircraft's mediocre performance. As we crossed the Italian Apennines at about 9,500 feet we became caught in a downward flowing standing wave over the mountains, and we needed maximum continuous power on those four Merlins for a full 20 minutes to get us clear of the downdrafts.

The heating in the Avro York seemed to be non-existent, and we shivered over Turkey when bad weather forced us to climb to 17,000 feet to clear mountains in the area. I tried not to even think about the disastrous consequences of engine failure as we bounced around in thick cloud with rocky crags buried in them passing below us. We all had oxygen masks hanging loosely in front of our faces. As I inhaled the life-giving stuff, I was the first to notice the smell of burning and alerted the Captain on the intercom. It was not long before smoke started to pour from a radio set opposite the navigator's position where I sat. I grabbed an adjacent fire extinguisher but fortunately did not have to use it, as the radio operator had hastily wrenched out the power supply socket and with the side windows open the smoke gradually dispersed.

That evening we really enjoyed a cool beer at Habaniya in Iraq, and the rest of the trip was fairly relaxing in between navigational duties. As we crossed the vast expanses of Arabia, India and Burma, there was even time to get through quite a bit of work on some pages for *Marvelman*.

At Rangoon the scene for me changed to engineering duties when one of our engines developed ignition trouble.

"Give me a hand to change the plugs will you, Mate?" said our engineer. I soon found out that there was more to this than met the eye as there were no ladders or trestles available. It was a precarious perch — a fall would have meant a few broken bones at the least — and with the cowlings off I handed Joe fresh plugs, taking the old ones, all 24 of them almost red hot.

Squatting up there sweating in the midday sun of Burma, I had time to reflect on the age of these aeroplanes; the radio set that through sheer fatigue had gone on fire over the Turkish mountains, these oil streaked cowlings, and the rattling and dented fuselage — perhaps I was better off staying with my present firm. Somebody must

RANGOON.... EN ROUTE SINGAPORE, WINTER 1956/7... HELPING THE FLIGHT ENGINEER CHANGE A SET OF SPARK PLUGS ON A MISFIRING MERLIN ENGINE OF OUR AVRO YORK.... SOME MONTHS LATER, HE WAS TRAGICALLY KILLED IN THIS SAME AIRCRAFT, IN A CRASH NEAR DELHI.......

have been looking after me that day in far off Rangoon when I made my decision atop the old York's wing because, by staying put, my company was taken over about 20 years later and seniority got me on to wide bodied jets.

Our trip out to Singapore went without any further hitches, and twelve days after leaving we were back in Wiltshire again; the old aeroplane even indirectly obliged by giving us all a laugh some time after landing. Our radio operator had been on a very heavy duty-free shopping spree while in Singapore. Japanese binoculars, cameras, watches, booze and cigarettes had been hidden carefully up in the wing main spar area where it ran across the cabin roof. The five of us crew members dutifully trooped into Customs and made our declarations; we had all paid a bit of duty, and I did notice that the R/O had paid his by cheque. We then went along to the RAF Mess to have a meal, and were getting to the end of it when two burly Customs officers walked up to our table. In a stern tone he called the radio operator's name. The man went as white as a sheet, swallowing hard and steadying himself with uncertain arms as he rose shakily to his feet covered in confusion. For sure, I thought, the cache had been found and the game was up — a full confession would be blurted out by the demoralized R/O at any minute now.

"You haven't dated the cheque," said the Revenue man.

An undisguised look of relief, that must surely have aroused their suspicions, spread across the miscreant's face as he eagerly seized a pen, dated the cheque, and with a nervous cough returned it. The York was later flown empty on a short hop back to base, after which our colleague's booty was unloaded at leisure and found its way safely home.

Over the years I was to notice a marked decline in such illegal importing operations by aircrew; the direct reason was the gradual

SURPRISE VISIT TO A FRENCH NUDIST COLONY NEAR BORDEAUX, 1957.

THE 'VICKERS VIKING' CABIN, WITH THE WING MAIN SPAR RUNNING RIGHT THROUGH IT..... A POPULAR AREA TO CHOOSE TO SIT TO WATCH THE MOUNTAINEERING EFFORTS OF THEIR AIR HOSTESS......

improvement in salaries, conditions of service and pensions, all of which could be forfeited if caught.

On return to the fold it was back to flying Dakotas and Vikings on less exotic routes, but still always full of unexpected surprises. It was Son Bonnet again, Palma de Majorca's old airport, and we had floated down through the hot afternoon air in our Dakota, over the olive trees at the end of the runway. The tarred strip was none too long, and on a hot summer's day was always slippery and molten. The Dakota had settled down nicely on the main wheels, and the tail was just beginning to settle, when out of the corner of my eye I glimpsed a figure on a bicycle. In horror I saw him cycle straight across in front of our aeroplane. He was wearing a floppy broad brimmed hat and perhaps that was why he had not yet seen us.

I started to put on left rudder to brake, and we began to pull over to the side of the runway; we could edge over no further because of the lights. We were still racing along, and I resigned myself to colliding with him. At that second he must have heard us or popped out of his day-dream for his head turned, and a look of blank amazement cracked across his face. With an absolutely frenzied effort on the pedals, which I was surprised did not snap the chain, he just managed to pass clear of us under the starboard wing tip.

When I had finished doing a Fred Astaire on the rudder pedals to get the aircraft back into the middle of the strip and she had slowed down, I grabbed the hand microphone as soon as my left hand was free. I was badly shaken, and found myself shouting into the mike at the Tower, demanding to know the meaning of what a cyclist was doing crossing the runway in front of our landing aircraft. This line of enquiry did not seem to do much good.

A CAREFREE SPANIARD CROSSING THE RUNWAY AT SON BONNET AIRFIELD, PALMA. PASSENGERS WONDERED WHY THEIR DAKOTA SWERVED SUDDENLY AFTER LANDING.

"What cyclist, Captain? We do not see any cyclist from ze tower Señor."

Indeed there was no cyclist to be seen; he had long since disappeared among the olive trees further along the strip.

The old aerodrome of Son Bonnet, a few miles NE of Palma, is well worth a visit, even perhaps today. The terminal building was built much on the same lines as Croydon, with the airline check-in desks bordering the central hall and adjoining this was a restaurant where, in summer, meals could be taken outside on a patio under the vines. When last heard of the building was disused, but it was at our ticket counter in the terminal that my education commenced on the complex problem of dealing with difficult passengers.

I remember walking across to the desk, and was soon engrossed in preparing the load sheet and attending to other documentation. I had taken little notice of a group of returning holidaymakers, who were being a bit noisy and looked as though they had been at the bottle a bit. I had just completed the paperwork when my uniform hat was knocked right off my head to the accompaniment of scattered laughter.

I turned round, beginning to look very foolish indeed, to see a large man with face wreathed in an oily smirk inspecting me from under a large straw hat. As he stood there unsteadily, I slowly replaced my pen in my coat pocket while taking note of the hat that was too good an opportunity to miss. Both of my hands shot up and firmly grasped the rim of the hat, pulling it downwards as hard as I could. It proved to be more effective that I could possibly have hoped for as our friend's head disappeared into the recesses of the hat and the sweat band seemed to pop into position under his chin sort of locking the head inside. Trying to act as nonchalantly as possible, I picked up my uniform hat, dusted it off, and placed it back on my head. Beside me, our obstreperous passenger was wriggling in twisted contortions as he struggled to extricate himself from the imprisoning hat. The party, who had been with our friend, were now roaring with laughter at the spectacle of the swaying figure, and I gave them a friendly wave as I attempted a dignified exit from that hilarious scene.

I had been lucky on that occasion as all the participants had taken it in good part. Incidents with unruly passengers that followed years later took an entirely different form, and I made a mental note not to try to push my luck that far again.

THE UNDIGNIFIED LOSS OF A HAT AND HOW TO DEAL WITH A MERRY PASSENGER.........

CHAPTER 7

Passenger loads were increasing, competition was hotting up, and the customers were going for quicker and more comfortable flights. Our old Vikings and Dakotas were becoming badly outclassed, and as usual hand-downs were becoming available. In those days the Independent Airlines would snap up the cast-offs of the State Corporations, who were themselves moving up the scale, and early in the year 1958 our company acquired one Airspeed Ambassador from British European Airways with an option on three more. Once again, like the Viking before, it was decreed that this was far too hot a ship for a Junior Captain to be let anywhere near. Certainly the aircraft was a big step forward; it was pressurized which was something new, the two staged supercharged engines were the ultimate in piston power produced by Great Britain, and the 4 bladed propeller had a massive diameter of 16 feet, but above all the aircraft had a grace of line that was beauty itself. The finely tapered wings were set above the perfectly streamlined body, which swept rearwards to the aircraft's three vertical fins. Passengers loved travelling in it with its unobstructed view downwards through the large side windows. The aircraft seated 55 passengers, and was an immediate success. The finance houses were persuaded to put up yet more money, and very shortly three more Ambassadors were acquired.

The story changed overnight; we would after all be allowed to fly the new aircraft sooner than expected, which was now a case of necessity. A hand-out of notes, some intensive study, followed by a technical examination, and flying training commenced. The aeroplane's performance was breathtaking compared to the Dakota, the steerable nose wheel made life very much easier, and because of this the pilots' seats were much closer to the ground which accentuated the extra speed even more.

Sadly to say, my flying training did not get off to a very auspicious start; on the second day of circuits and landings at Southend Airport, disaster struck. There had been five of us in the aeroplane; I had just completed my stint of flying, and was sitting down below the level of the pilots at the radio operator's desk while someone else had a go.

The Ambassador had just landed, and I could feel the brakes start to go on, when suddenly there was an almighty lurch followed by a jarring sideways crash. The air was instantly filled with the scream of grinding metal and the clanging of the propeller blades as they thrashed at the runway. The motion finally ceased, and as usual in such cases everything thereafter seemed to happen in slow motion. Looking upwards I saw the Training Captain, who was also the Operations Manager, reach out and snap off both fuel cut-off switches. Silence now reigned and no one moved. The first words to break the stillness sounded almost deafening. A rich Yorkshire accent exclaimed, "Thut's fooked it," adding, "we've got three greens?"

Sure enough, there were the three green lights shining at us from the instrument panel indicating that all the wheels were indeed safely locked down.

After that events happened fast. I grabbed a nearby fire extinguisher, and had the door open in a trice. Outside there was fortunately no sign of fire, but our fine aeroplane was now a sorry sight. We gathered dejectedly on the runway to inspect the damage; the propeller blades were all bent into grotesque shapes, the bottom of the fuselage and the engine nacelle were bent, and the collapsed main gear had pushed up a rod which had damaged the wing resulting in the wing-tip itself being twisted after coming into contact with the ground.

The cause of the trouble had been that part of the wheel casting had cracked, allowing the twin wheels to turn as the aircraft slowed. The strain had broken a down strut, which had then let the whole leg collapse. We sadly left the aeroplane in the hands of our engineers, who undoubtedly heard the cash registers ring for they were immediately put on overtime to get the Ambassador repaired in time to meet its summer flying programme.

Flying our new aircraft was a pleasure, but the company's schedules were sometimes crippling — starting at seven in the morning and finishing at ten at night, and in between flying no less than six sectors, was a regular occurrence.

In spite of her beauty, over the next few years, the aircraft was to give me some of my worst moments, and it was a great pity that in her later years she was to become a deadly killer because of a simple weakness in the design of her flap mechanism. However, that was all to come much later; in the meantime flying hours and confidence built up on this type.

We had not been going more than a few months when 55 passengers, 4 crew and myself came within a hair's breath of biting the dust. The 'someone up there' was cutting it very, very fine indeed on that day as we completed our take-off and climbed away out of Edinburgh Airport still under their control. Because at that time there was very little liaison between civil and military controls, the presence of a twin-engined Anson was not known to Edinburgh, and unknown to us it was heading our way.

The climb performance of the Ambassador was excellent, and she went up with a pronounced nose-up attitude which restricted vision a little through the very small cockpit windows. The co-pilot had his head down making a start with his paperwork, and as I flew the aircraft I looked up at the magnetic compass, which was mounted right in the middle of the front windscreen. The compass was a huge affair about the size of a large grapefruit with a mirror below it. As I glanced up into the compass through the mirror, I thought I noticed a movement at the side of the mirror. I moved my head sideways on impulse, and my blood froze. There coming straight towards us on a collision course was a twin-engined aircraft. Our closing speed must have been more than 300 m.p.h. They were upon us the next instant. My left hand had started to push the control column forward, and my right hand was darting towards the throttles to close them but it never even got anywhere near them. There was a sudden roar, above the noise of our own engines, and it came and went in a split second — in the blink of my eye I saw the metal rivets on the passing engine cowling.

The co-pilot jumped in his seat at the sudden noise and the passing of the dark shadow, as the other aircraft shot right over the top of us. I ducked my head instinctively awaiting the impact as we continued upward, but it did not come and we had been spared. For a few seconds we were too shocked to even utter a word. Words were spoken and reports were filed, and no doubt it all helped nudge the Ministry towards introducing better ground radar coverage over the years that followed. The RAF Anson must have cleared our propellers and triple tail fins by a hair's breath; a few feet lower and we would have been scattered over the Scottish hills.

Smooth though the Ambassador was, she was soon to bite me, and bite me very severely indeed. The situation crept up on me very subtly as they frequently do in aviation, and eventually built up to a desperate fight for survival.

BRUSHED VERY CLOSELY BY THE SHADOW OF FATE, AFTER TAKE-OFF FROM EDINBURGH... THE NEAREST MISS OF A FLYING CAREER.........

It all started on a return flight to Newcastle from Dublin. The weather was none too good; a complex frontal system covered the whole of our route over the Isle of Man and Carlisle with continuous heavy clouding extending solidly up to about 14,000 feet. The co-pilot was very experienced, but tended to be erratic in difficult situations and for this reason had not yet been promoted. The third crew member was an irrepressibly humorous Geordie named Bill, who was along to do the refuelling and to take care of any snags. In addition, we were carrying a radio/electrical man, who was aboard to observe and try to clear up a persistent radio compass snag on the aircraft, and he had been carrying out checks on the previous sector on the radio gear below and behind the pilot's seat. In the main cabin we had 50 passengers attended on by two stewardesses.

We took off from Dublin, climbing soon into the heavy clouds above us, and set course north-eastwards to pass over the Isle of Man. All seemed to be going normally, so I left the co-pilot to get on with the navigation and steer the aircraft through the automatic pilot, while I caught up with some paperwork.

About 15 minutes later, I sensed something amiss; perhaps it was the co-pilot nervously winding the radio compass tuning knob on the box above his head, with the electrician on his hands and knees on the floor. The co-pilot's reply to my query was unconvincing, "Still trying to tune Deans Cross beacon."

"It's a fairly powerful one — should be able to get it from here," I said.

After a further few minutes, the compass needle was still wandering aimlessly round the dial, pointing to nowhere in particular, so it was time I took a hand.

"Call Preston Control," I said. "Ask them if it's working." Very strangely there was no answer to that call — just silence. I turned round and looked down at the radio engineer, who now had panels off and was surrounded by electrical gear on the floor. Something was not at all right here. I leaned over to check the co-pilot's navigation log, and he was positive we had passed over the Isle of Man radio beacon at the time written on the log. I checked the aircraft's heading on both the gyrosyn compasses, one in front of me and the other on the co-pilot's side, and all was in order.

I then reached out for the mirror below the magnetic compass, and moving it I looked up into the compass. I nearly choked in horror, as the heading on the magnetic compass was about 60 degrees off what was at present showing on the two gyro compasses, which explained the silence on the radio — we were miles off course and out of range.

My throat suddenly went dry, and there was a dull pain deep in my chest; I had to force myself to fight back panic. Had the radio engineer disturbed the electrical supplies to the gyro compasses? How long had we been diverging from where we should have been? My best guess was that we must be far to the north. I had already turned the aircraft due east using the magnetic compass. Could the gyrosyn compasses be trusted any more? I told the radio engineer to cease whatever work he had been doing and put everything back to the state he had found it.

"Switch to the emergency frequency, and put out a call," I said to the co-pilot. We were still flying in thick cloud as I outlined my intentions to the crew.

"We'll fly for 20 minutes due east and then start a descent. We should break cloud over the North Sea; then we'll fly due west and try to locate ourselves on the coast."

The co-pilot's face seemed to be taking on a blank expression, so I told him to plot our assumed course on his chart and to keep calling on the R/T. There was no point in holding a court of enquiry now; we had to extricate ourselves somehow from this very serious situation.

The radio compasses were dead, even when tuned to powerful ground stations in the area of NW England. Radar on the ground or radar aboard our aircraft would have solved our problem immediately, but that was years away. All I could pin our hope on was the magnetic compass, and aviation experience had taught that this basic instrument rarely failed unless someone had put down a beer tin or other ferrous metal next to it.

Looking across at the co-pilot I could see that work had not yet started on his chart — books, dividers and paper lay about as he looked across at me.

"Can't find my protractor, Arthur."

I was beginning to lose my patience as I reached into my briefcase, pulled out my own, and slapped it down rather perfunctorily on the pile of paper on his lap.

We were still ploughing along through thick cloud; just one break in it would have served us fine, but none came. In the meantime the co-pilot's hasty air plot confirmed my guesses, and we continued on our 20 minutes of easterly flight. It was almost with relief that the time came for descent, and the hoped for sight of the sea far below the cloud. If wrong we were all perfectly well aware of the peril we faced with a sudden final rush into a Scottish mountainside. Back came the throttles, and we started on our way down. The deep throated howl of the huge Centaurus engines eased as the superchargers were taken out in turn.

We descended through 10,000 feet still flying blind, and the altimeter needle continued to unwind through 5,000 feet. The cloud was getting blacker but wisps of it were flashing past the cockpit windows.

"Could be breaking up," I called.

Then suddenly we flashed into a small clear patch.

"Christ," I shouted, "mountains!"

It was a shattering blow — rocky hillsides where there should have been sea, and that pain in the chest had returned. Four pairs of eyes were now straining to see what lay ahead through the small cockpit windows.

I had already started to open up the throttles, uttering a choking profanity, and adding, "We'll have to get back up again." I cringed at the thought of climbing back up into all that solid accursed cloud.

At that moment one of the stewardesses entered the cockpit, having heard the power go on, quite understandably she wished to know what was going on. She was a very efficient and well respected girl, and I would not have dreamed of being on anything but my best behaviour when addressing her, but these were far from normal times. I remember replying to her query out of the corner of my mouth as I desperately concentrated on peering ahead.

"Alma, I'm afraid we're in the shit."

For that ungentlemanly remark, I was to later apologize most profusely, but for the moment my eyes were on the instrument panel as we climbed in cloud once again.

Then quite unexpectedly we flew into another clear patch. I levelled the aircraft at 4,500 feet which should take us safely above any mountains on offer in Scotland. Over to starboard of us, through very ragged black cloud, a glimpse of water was just visible that looked very murky indeed under there — was it one of the Scottish lakes and a dead end surrounded by mountains, or the open sea? We were all looking at it now as I banked the aeroplane towards it.

"I'm going to go down through that hole. Everyone happy?"

I got a chorus of unenthusiastic assents. Back came the throttles, and down we went once again.

It got blacker and blacker, but we managed to keep contact with the water. The Ambassador was now slipping along below the general cloud layer at about 500 feet, with rain falling in patches all about us. We seemed to be flying in an estuary. There were foreboding black mountains over to our left partly obscured by rain, and ahead of us stretched that blessed sight — the sea — just visible through the patchwork of showers.

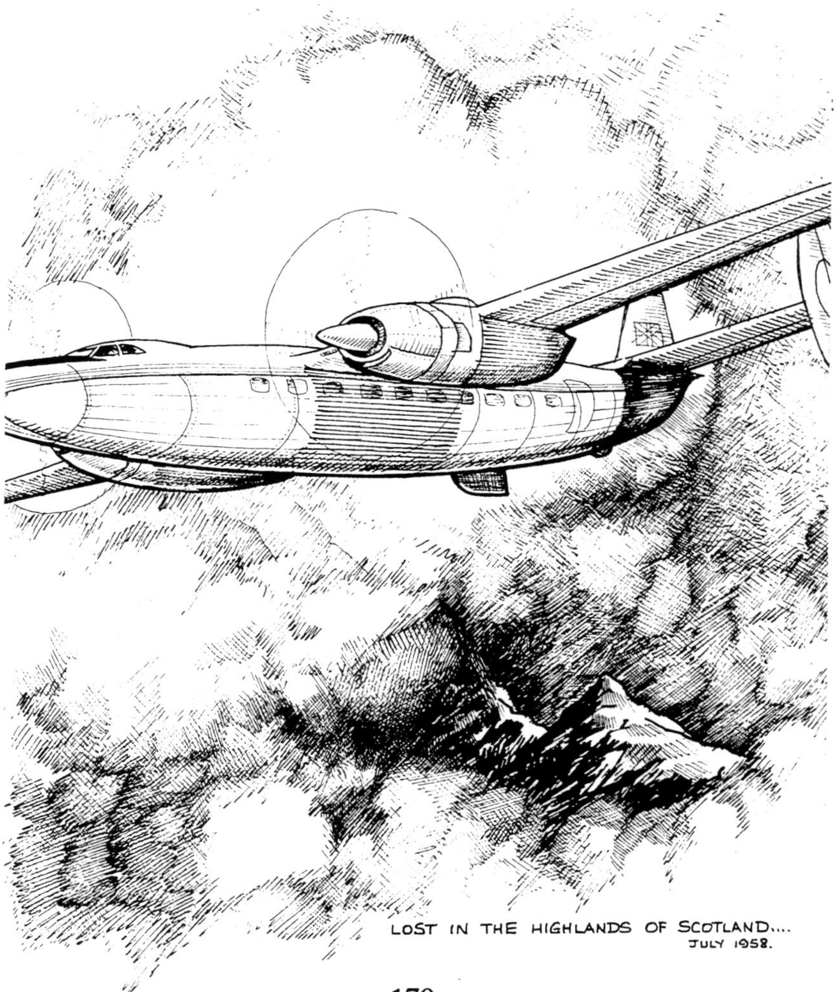

As we swept along towards the open sea, there was no time to waste — we must find out where we were. With both windscreen wipers working furiously on the glass in front of us, I banked the aircraft to port and headed back westwards towards the land. The two engineers were now clinging to the backs of the pilots' seats and peering over our shoulders, one was standing on the radio operator's table and the other on part of the seat platform. All eyes were peering ahead through the murk, and a long low bridge could just vaguely be made out coming up in the distance.

"Well, that's not the Forth Bridge," I exclaimed.

The co-pilot must have misheard me, or perhaps he was clinging to a straw. In an excited tone, he shouted almost triumphantly, "It's the Forth Bridge."

For the second time that day I lost my patience with him and raised my voice, "Don't be a bloody idiot. You've seen the arches of the Forth Bridge enough times."

Which bridge was it? No inspiration at all came to my numbed mind and as we continued to race over the water towards it, a voice came from behind me.

"I think it's the Tay Bridge, Arthur!" It was Bill, our flight engineer, still hanging on behind the co-pilot's seat. We swept low over the bridge, and buildings and roofs of what looked like a large town could be seen on our right.

A few seconds later, a female voice spoke into my ear.

..... FOUND AGAIN! IDENTIFYING THE TAY BRIDGE.....

"I've just seen Dundee Cake Works written in large letters on a factory roof."

I smiled in appreciation. "Good for you, Alma." Little did she realize how much help that confirmation had been. She had slipped back and had had a look out of one of the cabin windows. What it was to have help when needed! Dundee and the Tay Bridge it was, but we were flying up a dead end with hills coming up again through the murk ahead. I wheeled the aircraft left, and headed south-eastwards.

What a relief it was to know where we were once again. Shortly afterwards we got our first answer on the emergency frequency from RAF Leuchars, and asked them to relay a message with our position to our destination: Newcastle. We continued along the Scottish coast, our altitude never more than 1,000 feet, carefully map reading and never out of sight of the coast. As we crossed the border, visibility started to get worse; meanwhile in the cabin our two stewardesses, who had been keeping the passengers informed, were able to tell them the good news that we should be down in 15 minutes.

As we approached Newcastle, the coastline could barely be seen now looking nearly downwards, and at this point we climbed to enable the airfield radar to identify us. The airfield in these times was surrounded by fairly high slag heaps from the coal-mines; the huge black pyramids have long since been sold off very profitably for roadmaking, but before that were treated with great respect by pilots. The radar operator, who talked us down that day, was a young lady with a very high reputation for skill, and she did a first class job as our steering was somewhat erratic.

As we taxied in, we were well over an hour overdue and, up until that time in my aviation career, I had never experienced such fear as on that flight. I could now begin to appreciate how my Captain had felt when we had been lost over the Sahara between Kano and El Fasher many years before.

Our near disastrous exploit had no repercussions; various reports had to be filed, and I was relieved when no blame was attached to myself.

When I climbed out of the aircraft at Newcastle late that morning after my harrowing experience, I could have done with a week off. All that happened was that I found myself completing the rest of my day's flying programme, missing my lunch and again going to Dublin but happily in a different aeroplane.

My stars during the month of July 1958 must have been extremely badly placed, because before that month was out I was again involved in another adrenalin stimulating exercise. We were flying the flagship of the fleet, the same Ambassador that had dumped us unceremoniously on the runway at Southend when her starboard undercarriage had collapsed. Her registration was G-AMAD and we referred to her respectfully as 'Alpha Delta'. This night in July, we brought her back through difficulties to a safe standstill on terra firma at Heathrow to a spot on the grass where Terminal One now stands. That same spot was within feet of where she was destined to end her flying days, with a final death plunge into the then as yet incomplete terminal building 10 years later almost to the day.

Our problems had started at the end of a long day, slave labour by today's standards, with a duty day of 19 hours and 30 minutes over five sectors of flying. It was the sort of duty time that would probably put today's airline Captain in prison for breaking the law! We had started at Southend, had been to Toulouse, Palma, Toulouse, and were now wending our way northwards in darkness with the lights of Paris just coming into sight. Aboard were 55 passengers returning from holiday. I was looking forward to getting back to Southend, having a beer or two, and then getting home.

There were four of us aboard: two pilots, a radio operator and an engineer, who was none other than the Chief himself, which was very good because the 'technical difficulties' that were shortly to follow could be observed at first hand. Quite by chance I happened to be the first one to observe the fault. It was usual during flight for an electric motor to cut in at intervals to top up the hydraulic pressure, and this made quite a racket. It had not happened for some time, so I leaned across towards the co-pilot's lower instrument panel and pressed the override button to do the job. Nothing happened! I repeated the operation, but still not a peep out of the motor. I could not believe it — the switch was supposed to be foolproof! I was exceedingly tired after our long day's flog, so was quite content to turn to Johnny, our chief engineer, and leave the problem to him, but it did not look good.

Johnny was a man of massive proportions; 'hands the size of hams' must have been coined with him in mind. He had a reputation of getting a sick aeroplane serviceable whether the aeroplane liked it or not. With an amiable grunt, Johnny tried the button again; an enormous forefinger stabbed down on the button once more, but it was as dead as a doornail.

With the twinkling lights of Paris now spread out prettily below us, the implications of the fault struck home — we were going to be without our main wheel brakes on landing. The Ambassador was a very sleek aeroplane indeed, presenting very little frontal area once on the ground except for her flaps. The aeroplane had originally been built with reversing propellers, but they had long since been withdrawn due to unreliability. To make matters worse, the touchdown speed was high, and the brakes were therefore the only means of bringing her to a standstill after landing. The needle of the pressure gauge was now reposing uselessly on zero. There was a back-up system that was designed to give six applications of brake when fully charged, but this was topped up by the same motor and, even worse, was steadily leaking away before our very eyes.

A few minutes before, I had been pleasantly relaxed gazing down at the lights of Paris, and now with the adrenalin jolted into full flow a frantic hunt for an escape route commenced. To continue to Southend was now right out of the question — the fairly short runway was always an adventure getting into at the best of times. There was a menacing bunker at one end, designed to stop aeroplanes overrunning the road beyond, and a steep ditch and a railway line at the other end. To make matters worse, rain was reported sheeting down all over the south of England. We were going to need the longest airfield available.

While checks on the fuses were being made by our engineer, we were now nearly across the Channel. I informed the controller of our problem, and told him that we would be diverting to Heathrow. Descending through the stormy clouds, we commenced our re-routing. The aeroplane was now bumping around in the turbulence of the lower levels, and the glow from the instrument panel fell on eyes and hands while voices were busy making preparations for this last minute change in plan. The needle of the reserve accumulator, on which we were relying, was creeping ever lower; I had to force myself not to dwell on it too long.

As the ground controller gave us radar headings to steer, a steady downpour of rain was drumming against the cockpit windscreens. A last final turn put us on the extended centre line of the runway, and we began our landing run in, using the Instrument Landing System centre and glide path beams. We were descending steadily but during all this our radio operator, sitting behind and below me at his desk, had decided to check and retune the radio beacon using the remote tuning facility near his desk. The wrong time to be doing this in any case, but when he had finished, he inadvertently pressed the wrong selector button.

"Bloody hell," I shouted in dismay, "we've lost the ILS."

The two bars, that I had been concentrating on keeping in the central spot on the instrument in front of me, flew off the scale. Our chief engineer took it up instantly. He was standing between the co-pilot and myself, peering ahead through the blackness and sheeting rain, and had fortunately spotted the movement of the radio operator's hand. There was a loud exclamation near my right ear.

"Cunt," and this was followed by a thud, as Johnny's massive hand batted the unfortunate R/O across the head. The ILS instantly came back on again, and a quick adjustment, as we descended earthwards through the blackness, brought us back onto our approach path.

All this had taken place at about 600 feet, and shortly afterwards we began to see the occasional light float past below us through the rain. At last the runway lights came into view through the arcs of wet glass that the windscreen wipers were slashing away at trying to keep clear. As we crossed the runway threshold, I pushed the aircraft down early so as to take advantage of every foot of concrete. The main wheels splashed down, and I followed this by lowering the nose wheel as quickly and gently as possible on to the streaming runway with the control column.

The moment of truth was now upon us as I steadily depressed the tops of the rudder pedals to apply the brakes, and we began to slow down. We were still doing about 80 m.p.h. when, to my dismay, the pedals went slack, flopping forwards. That was the end of our brake pressure; the wretched system had not even given us a fraction of what we had expected and we were still going far too fast. The tower had previously advised us that, if we were going to leave the runway and had any control over this, they then would prefer we did so to the right as there was more open space available there. The rain-soaked grass would do a better job slowing us down, so while we still had rudder control, I started to edge on right rudder and we gradually drifted off the runway.

Thoughts raced through my mind; it would be useful to keep the engines idling in case a burst from either was needed to keep us clear of any obstructions, but we would slow down a lot quicker with them stopped. Still some distance away, I could just make out two brick

BRAKE FAILURE ON A STORMY NIGHT...... FOLLOWED BY AN UNCONTROLLED RUN ACROSS GRASS AT HEATHROW, WHERE TERMINAL BUILDINGS NOW STAND........

huts, but it looked like we should clear them or even stop before then. I also thought of my trump card; we could deliberately retract the wheels — that would stop us soon enough if we were going to hit anything!

"Cut the engines!" Both the fuel cut-off switches were snapped off, the two big Centaurus engines immediately faded, and the propellers started to run down. Now there was silence, and very alarming it was to be running across an airfield in darkness and rain totally out of control. I placed my right hand on the undercarriage lever with its nearby override switch, and this gave me a lot more confidence as I watched the brick huts getting closer. It became a case of 'will we hit them, will we not'. The three of us, peering through the cockpit windscreen, watched spellbound as the nearest building just cleared the port wing, and our aeroplane finally stopped.

The usual procession of fire engines and ambulances arrived on the scene, and then departed after checking that all was in order. The aircraft's emergency lights were turned on to illuminate the main cabin, and just the sound of the rain falling on the aeroplane broke the silence, until eventually a coach arrived and the passengers were disembarked.

My attention now turned to less, or more important happenings depending on viewpoint, namely six large bottles of Bacardi rum. As a special concession, HM Customs at Southend kept a book allowing aircrew based at Southend to bring in a bottle a month, and unfortunately we had chosen this flight to ship in our quota.

"Sorry," said the Heathrow Customs Officer, "either pay the duty or the stuff goes into Her Majesty's Warehouse."

The fact that we had just survived an emergency landing meant absolutely nothing at all to these gentlemen of the Revenue; no amount of supplication would prevail, and our bottles disappeared from sight. Our litres of Bacardi had cost us each a mere 7 shillings and 6 pence, and the duty required was an enormous £2 — clearly an uneconomical proposition, and it put the final damper on our trip that night.

Later, on return to base at Southend, I was shown the cause of our trouble; a small brass contactor, no bigger than a finger nail, had snapped. Our experience was of benefit to all other operators of these aircraft, which were all quickly modified to prevent this sort of thing ever happening again.

It was just as well that I had not known it at the time, but to my mortification the makers confirmed that their Ambassador's wheels could not be retracted while the aircraft was on the ground. It had been just as well that we did not run into those brick huts after all!

Pay and conditions of service in the Independent Airlines were poor in comparison to the State Corporations; this is mentioned by way of offering it as an excuse perhaps for the other liberties that we took. We were in many ways not hampered by the restrictions that existed in the State Airlines.

Personally, I tried never to miss any opportunity, when flying an empty aircraft or carrying freight only, to indulge in a little bit of low flying. Most pilots love the sheer exhilaration of skimming low over land and sea, but are deterred by the thought of getting into trouble — the trick of course was not to be caught at it. This sometimes required a certain amount of wariness or cunning. For example, when over water, avoid flat calm conditions because of the dangers of optical illusions; also avoid Customs, police or pilot boats like the plague. Likewise never fly low over a built up area, keep clear of Coast Guard Stations, and when approaching an airfield regain a respectable altitude before coming into view. These were but a few of the implications, and aboard it was essential, if not just plain consideration, to obtain the assent of all crew members before going down low. I never ever met a crew member who did not thoroughly enjoy one of these excursions; co-pilots would often ask to have a go too, and I was able to pass on tips that had been handed down from Captains, such as Wally in India.

How well I remember, for example, the maestro years before instilling into me the importance of always trimming the elevators so that the tail remained heavy on the control column; that way there was a continual tendency for the nose to rise to keep the aircraft out of danger during any moment of inattention. A great time was always had by all, and it is perhaps a sad thought that most of the young pilots in airline service can never experience the delights of a 'beat up', as

THROUGH THE PENNINES BY ROAD... ALSO.....

ON A LONELY HEADLAND ON THE ISLE OF MAN..... WE WONDERED WHAT WAS SAID BETWEEN THE COUPLE LATER ON?...........

present day flight recorders automatically highlight any such diversions from normal operations.

A new trend was becoming commonplace in our passenger carrying operations, and that was night flying to try to get round the clock utilization of the aeroplanes. Moonbeams must have been slanting through the cockpit windows, for romance seemed to be in the air as one of our Ambassadors crossed the Bay of Biscay from Portugal. A good friend of mine, flying as co-pilot, was in his seat in the darkened cockpit as the aeroplane winged northwards. On his lap sat one of the two stewardesses aboard, as the autopilot flew the aircraft. In the main cabin, the lights had been turned down, and the 55 passengers slumbered peacefully lulled by the smooth sound of the two Centaurus engines. The Skipper, another long standing friend of mine, was elsewhere. It so happened that his steady girl-friend was the other stewardess, and he was enjoying a spell off with her in the galley compartment, while the other side of the cockpit door happy cuddling continued. However, all good things must eventually come to an end.

"Must go back and see if any of the passengers need anything," she cooed to the co-pilot, and having said that she reached for the nearest object with which to pull herself up off his lap. Unfortunately this happened to be the two prominently mounted throttle levers on

AN ILL CHOSEN HANDHOLD DURING A NIGHT FLIGHT.....

the pedestal between the two pilots' seats. The result was very spectacular and very alarming as a combined 5,600 h.p. died suddenly to practically nothing. The Ambassador did its best to stop in mid-flight. It was not very comfortable for others too; the Captain nearly jumped out of his skin, 55 passengers became instantly awake as their heads nodded forward, and the co-pilot nearly had a stoppage. He grabbed the throttles as quickly as he could, while his girlfriend stepped sedately away, and pushed the two levers back up again. The Captain burst back into the cockpit, just as the engines surged back to cruising power. Meanwhile in the cabin, 55 now wide awake passengers were sitting bolt upright, wondering what had happened.

What does one tell people at a time like this? Not the complete truth, I rather imagine: "Nothing to worry about Sir! They're just changing over the petrol tanks." Or perhaps, "One of the superchargers giving trouble. Go back to sleep, Madam, still a long time to go before we get to London."

Along with flying passengers, the company had built up a steady business transporting racehorses. The aircraft used for this was a Bristol Freighter, as blunt and chunky an aeroplane as the Ambassador was sleek. The Freighter, also known amongst pilots as 'The Frightener' or 'The Frightful', could manage up to six horses with their grooms and equipment. We were all eventually roped into flying the Freighter in turn, and I was no exception, in fact it sometimes made an interesting change to the passenger schedules.

However, the horse traffic used to diminish somewhat during autumn and winter, and to keep the aircraft employed the company also ran a contract to transport cars and spares from a motor manufacturer at Luton in Bedfordshire to a subsidiary company across the Irish Sea to Belfast, Northern Ireland.

It was a misty night when I turned up for work at Luton at 9 p.m. and, as was the usual custom, I went up to the tower to have a cup of tea, a chat with the controllers, and to check the paperwork and weather. The whole of the South of England was out in thick fog, which did not surprise me, because I had had a job getting to the airfield on time through the murk. The co-pilot had joined me, and when we had finished our tea we said our goodbyes and walked out to the aeroplane.

Loading had just been completed — three cars stood bumper to bumper inside the Freighter and below the cars, under specially constructed ramps, were packed large quantities of spares, every last ounce of carrying capacity was to be utilized on this flight. In the fuel tanks was sufficient petrol for the 2¼ hour flight across NW England and the Irish Sea, with scant reserves for diversions. Satisfied with the loading, the two big bulbous front doors were closed and locked, leaving the two of us inside to get the show on the road.

As I climbed the ladder up to the cockpit above, little did I know that this flight was going to turn out to be a nightmare. It had been a little over a year since my hair-raising flight, lost in Scotland, and my turn had come round again.

The cockpit was cold as we strapped ourselves into our seats, damp and condensation was everywhere, and outside the fog drifted in patches. We were anxious to get started and be away as soon as possible before it got any worse. The starters whined and in turn the two big Hercules engines coughed smoke and flame from the exhaust stacks just outside and below the cockpit, then burst into life and settled down to a steady crackle. Not having far to taxi, as Luton in those days had no runway, we ran up the engines and duly got clearance to take-off.

With both engines roaring at take-off power, we went lumbering across the damp grass into the darkness and mist. The tail was already up when we started to run into thicker patches of fog, and I had to switch my concentration wholly on to the glowing instrument panel in front of me to keep the aeroplane straight on her take-off run. We raced across the airfield completely blind, and after a few final bumps I hauled the Freighter off the ground as early as I dared, and we rose up into the fog shrouded night air.

"First course for Daventry is 317 degrees," called out Reg, the co-pilot. What a relief it was to be out of the fog on the ground. As we approached 1,000 feet I started a climbing turn to the left to head away towards the north-west. The heavily loaded Freighter's rate of climb was noticeably poor; the block shaped flying machine had succeeded in staggering up to about 4,000 feet, when suddenly it happened.

There was a chuffing noise, and then a loud bang which shook the whole aeroplane roughly. The oil pressure gauge on the port engine fell abruptly to zero.

"Feathering the port engine," I shouted, and with the help of the co-pilot pulled back the propeller pitch, throttle and fuel cut off levers as I pressed the feathering button. Power was immediately increased on the remaining live engine, and the strain on my right leg on the rudder pedal relieved by winding on rudder trim.

During all this very urgent activity, we had lost a valuable few hundred feet of height; a hasty glance, into the blackness out of my side window, dimly revealed the four big blades of the propeller now facing into the slipstream, which greatly helped to reduce the drag of that unwieldy aeroplane. At this moment Luton called us on the R/T, speaking to Reg with a message for me.

"Will you tell Captain Whitlock that he's left his gloves up here

OVER AN HOUR OF SHEER COLD FRIGHT... OVERLOADED, ON A FOGGY AUTUMN NIGHT.

in the tower."

The co-pilot looked across at me sitting crouched tensely over the controls with sweat gleaming on my brow, and answered, "I think he has more important things on his mind right now. We have just lost an engine. Would you hang on to the gloves? Thanks."

The remaining 1,980 h.p. Hercules engine was straining away at maximum continuous power; its oil temperature and propeller r.p.m. were right on the top limit, and we had no option but to continue north-westward.

The co-pilot had been busy checking the latest weather, and there was now not a single airfield unaffected by fog in the south of England. Our attention focused on our air speed; it remained hanging several knots below the minimum single engine safety speed.

"I think it'll be worth trying a shallow dive to see if we can build it up a bit," I said to Reg. He agreed, and I eased forward on the control column. While we squandered about 500 feet of valuable altitude, the speed rose a few knots, then settled back to what it had been before. I cursed silently — so much for that idea — we had high ground and television masts in the vicinity up ahead. Below us in the pitch blackness, fog swirled and our struggling Freighter was now flying level at a shade under 3,000 feet, as we slowly progressed north-westwards passing fog shrouded Birmingham.

Then it happened; the straining roar of our remaining serviceable engine cut sharply in a series of banging coughs, and the aeroplane immediately pulled off course starting to drop. That old pain hit me in the chest, and my throat went bone dry. I grabbed the starboard throttle, pulled it back, and then eased it hopefully forward.

"Keep running you bugger," I choked, as I heard in my head sets Preston Air Traffic Control call with a note of anxiety:

"Lima Juliet. Have you altered your heading?"

That enquiry went unanswered as I opened the starboard throttle up again, and mercifully the engine surged back to a full-throated roar, but for how long I wondered?

We turned back onto course, and informed the controller what had happened. The engine coughed again, but did not cut. I began to fear the worst that we might be faced with a crash landing, and under the worst possible conditions — darkness and fog.

I shouted hoarsely to the co-pilot, "Reg, if we have to force land, I'll fly her down straight ahead, as slow as possible, just above stalling speed, and you do landing lights, fuel and ignition off."

THE REMAINING ENGINE CUTS..... BRIEFING THE CO-PILOT FOR THE EXPECTED CRASH LANDING IN THE DARKNESS AND FOG............

The engine had coughed some more times, and it was keeping me in a permanent state of dread. Picking up my microphone and steadying my voice as best I could, I informed the controller, "Our good engine is still acting up. Can you get us into anywhere near by?"

There was a silence, and then, "RAF Shawbury. Stand by for their weather — I will call them by telephone."

It seemed like an age, but he came back remarkably quickly.

"Shawbury has poor visibility with drizzle, and Manchester has visibility of one mile with drizzle."

We were now very nearly past Shawbury, and as neither of us had ever been there and we had no information on the place, I therefore elected to carry on to Manchester which was only about 35 miles away.

At long last we started our approach. The hollow feeling in my chest and stomach began to ease as we turned and descended under the instructions of the radar controller. Everyone involved knew very well that there would be no going around for a second attempt once we were committed on the final descent. Down we came into the murk; rain began to hiss and run across the windscreens, while the night outside was very black. I followed the controller's instructions on heading and rate of descent concentrating as I had never done before. At about 500 feet, through the cloud and rain, I saw the occasional light drift by below us, and a little later the blurry glow of the runway lead-in lights came into view dead ahead. Our man on the radar had done a marvellous job and, with windscreen wipers slashing away and landing lights probing ahead, we finally crossed the rain-soaked runway threshold.

As I pulled the power off our faithful remaining Hercules, it crackled and backfired almost happily as we flared for the landing, and the main wheels brushed on to the runway. It was the end of 1 hour and 10 minutes of one of the worst flights I ever experienced, and it was a wonderful moment when we got our aeroplane safely back on the ground. The wheels had not been on the ground seconds, and my relief was so great that I shouted across the cockpit to the co-pilot, "We've made it, Reg! Shake on it man!"

We were indeed shaking hands in triumph over the throttle pedestal, when I realized that the old Freighter's tail wheel was still in the air. We completed the landing run, and cleared the runway with some difficulty with only one engine.

On the tarmac we shut down and climbed down out of the cockpit. It was great to be able to stretch my legs, and to savour the delights of the fresh air and terra firma despite the drizzle. I next went round to examine the port engine; it was a grim sight, the cowlings, nacelle, wing and even the tail were blackened by crankcase oil. A piston had smashed a cylinder up after its sleeve valve had disintegrated. The feathered propeller, high above me, completed the grim scene. I had had enough; turning to our handling agent, I checked that signals had been sent to our base, and then enquired into which hotel we had been booked.

"Well, I'm ready for that beer," I exclaimed, as the two of us lugged our bags over to a taxi, and later retired to bed with the memories of that flight well pickled in beer.

A party of our engineers drove up from Southend in a lorry with a spare engine. The lads worked a 'ghoster' through the night and into the next day, and we were ready to continue on our way early the day after.

CHAPTER 8

"What a damned easy life that lot have! — overpaid, oversexed, and underworked," an oft heard verdict on pilots, and an opinion readily endorsed by some visitors to the flight deck, observing the apparent inactivity. It would need only the entrance of a pretty stewardess bearing refreshments and perhaps some light-hearted banter to harden the opinion into a conviction. It had all been said before of previous generations of pilots, but the reality in the past was sometimes far removed when I recall the many who fell by the wayside purely because of lack of skill. Whereas the vast majority of today's lame duck pilots are weeded out at scratch or ruthlessly at any later stage in their careers, their older contemporaries were not. Some of this very small band survived by being carried along by the loyalty of colleagues, misguided as they were by present day practices. It all should have come under the heading of 'Lessons Learned in Aviation', and a case that amply illustrated this point developed parallel to my own career in the company.

When I had joined our Southend based firm in early 1953, it was not long before I was to meet a certain fellow co-pilot, who was senior to me in the company and older by several years. Highly educated, he came from noble Belgian stock and was a Baron by rights. He had just been old enough to catch the tail-end of World War II as a Junior Officer in the British Army; a big-hearted guy in all respects and an absolute gentleman. He was as keen as mustard on flying, yet he just did not seem to be able to quite get the hang of it consistently. In due course, I was promoted to Captain over him, and it was not long before he was crewed as co-pilot with me. This produced not even the slightest signs of rancour, having to fly with one younger and more junior to himself.

We got on well, and I set about doing my utmost to try to get his flying up to scratch. It became a sort of challenge, and apparently did not go unappreciated. "Here you are," he said to me one morning, handing me an Italian belt in superb quality black leather. "It's a spare one I had — you're welcome to it. That brown one you wear with your uniform looks an eyesore."

Being aware of the Baron's impeccable Saville Row wardrobe, I knew this was not any old cast-off with which he was presenting me. So it was, as I accepted the belt, that I acquired an item of garment which was to last me very well for the next 30 years of airline flying, such was its quality. To tell the truth, as the years went by, I came to regard the belt as a good luck mascot. It certainly seemed to work thus, which was unfortunately more luck than eventually befell its donor.

Cross wind take-offs and landings seemed to be the area that gave my problem co-pilot the most trouble; once in the air and away from the ground, he would cope well enough, but get him back towards earth again and things would invariably start to go wrong. On today's heavy jets, he might have made better going of it, but handling a Dakota in a cross wind on take-off or landing was an entirely different kettle of fish. Instruction was freely given to my keen co-pilot on every available occasion; demonstration followed upon demonstration with blow by blow analysis of rudder pedal action and aileron deflection, and this went on for months. Just when I would be starting to think that his problems were licked, he would unexpectedly have a lapse, and this would sometimes necessitate nerve jangling recovery action by myself.

"Here you are," I said one day at Leeds. "A nice cross wind take-off for you to practise. Let's make a new start of it today."

We climbed into the Dakota, and as we sat in the cockpit doing our checks and awaiting the passengers boarding, I again went over the exercise to refresh his mind. He was full of enthusiasm and raring to go as he taxied out to line up on the runway.

We could not have had a better day for it; the sun was shining, we had both had an excellent breakfast at the hotel, and as the bright orange wind sock in the centre of the airfield bellied out, we began our take-off run with a roar as the engines were opened up. The Dakota surged forward, and the tail was raised. Good footwork on the rudder pedals was keeping us nicely straight on the runway. Had he cracked it, I thought? Now all he needed, as we gathered speed, was a progressive deflection of the control wheel to keep the 'into wind' wing well pinned down.

Oh! no, I groaned inwardly. He was turning the wheel the wrong way. I poised myself to grab the controls in an instant, but then decided to let him continue as much as I dared so that he could learn by the mistake. The cross wind started to lift the wing, and the Dakota lumbered into the air in a half-cocked attitude. Still I refrained from interfering and the aeroplane, now free of the ground, drifted off downwind over the grass as we diverged from the remaining part of the runway over which we should have been. The co-pilot was obviously ill at ease with sweat beginning to show on his brow, but I let him get on with it, and when he had eventually settled down in the climb I asked him what he thought had gone wrong. "Must have had the wrong wing down," he replied, after some reflection.

I would have liked nothing better than to have got back down on the ground right then, and to have repeated the exercise once again, but such opportunities had to be taken only when they presented themselves. Months went by, as he flew with others, and remained a co-pilot.

It was in the early summer of 1960 that he again flew with me, this time in a Bristol Freighter. This particular aircraft had been leased from another operator. It was an early production model, and the main difference was that it was fitted with the older type of differential pneumatic wheel brakes. However, we had both used the system many times before, and it came to my friend's turn to fly out of Liverpool to Dublin.

With our load of three cars aboard, and the passengers in their rear cabin, he taxied the aircraft away from the terminal building out to the runway. We were making our way along a rather narrow stretch of taxiway when events started to get out of hand. We had come to a halt with one of the wheels quite close to the edge of the paved surface. I glanced across at the co-pilot who was beginning to look quite tense. He had already started to open up one of the engines to help swing the aircraft back. I had hoped that he would have been able to sort it out for himself, but with the Freighter still stationary he was increasing the power of the engine still further. I was amazed at how quickly he had let the situation develop; his left hand was clamped on the control wheel with thumb pressing hard down on the brake lever, while his right hand clenched the throttle lever trying to bend it still further forward. His face was now covered in beads of perspiration, and veins were standing out on his temples and neck. The engine, very nearly at take-off power, was shaking the airframe alarmingly.

My instincts told me that if he released the brakes now, with so much power, anything could happen. Mustering as calm a voice as I could, I said, "Relax man. Take the power off."

This he did straight away, but his thumb still remained pressed so hard on the brake control lever that the needles of the pressure gauge were hard up against the stops.

"Look at the pressure you've got on those brakes!" I added.

"Oh! Christ," he exclaimed, as the metal bending thumb pressure was relaxed. It was obvious that he had become confused, and I felt very sad to see it happen to such a good guy.

There were no training establishments in existence in most of the companies operating then, just a few Captains licensed to carry out instrument ratings and six monthly checks, and a Chief Pilot to decide on promotions and other matters. It was left to such Captains, who took sufficient interest, to help co-pilots, where necessary, with practice and instruction. So it was about a year later that the Chief Pilot, after due consideration, made a decision to promote the Baron. It was felt he had been a co-pilot for so long that perhaps being on his own would be the right tonic. The decision was unique in that he was given his command but only to fly freight aircraft; moreover the company would as far as possible make sure that an experienced co-pilot was crewed with their new Captain. I was happy to hear the news and certainly hoped that my old colleague would make good. Life in the air must have gone reasonably well for him for some time, although there was the occasional story repeated by crew members.

I became directly concerned again one afternoon at Luton, having arrived at the airfield by road to take over a Freighter from an incoming crew and fly it over to Northern Ireland. The aircraft was not yet in, so after attending to the necessary pre-flight paperwork and with time to spare, the co-pilot and myself decided to visit the control tower to watch the Freighter land. Unknown to us it had landed by the time we laboured up the umpteen flights of steps to the top of the tower, from where we saw our mount parked far below us with engines switched off.

"What are they up to around that wing?" I asked the co-pilot, as I gazed idly down.

"Looks like they've got some trouble with the flaps," he replied. A small group were now standing under the wing, and then I saw the incoming Captain climb up a small trestle, apparently trying to get a closer look.

"It's the Baron," I said. "Very conscientious of him checking over an aircraft after a trip instead of just leaving it to the engineers."

The crew were preparing to leave for home when we got down to the Freighter.

"Just some reported damage to the flaps," said the Baron, "but they are perfectly OK."

After some pleasantries, we said goodbye and climbed aboard, while loading was completed.

As we sorted ourselves out in the cockpit, the co-pilot leaned across with a chuckle and casually mentioned, "I've heard a whisper that they might have brushed a tree on landing." So that was why he had been so interested, I mused. "Crafty devil, not letting on."

The new concrete runway at Luton had just been completed, and the trees at one end had not yet been fully cut back.

"Easy enough to do, perhaps," I said, "but still no excuse to try and complete the cutting job with our aeroplane!"

However, we started up and taxied out, but as we turned about at the end of the runway there was further evidence of our Freighter's recent arrival.

"Look at that," said the co-pilot pointing at the branches and foliage strewn about on the concrete.

"They must have really gone through those trees."

We had a further laugh, did our checks, and then went roaring off down the runway.

I started to lift the tail, glancing down at the airspeed indicator, and had to blink twice before looking again. We were accelerating away at the Freighter's usual lumbering rate, but my airspeed indicator needle was still resting solidly on zero. It was, strictly speaking, an abort situation, but the co-pilot's gauge was working so I shouted to him, "Call the speeds, will you? We'll continue."

With a few final bumps we were into the air, and as we climbed we had time to reflect.

"This has got to be something to do with those trees," I said, and added, "and if it was, just as well we carried on otherwise someone might have had some explaining to do!"

The co-pilot was adamant that, during his pre-flight inspection, he had seen no debris near the Pitot tube under the wing, from which came the air pressure to show airspeed. The co-pilot did the landing at our destination, and on closer examination from the ground the Pitot tube was found to be clogged up with bark.

I could not help but see a funny side to the incident when, some months later, I was having a conversation over a beer with the co-pilot, who had been aboard the Freighter at the time it had been flown through the trees. "I had just joined the Company," he said. "It was my first trip on a Freighter, and it was obvious we were going to hit the treetops. I thought this was the sort of low approach that all the company Captains made!"

The saga of the ill-suited Captain was, very regrettably, not over by any means. The telephone rang one day on my day off. It was Southend on the line.

"Can you help us out, and get on the late morning BEA flight for Belfast? The Chief Pilot should be on it too — he will explain."

We both caught the flight with not too much time to spare, and while we rode across as passengers I learned that, alas, it was my old friend, the Baron, in trouble again. His aircraft had become bogged down just off the main runway at Belfast's Nutts Corner Airport. The airport had had to be closed, and numerous scheduled flights diverted while the aircraft was dug out. But far worse still for the luckless Captain was the fact that the Managing Director just so happened to have been on the spot, and witnessed the whole incident. He was furious; it was as though he had been personally humiliated, with one of his aircraft standing wing down in the bog blocking all air movements. His reaction was predictable, and instantly the Baron was suspended, pending enquiry. This was where the Chief Pilot, now sitting in the next seat to me, was coming in.

It was not difficult to guess at the cause of the mishap, and so it turned out that the trouble was the Freighter's, by no means foolproof, tail wheel lock. It was a wretched device, and needed to be watched like a hawk. If the wheel was not locked for landing, then it would shimmy like mad and the tail would hop around after touch down like a jack rabbit, which was very embarrassing. On the other hand, it was often difficult to release the lock after the landing run, and to start a turn on the ground with it still in only jammed the lock still further.

The enquiry inevitably revealed the Captain's frenzied struggle to free the forgotten tail wheel lock, which would not have disengaged in any case as they were trying to turn off the runway at the time.

As I flew the aircraft back later in the day, I felt very sorry to hear that he had been fired, but about a week later the grapevine gave forth further news. I was very pleased to hear then that the Baron had been able to get another job with a company also based at Southend. Within a very short while, he was checked out again as a Captain — perhaps the change of scene would be for the better.

Unfortunately it was not to be. I picked up my newspaper one morning, and had to swallow hard as the headlines of an air accident stared me in the face: 'Dakota crashes on high ground above Ventnor, Isle of Wight'. The report made tragic reading. The aircraft belonged to the company our recently sacked pilot had joined. Only one person, the stewardess, survived the impact and she died later in hospital. The rest of the crew and all the passengers were killed. The aircraft had been on a relatively short flight from Jersey to Portsmouth, and had been exactly on track but had started descending through cloud too early. As I read further, the name I feared I would find heading the published crew list was indeed there. It was a sad moment; my old colleague, the Baron, had made his last mistake.

It was lessons such as this, which gradually got through in the aviation world, that no longer would a pilot of marginal ability be allowed to slip through the net to jeopardize the lives of passengers. As aeroplanes became more costly, even the insurance companies would bring pressure to bear.

"Would you trust your wife and kids to fly with him?" was an oft heard question, and it took on real meaning sometimes. An operations manager in our company, who was going on holiday with his wife to Klagenfurt in Austria, once went as far as to substitute another Captain to fly the aircraft. The airfield was a difficult one situated in a valley with quite high mountains near by, and the original pilot programmed had notched up a chequered career. It was only much later that this same Captain was demoted, and then eventually dismissed.

In those earlier days there was many a dubious character still floating around. One very blatant case, carried along for years, was the same pilot mentioned earlier, who had succeeded in stopping both engines of a Dakota flying over Wiltshire and then did some gliding. He had been demoted back to co-pilot, and as such our paths inevitably crossed.

It was only fair to let him do some flying at least to keep his hand in, but to do this was to place one's own neck at definite risk, particularly when it came to him doing a landing. His hands often shook so much that it was difficult for him to hold a cup of tea — only a beer after a flight seemed to be capable of steadying them. In the cockpit, after a stewardess had handed him his tea, the cup would progressively start a little dance in the saucer. The contents would begin to slop out of the cup, and get slowly worse until the cup was half-empty with most of the remainder sprinkled over his uniform; whatever small quantity survived all this eventually was drunk.

It was for such reasons that he was posted permanently to flying freight only. He eventually succumbed to a nervous breakdown and left flying altogether, but not before he had badly frightened quite a few of us.

My worst experience with him came one fine English autumn evening while returning to Luton. It was just getting dark as the Freighter motored down towards the runway in calm conditions. At the controls, and no more than usually ill at ease, sat our friend, flying from the Captain's left hand seat. For some unknown reason he was going far too fast.

"You're a bit fast. Will you get the speed back?" I called. He pulled the throttles back a bit, but the airspeed was still a good deal above normal as we crossed the runway threshold. The runway was long enough, so I decided to let him continue, but as we swooped on to the concrete, the landing suddenly started to go badly haywire. The big bulbous nosed aircraft touched down first on one wheel and then the other, and at the same time started to drift sideways. It was as though there was no one at the controls.

"Keep her straight," I bellowed, but too late, we were now heading off the runway. The paved surface had not long been down, so the adjoining ground was still rough from where the bulldozers had been at work. It all happened so very quickly. The aircraft began to bump as we ran over the ruts, and I cursed the wretched man as I screamed out, "I have control."

From the right hand seat, I reached over and opened up both throttles against the stops; my instincts told me that we were still going fast and should be just about able to stagger up into the air again.

"Flaps up," I shouted. There was a roar of engine power, a bang and a blue flash from outside the cockpit. In the semi-darkness ahead and to the right, I was aware of the dark shapes of trees, and my limbs were stretched to their limits. My left arm was extended fully forward holding the throttles open, my left leg was ramrod straight straining against the rudder bar with full left rudder on, and with my right hand clutching the control column, I suddenly realized we were not getting anywhere — only the left engine was flat out. The bang and the blue flash had been the starboard engine cutting, and it was only now building up to full power. In those split seconds, I realized something else; the brake pedals under my feet did not feel right — the co-pilot in his panic had both his feet still on them with both brakes locked fully on. This was no time for niceties, "Get your feet off the bloody brakes, you idiot," I screamed frenziedly.

The dim shapes of the trees looked menacingly nearer now. It was hopeless, if we were going to hit them, better to do so as slowly as possible. I slammed both throttles shut as the terrible bumping over the unmade ground got worse, but now with the co-pilot's feet off the brakes, the aircraft was beginning to respond to my full left rudder and brake. Slowly the Freighter began to drag back towards the safety of the runway somewhere vaguely to our left. How the tyres were standing up to this torture, I just could not imagine.

We were right down at the far end of the field when we eventually got back on to the runway, and there was precious little of it left. The aircraft finished up in a series of diminishing swerves, with squealing howls from the tyres, as I damped the swings down with vicious use of both brakes in turn. We came to a halt right at the end of the strip, but with sufficient room to turn the aircraft round on the concrete

INTO A TIGHT CORNER AT LUTON ..... AUGUST 1960.

to taxi back. Livid black skid marks on the new white concrete bore testament to our recent arrival, and they continued to do so for months afterwards.

As I taxied back, I felt myself shaking from the effects of the ordeal, and the co-pilot did not escape from the reaction that followed. Unprintable profanities flowed forth at him across the cockpit, and by the time we had reached the tarmac area he must have been in no doubt as to what I thought of his performance. It was unbelievable that a pilot, who had once captained a 4-engined Halifax and had reportedly reached the rank of Group Captain during World War II, could deteriorate to such a state.

Utterly disgusted, I climbed down the ladder from the cockpit to examine the damage. Both the Freighter's large main tyres were cut to ribbons, one worse than the other. How they had not burst was nothing short of a miracle. They were of course fit for nothing else but scrap, and it involved the company in considerable expense changing them. It was one time that I had no compunction about reporting the incident.

I had good cause to reflect on our lucky escape, several years later. I had just landed at Dublin, when word reached us almost immediately that there had been a very bad accident a short while previously.

"Just walk across and look behind that building, Captain," said one of our ground handlers as he relived the moment.

"It was a Freighter. He came right across our heads, and missed a BEA. Vanguard loading passengers by a few feet before hitting the building."

I walked across, and it was not a pretty sight, just a tangle of wreckage wedged between two concrete buildings. The three crew aboard had been killed instantly. They had been trying to climb back into the air again after landing. But for the grace of God that could have been us at Luton.

Over a beer one day with a good friend named John, a fellow Captain, I was relating my recent excursion off the runway, and then in turn I listened to an account of his. Although it was told in a humorous vein, it might not have seemed funny to some of the participants at the time. The villain of the piece, as nervous as usual, was again having some practice.

"We were landing at Dublin," said John, "with six racehorses and their grooms aboard, and our friend at the controls," he added, taking a pull at his beer almost as though he needed it.

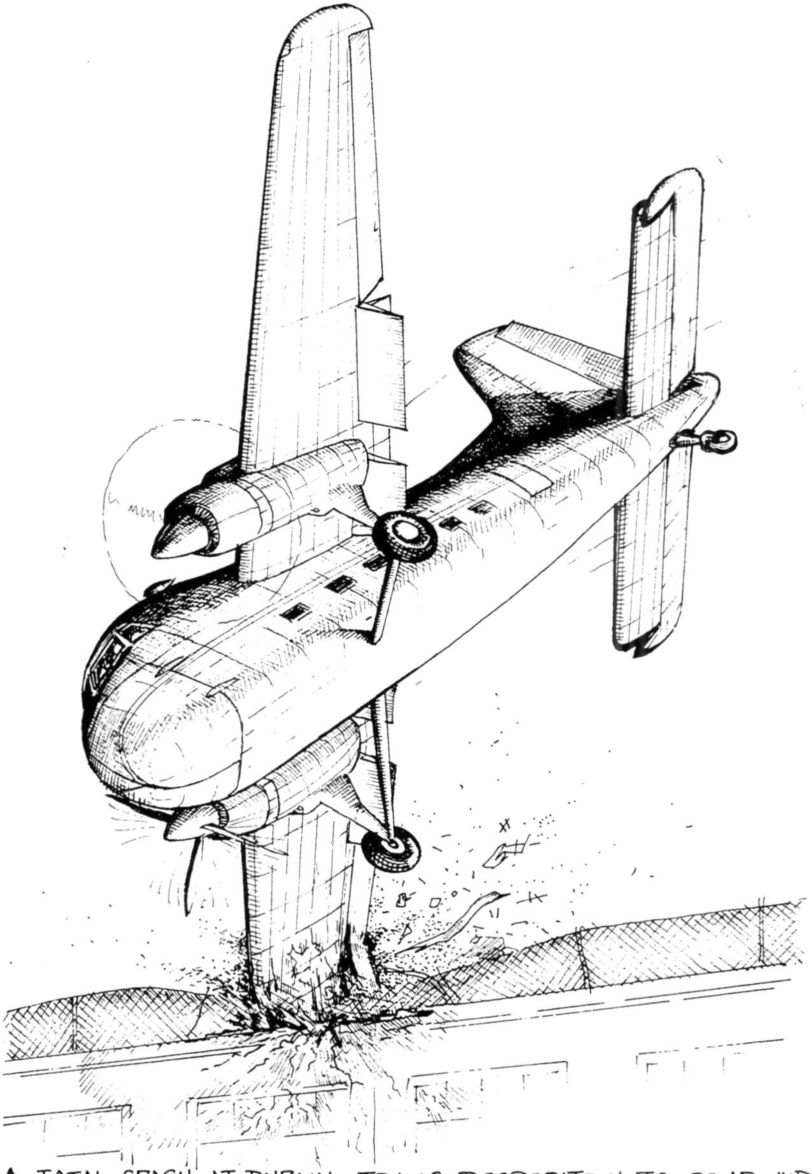

A FATAL CRASH AT DUBLIN... TRYING DESPERATELY TO GO AROUND ON ONE ENGINE. A SIMILAR FATE COULD HAVE BEEN OURS AT LUTON.

"He hit the ground pretty hard, and went sailing right back up into the air again. The head groom felt the bump and stood up exclaiming to the rest of the group, 'we're down boys'. In actual fact we must have been 20 feet up, and I just had time to put on a burst of power, but we hit the ground so hard it was a wonder the undercarriage took it!"

John went on to describe how the grooms had had to pick themselves up from out of the hay, all except one who had to be carried away with a badly sprained ankle. The horses had stood up to the impact remarkably well, and were all able to walk away when unloaded, but a heavy landing check had to be carried out on the aeroplane by the engineer.

The spectre of bankruptcy had been flitting around behind the scenes during these times of the early 'sixties. The company had perhaps overstretched themselves trying to develop new scheduled routes and rumours were rife. It was going to be a case of history repeating itself, for these events followed a pattern that has often occurred before in aviation. It usually went as follows — while in financial difficulties a company aircraft crashes, insurance pays out, creditors swoop, and the company folds. Ours unfortunately started to go the same way, after tragedy struck from a cloud shrouded fell in Cumberland. Murphy was in full cry that day, and what could go wrong, did go wrong.

It was an early start, with grim weather as the Dakota struggled north-westwards from Leeds bound for Carlisle, flying into the teeth of a head wind ripping in from the Atlantic and the western Isles. Total cloud cover blanketed the route. Aboard were the Captain and three crew. As well as the co-pilot and Stewardess, they had with them a very keen newly joined trainee pilot, who had made special efforts to change with a colleague to get on to that trip.

At Carlisle, to help them through the cloud and to stay clear of the nearby mountains and rising ground, they would have to rely solely on the radio bearings given to them by the lone operator in the small control tower. Was it early morning bleariness? There was a mix-up of bearings to the aircraft as it transmitted its signal, and that relentless north-west wind did the rest. The Dakota ploughed into the side of Croglin Fell, and all four aboard were killed instantly. The passengers, waiting on the ground for their aeroplane to land, heard the news in stunned silence, and not without relief that the tragedy had occurred prior to their boarding.

At the Public Court of Enquiry, evidence was given about how, as the Dakota descended through the cloud, with the co-pilot's voice calling for and repeating back the bearings being given to him from the tower, the Captain's voice suddenly cut in. He had sensed something was not right and the interruption was made in a tone of urgency. He was an old friend and a skilled pilot, and it was widely believed that the bearings were the opposite to what they should have been. The findings of the court were eventually published, and it was one of those rare events where pilots, no longer able to defend themselves, were not blamed.

The probationary young pilot, who had swapped places with his friend on that fateful flight, eventually flew with me on several different types of aircraft, and eventually became a Captain of a wide-bodied Tristar.

INCORRECT BEARINGS FROM A GROUND STATION... OUR COMPANY DAKOTA PLUNGES INTO CLOUD SHROUDED CROGLIN FELL... CUMBERLAND.... OCTOBER 1961.......

Aviation accidents, where the crew no longer lived to tell the tale, had long frustrated investigators — until, that is, the 'black box' flight recorder and the cockpit voice recorder came upon the scene. Before this, however, it was often a very different scene. It was sometimes all too convenient to call it pilot error, especially if they were not around. But there were many investigators who did the job extremely conscientiously; they built up great experience in ferreting out even the most insignificant detail in their quest for the facts. However, there were others who took a far different approach.

"Survive a serious accident, and you've really got big problems, boy!" said a friend to me one day, and I had no reason to doubt him because I knew he spoke with good authority.

He had been a Captain with the State Corporation, and had been in command of one of their Ambassadors (also called the 'Elizabethan') on a flight out of Dusseldorf in Germany. It was in the early days of the airliner's introduction, and in many ways it had several radical features, along with the usual crop of bugs. As his hair-raising account unfolded, it became more and more incredible.

Their take-off in the beautiful airliner had been normal, and as they continued their climb, suddenly, one of the huge 16-foot diameter four-bladed propellers went haywire. At first, the pilots just could not believe what was happening. They feathered the propeller, and carried out the rest of the drill immediately. But it made no difference at all; the prop stayed stubbornly in reverse, and continued to rotate giving them an almighty burden of drag. They increased power on the good engine, and then more power and even more power, until they had all it could give, and yet they were still coming down. They feverishly tried everything they knew, including varying the air speed. Murphy had chosen the right day as well — a heavy mist shrouded the countryside below. They were still descending rapidly, when they got a brief glimpse of the River Rhine down through the murk as they passed over it. There was absolutely no chance of making it back to Dusseldorf Airport.

Desperate measures were now called for as it was going to be a forced landing in a field, that is if they could find one in the murk. Meanwhile in the cabin, the passengers were being prepared for a crash landing. The live Centaurus engine was thundering at full power with the throttle hard against the stops; it was only its tremendous power that was now keeping them in the air, but only just.

As the airliner sank inexorably lower and lower towards the ground, the two pilots were having great difficulty seeing what lay ahead. Only seconds remained now. What looked like a decent sized field came into view hazily before them. My friend had time to bank towards it, but this was not their lucky day. Power lines stretched right across the field suspended from towering pylons just coming into view. The ground was coming up rapidly, and they were committed.

With brilliant airmanship and split second dexterity, the Skipper called for flap and at the same time eased back on the control wheel. The Elizabethan rose upwards and staggered across the deadly cables with inches to spare, but she was very nearly out of flying speed. In a semi-stalled condition, she mushed back towards the field and struck the ground with a bone jarring crash.

The entire port wing was torn off along with the engine on that side, and the passenger cabin changed shape, squashed to the extent that the tops of most of the seats now touched the cabin roof. The passengers were very badly shaken, but miraculously none were seriously injured. Outside the scene was one of devastation. Bits of the once gleaming 'Silver Wing' Elizabethan were scattered round the main wreckage. The beautifully styled triple finned tail still hung on to the mangled fuselage, but was twisted to a grotesque angle.

Ambulances arrived fairly quickly and rapidly had the injured on their way to hospital. They were in good hands as the German doctors soon had their cases well under control. The Captain had back injuries but, in the next bed, the radio operator was in a much poorer state.

It did not take long for the Ministry Accident Inspectors to get across from England, and they made for the hospital where there were, after all, surviving pilots out of whom they would soon get to the truth. The doctor-in-charge reluctantly agreed to let them question the injured Captain. The investigators eagerly started a barrage of questions directed at the figure painfully propped up in bed.

It soon became apparent to the Captain, from the way the questioning was going, that the inspectors were seeking to blame him for mishandling the emergency. However, he was not only an above average pilot, but knew the technical side of the aeroplane inside out. The questions kept coming at him in rapid succession, but were parried with logical answers. The fact remained that the propeller had gone suddenly into reverse in the air in spite of the safeguards to prevent this happening. The reverse facility was designed to operate only on the ground to slow down the aeroplane after landing. It was as though the investigators were trying to justify the design that their Department had approved, and it just could not have gone wrong; it must be the pilot who had slipped up somewhere.

"Captain, had you thought of trying this?" or "Did you do that?" The inspectors seemed to be under the impression that the two pilots had all the time in the world to work through the endless possible permutations. My friend was beginning to become more and more irritated by their attitude. The German doctor, hovering near by, was showing signs of increasing concern over his patient's welfare. The questions were becoming more antagonistic, and the Captain's answers more heated in reply.

The doctor at this point warned the investigators, "Gentlemen, you will have to leave soon." The questioning continued, when one of the investigators, perhaps wishing to try another tack, asked oilily, "Captain, before you crashed, can you tell us if you noted what the Outside Air Temperature Gauge was reading?"

That was the last straw. Forbearance at an end, the patient painfully raised himself from his pillow and shouted at his inquisitors, "You stupid bloody idiots! Do you think I had time to look at an insignificant item like that?"

The German doctor cut in, "Raus! Raus! you will go now," as he hustled the investigators out of the ward by the arms. The Captain was still spitting with anger. I remember him telling me that if he had been sufficiently mobile, blows might have been struck.

What had been in the questioner's mind at the time is difficult to say; perhaps he had been angling on the possibilities of icing which was not a factor on that day. The temperature gauge in question was the smallest, least used and most remotely sited instrument on the panel, and it would have been ridiculous to have expected either of them to have taken note of temperatures at such a moment.

In appreciation of the exceptional handling of the aircraft, the corporation took the unusual course of making an *ex gratia* payment of a lump sum to their pilot.

After the Carlisle Dakota crash, the company staggered along shakily for a while, on the verge of bankruptcy, and so did most of us, the employees. The Receivers were called in, belts were tightened, we paid our own pension contributions, and thankfully, quite beyond our control in any case, the situation gradually improved.

Fate often played some cruel tricks, but I found it difficult to imagine anything as hard as in the lines of a letter I was shown which had been sent from Morocco.

Standing at the refreshments counter, drinking a last minute cup of tea before a flight from Southend, a voice called from across the floor of the departure hall. It was Gerry, who would be flying as co-pilot with me on the trip. "Just take a look at this, Arthur," he said, handing me the letter he had just collected from the Flying Club where he had once worked. The letter had come from an Airport Agent at Agadir in Morocco. It was not more than a dozen typewritten lines in broken English. The man in Agadir wanted to know who would take responsibility for a small twin-engined Miles 'Gemini' that was standing on the airfield.

The letter went on to describe what had happened to the two pilots who had flown it there. The two British pilots had landed at Agadir on their way to Southern Africa, where they intended night stopping and then continuing the next day. They had gone into town on the one night in a million that the great earthquake had struck. On that fateful night in the very early 'sixties, Agadir was virtually razed to the ground, and they had been lost without trace under the rubble of the smashed city. The aircraft was noticed standing unattended day after day, and it was only then that it had been realized what had happened.

Many times while flying over Agadir, I looked down on the rebuilt city, and wondered what had been the sequel to those strange workings of fate that brought two aviators to an untimely end at the hands of nature in that far off city.

In all branches of aviation, a taxiing accident has always been judged with extreme seriousness. It is always treated as carelessness, and severe disciplinary action against the pilot involved is invariably the result.

It was against this sort of background that I came to be involved in a taxiing accident myself, and it was the only occasion in my civil aviation career where I was responsible for bending a part of an aeroplane in my charge. Murphy, of course, played a prominent part in the affair, throwing in for good measure a traffic officer who did not stick to procedure, a student working during his holidays handling a ground power unit as well as a tractor, and various other factors.

We were about to depart from Jersey, and aboard our Ambassador were 55 holidaymakers about to return to their homes in the North of England. The traffic officer had given me the 'all clear' to start both engines, and the two big Centaurus radials were now burbling away smoothly while we carried on with our after start checks. The stewardess popped into the cockpit.

"Fifty-five passengers strapped in Skipper. All checks complete," sang out a cheery voice.

"Thanks," I said, and looked out of the small cockpit windows. The traffic officer was no longer in sight, and neither could I see anyone else outside.

"Ask for taxi clearance, please," I said to the co-pilot, and in reply the controller in the tower, overlooking the spot where we were parked, gave us the necessary permission. There was still no one to be seen outside, so out of sheer habit I checked with the co-pilot.

"All clear your side?"

His head moved nearer the small sloping side window.

"All clear my side," came his reply.

I released the parking brake, nudged forward the throttles, and the Ambassador started to roll forward. Almost immediately there was a stomach churning grinding and clanging of metal from the co-pilot's side. My heart sank.

"Christ! we've hit something," I groaned, slamming the throttles shut, pulling on the parking brake, and hastily shutting down both engines. My pulse was racing as I released the safety harness, and leapt from my seat. A single bound took me through the flight deck door, and I had the forward door in the galley area open in a trice. A good shove sent it outward and up, while holding on to the door frame I peered out.

A scene of destruction greeted my eyes — fragments of metal lay scattered about the tarmac. The huge four-bladed propeller had chewed its way up the ground power unit and as far as the farm tractor's oversized rear wheels. My first concern was for the driver, but the young lad was standing with a broad smile on his face regarding the wreckage. Not waiting to fit the step ladder in position, I jumped to the ground and ran towards him.

"Are you all right?" I asked, grasping his shoulder.

"Sure, Skip," he said. "I'm extremely sorry to have got in your way — had difficulty starting the tractor." I was never so relieved to see someone standing unhurt in all my life — the propeller must have missed him by inches.

We had been very fortunate, and the inquiry that was set up recommended an immediate review of ground procedures: traffic officers were to stand in full view of the pilot until ready to taxi, tractors were to be parked where they could be seen from the cockpit, and finally the nose wheel chock was to be the last item of

TAXIING ACCIDENT AT JERSEY..... AUGUST 1961.

equipment removed. Although not blamed myself, while filling in insurance papers and attending endless interviews, I had ample time to learn my lesson — any delay getting away would be acceptable in the future, rather than hear that terrible grinding noise again and worse still the injury or death that could have resulted.

What better than a little extra flying on suitable free days, weather permitting, and a welcome payment in cash for a few hours work. An Australian pilot friend was in a partnership running a Charter Airline, and they had purchased some Ambassadors which had come onto the market. At that early stage, they had no one licensed to fly the aircraft, one of which required ferrying north from Gatwick to Wymeswold in Leicestershire.

The flight turned out to be more than I had bargained for because an emergency occurred, the exact like of which had once won a BEA Captain a 'Queen's Commendation for Valuable Services in the Air', but unfortunately in this particular case did not come to the attention of Her Majesty!

At Gatwick, a burly ruddy faced figure, complete with homburg and overcoat, met me. He was a qualified pilot and, although he had never flown an Ambassador before, would sit in the co-pilot's seat to help out where necessary and also would be taking care of arrangements at the other end.

A farcical side show next developed over the question of my fee. As casually as I could manage, I said with a smile, "You've brought along cash for this trip, I hope?"

Clearing his throat, he answered, "There were some problems. I've got a cheque for you — it'll be OK — don't worry."

This was completely contrary to the arrangements we had made on the telephone, and I had good reason for insisting on cash. The financier, who was backing the deal, had recently been involved in some dubious deals, and there had been talk of bankruptcy proceedings.

"I'm not happy about this," I said. "You assured me it would be a cash deal."

I happened to be holding a pair of radio headsets, which he had just handed me for use on the trip, and I knew they were quite valuable.

"You won't mind if I hang on to these until the cheque is cleared, will you?"

It made me feel a bit of a heel, but the outcome of the little discussion ended up with my new found friend disappearing for a while and returning with my £75 in crisp fivers. We set to work at once.

Before climbing aboard, I was handed an indemnity form to sign. The conditions, for one flight only, required that the aircraft was not pressurized, the wing anti-icing would not be used, and lastly that the undercarriage would not be retracted. The engineer-in-charge suggested that I might like the undercarriage ground locks removed just in case we needed to raise the wheels in an emergency or an engine failure to reduce drag.

"Good idea," I said. "I'll leave you to do the necessary. Thanks."

Little did I realize it, but with those words I set a neat trap for myself.

The Ambassador had not been flown for a good while, and it took some time to get the two big Centaurus engines started and running evenly. Chocks were waved away through the small cockpit sliding windows, and we were on our way.

I intended enjoying myself on this flight. The Ambassador was a real pleasure to fly, the weather was fine, and I planned to 'visit' my home *en route*. My two sons had been told to be on the look-out for a fairly low fly past, as we would be passing that way.

We swept away down Gatwick's runway, and the graceful airliner lifted smoothly into the air. I commenced a climbing turn off the runway, my right hand flicked the undercarriage lever up, and then raised the flaps. Yes, this was going to be pleasurable, flying for a change off the airways, and with a beautiful sunny day to enjoy the countryside below from not too high an altitude. I levelled off at 1,000 feet, reduced the propeller r.p.m., pulled back the power, and commenced cruising in level flight. The Ambassador, with its characteristic whining drone, winged north eastwards towards the London suburb of Bromley.

Scanning over the aircraft's long streamlined nose, I saw the house coming into view.

'Wonder what the kids are going to think seeing the aeroplane going past with the landing gear down?' I thought.

"The wheels!" I cried, causing the co-pilot to jump in his seat. I had done it so automatically that I had not even realized it at the time.

"Bloody hell! I've raised the undercarriage," I said, looking across at the owner's representative, who stared back at me blankly.

I seized the undercarriage lever and thrust it back down. My heart sank, and there was a dreadful dryness in my throat. All thoughts of a fly past for the benefit of my young sons vanished immediately because the lever, held firmly down with my hand, produced no results at all. A lot of things normally happened when that handle was selected down. The nose wheel doors below the pilot's seat could be heard to clang open, there were considerable air noises, there were various jolts felt as the mechanisms locked down, and the aircraft would skid, having to be retrimmed because of yaw caused by the large main legs hanging down into the airstream. This time there was nothing — nothing at all — just a deathly silence, and a decidedly sinking feeling.

In the forlorn hope that at least the main wheels had come down, I said to my friend, "Will you walk back into the passenger cabin, look out of the windows, and see if they're down please?"

He returned to the cockpit a short while later, and I turned round anxiously. There was no need for words; his normally ruddy face was now a pale grey, and it was being moved solemnly from side to side.

"Shit," I exclaimed. "Looks bad, but we've got some more cards to play yet. Will you fly her for a bit?"

He climbed back into the co-pilot's seat, and I hastily handed over control to him with a quick word on a new course to steer. This was going to be the moment of truth. I was going to have to use the emergency systems, and I had never done this before in anger. Would they work?

Unfastening my seat belt, I climbed down from the seat and walked back to the passenger cabin, looking up at both engine nacelles in turn through the windows. They revealed no sign of the wheels, which were still tucked firmly inside. My attention next turned to the emergency up-lock release and the lowering handle. They were hidden away behind panels in the roof where the wing centre section ran across the cabin roof. Half-hidden among sound proofing, I found the lock release and pulled it, followed by the other handle on the opposite side. Through the adjacent window I saw the long port main leg swing straight down and lock, but no such luck with the starboard leg. It was sticking down into the air stream at a half-cocked angle, neither up nor down. There was no going back now, and no other system was available. I had made the mistake, and if I could not extricate myself, big trouble was in store for me.

With heart in my mouth, I went back to the lever in the roof and pulled it again with eyes glued on the landing gear leg through the window. Mercifully for me it moved a little way further downwards; more frantic tugging and it moved down still further. The 200 m.p.h. slipstream was at least on my side as it pressed against the big metal casting of the leg. As I continued pulling the lever, there was still further rearward movement until, to my immense relief, the undercarriage leg finally reached the limit of its travel.

The aircraft was fitted with mechanical locking indicators designed for emergency use if the normal electrical system did not work, and these were in the form of metal pointers visible through the forward cabin windows. On either side both these needles now rested pointing between the letters 'E' and 'L', and that meant the main wheels at least should be safe for landing.

Back in the cockpit, some colour returned to my companion's face when he heard the news. He seemed to be coping quite well with the flying, as I added, "Now for the nose wheel. Keep your fingers crossed."

Without further ado, I was down on hands and knees with a panel opened and groping below floor level for the emergency nose wheel release handle. A firm pull produced some noise and movement from below, but my senses warned me that it just did not sound right. The final jolt, which I had felt so many times before, was missing. My attention now focused on a little green plunger, below the co-pilot's seat, which was supposed to stick up when the nose wheel was safely locked down. It was barely visible and I did not trust it at all.

"Just my bloody luck," I said, climbing back into my seat and unfolding the map. "We'll deviate slightly off course, and fly over Luton."

I was soon talking to the Luton controller on the R/T, telling him of our problem and arranging to fly over the field for them to examine our nose wheel through their binoculars. We eventually came within sight of the airfield, and the tower could have had no excuse for not getting a real close up as I shaved the Ambassador past with our wing just clear of the tower's aerials.

"Hey, we didn't mean that low a fly past," rang in my earphones, but the verdict was negative.

"The nose wheel doesn't look as though it's fully extended, but we can't say for sure."

Well that proved nothing for us as we continued northwards towards Wymeswold, which we had no difficulty in finding on such a fine summer's afternoon. On receiving our first radio call, their reply was by no means welcoming.

"Suggest you return to Gatwick, Zulu November."

They might just as well have said, "Buzz off — we don't want a crashed aeroplane on our airfield!" and their suggestion was firmly refused; besides we did not have sufficient fuel for a return south. I informed the tower that we intended doing some high speed dives and pull ups in the hope of forcing the nose wheel backwards and down.

.... AND ATTEMPTING TO SHAKE IT LOOSE.....

The three dives that we did proved more alarming than bargained for as the aircraft screamed down, and the blood drained from our heads during the pull ups, wondering all the while if the tortured wings would stay on. Handing over control to my assistant and back down on my hands and knees, revealed that nothing had changed. It was a bitter disappointment, and there seemed little point in trying any more of the dives on which I had been pinning my hopes.

My mind was desperately searching for any other course of action as we circled the airfield, while discussing the most suitable grass area, off the runways, on which to run on to to minimize damage. While all this was going on, I still was feverishly searching my imagination for something else to try, and an idea came to me.

It was going to be cutting things very fine, but might just work while our diminishing fuel supply lasted, but in any case the less we had of it aboard the less the fire risk. I requested to speak to the chief engineer of the company involved, who was in the tower as well, and he came on the air asking me to go ahead with my message. Doing my very best to steady my voice, I transmitted, "I'm going to make a touch and go landing with only 20 degrees of flap to try to brush our nose wheel on the runway in front of the Tower. Will you use the binoculars and tell me what happens?"

I brought the Ambassador round on a flat approach, and at a higher than normal speed, as the intention was to go around again. Skimming the boundary fence and grass, I put the main wheels down early on the first part of the runway, and immediately started to gently lower the nose wheel. Gingerly it was dropped further and further, with the throttles slowly being advanced to keep the speed up. My throat was as dry as a bone, when an urgent shout came through my earphones, "The wheel's collapsing! Overshoot!"

I knew before I heard the call that we were sinking too low, and if the nose went down any further the propellers would touch the ground. In bitter disappointment, the throttles were pushed open, and we roared up into the air again.

As we climbed away, our man in the tower was back again on the R/T, "Zulu November — can't be sure, but I think the nose wheel moved back slightly further as you left the runway."

We would try once again. I was clinging to the hope that the tyre friction on contact with the runway would force the leg backwards and lock it.

We prepared to try once again and this time, as the nose wheel skimmed and touched the concrete without weight being lowered onto it, there was a definite 'clunk' from below our seats. A rather jubilant sounding voice echoed in my ears, "I think you've done it — the nose wheels moved right back."

But we were already away again, and the nose had not sagged downwards this time.

"Fuel's getting on the low side," I said to my assistant, as the Ambassador was flown round the airfield's circuit.

"Take her again, will you please — I'm going to check our little green button!"

On my knees once again, the all important button looked as though it had risen somewhat, but for the life of me I could not remember how far it normally protruded. However, the thud we had felt had been reassuring enough, and I now decided to chance a landing for real.

My thoughts raced: what else could I have tried, would I be able to run her onto the grass if the nose wheel started to collapse? I would soon get my answers because the moment of truth was about to arrive. As the main wheels made contact yet again with the ground, I delayed bringing down the nose until we had begun to slow up and then, with a dreadful feeling of apprehension, I lowered the unwilling twin tyres on to the runway. Cowering inwardly, I waited for the cockpit to sink to the concrete with a crash, but it did not happen. My efforts had got me off the hook and the Ambassador continued her landing run as I gently applied the brakes.

There was a lusty shout from my companion, and his hand thudded on to my shoulder, "Well done boy, you've done a bloody good job!"

I permitted myself a wry smile, thinking that, as it had all been my fault in the first place, the owner's representative was being quite charitable. Later that afternoon, on the way back south by train from Nottingham, my friend showed an undisguised sense of relief at the outcome of the flight, and what was more bought me several drinks on the strength of it.

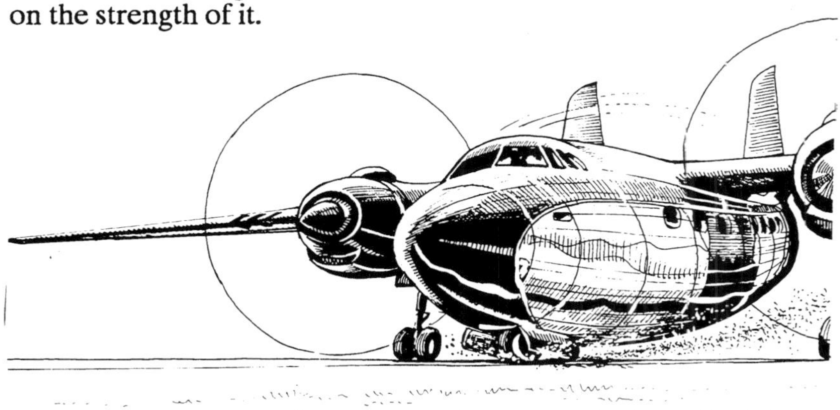

A NOSE WHEEL THAT WOULD NOT LOCK DOWN.

As I had been moonlighting when the incident at Wymeswold occurred, I had to be careful that it did not get back to the ears of management. However, I did recount the experience to a co-pilot friend when I was back flying with our company. By pure chance he was on a flight some weeks later, flying as co-pilot, with a Captain who was an old time veteran and much respected, but who was still smarting because he had received a severe written rebuke from the company over a similar nose wheel emergency, with a full load of passengers aboard, some months earlier. They had lowered it using the emergency release handle, but had requested the Fire Service to stand by just in case. Everything had turned out OK, but the local paper, perhaps being a bit short of news that evening, had given the incident front page space fully dramatized. The firm had been very vexed, the letter had followed, and far worse a dreaded copy was to remain in the personal file of the unlucky Skipper. Now, unbelievably, the two of them were due to land at Newcastle, with yet another nose wheel emergency and with passengers aboard.

So the wheel was lowered, a green light on the instrument panel was absent, but the green button protruded. The co-pilot counselled caution, but the veteran Captain produced his rankling letter and quoted, "The company do not appreciate unfavourable publicity — if the green button protrudes, then you should know that a safe landing can be made."

"But Skip," interjected my friend, "Arthur told me that he had this very same thing happen to him at Wymeswold a few months ago ... " He was cut short.

"I have my letter," said the Captain. "If the button is visible, that's it according to them."

They came in and landed. The nose leg collapsed, and sparks flew as the belly scraped along the runway with a rending of metal, together with a fearful racket as the props flailed themselves on the ground. Above all this noise, as the Ambassador slid along, could be heard the almost delighted cackle of the old veteran saying, "That will teach them to be so clever."

The aircraft now rested in a drunken nose-down attitude. The

AN AEROPLANE LOAD OF PASSENGERS, COME TO REST WITH MORE NOSE WHEEL PROBLEMS.

two switched everything off, and the co-pilot opened the front door and stepped out. In the cabin, the two stewardesses, realizing what had happened, told the passengers to collect all their belongings and leave by the front door instead of the rear, which was now perilously high above the ground. Some of the passengers even confessed later that they thought this was all part of a normal flight, sparks and all!

Everything was proceeding in an orderly manner in the cabin until, that is, the arrival of a lone fireman. Wielding an axe in one hand and an oversized torch in the other, he literally shoved the co-pilot bodily aside saying, "Get out of my way."

Inside the darkened cabin, the passengers were making orderly progress, when suddenly the wild helmeted apparition burst in upon them.

"Don't panic! This is an emergency! Evacuate the aircraft!" he bellowed at the top of his voice. That did it; arms and legs started to fly and chaos reigned — there was a mad rush for the exit.

The beautiful but forlorn aeroplane's troubles were by no means over. The triple finned tail, now sticking ignominiously skyward, had to be brought down so that the nose leg could once again be lowered. The station engineer had the answer: add sandbags to the rear cabin and let gravity do the rest. The plan was put into action and, when sufficient bags had been loaded aboard, the tail started to move downwards, very slowly at first but quickening rapidly to slam into the tarmac with a sickening bang. Repairs to this second accident were far more serious than the first, and many agonizingly searching post-mortems followed.

The cause of all these problems was eventually traced to nothing more simple than a few dried coats of green paint! The green button should always have been pushed up by a rod from below, when the nose wheel was safely locked down. The button had been painted so many times that it had stuck permanently up. Murphy had struck yet again.

The breaks away from scheduled flying were very frequent during these years. The tempo of life slowed noticeably as one bumbled through the skies at a leisurely pace with no really rigid schedules to keep, and even a very welcome extra livestock allowance of ten shillings per hour was payable for putting up with the farmyard smells. The Bristol Freighter had been originally used a lot as a car ferry, but came into its own as a 'flying horsebox'.

Motoring about Europe to some fairly outlandish aerodromes

with some of them just grass fields, the aeroplane could also let one down unexpectedly. Until it was modified, one of the aircraft's weaknesses was the brake system. To apply the brake, a bag or 'sack' inside the wheel assembly was inflated by air, and the designer must have forgotten how hot things got down there because they were always bursting.

At Le Bourget, coming in with some valuable horses to race in Paris, I was giving a very raw first officer some training and practice. He had just done the landing and had now finished taxiing down a straight stretch about a mile long with the wind blowing right across the track. The co-pilot had been using the left brake quite a bit, as the cross wind pressed against the large slab sided tail that caught the breeze better than any windjammer's sails. We had just entered the terminal area with gleaming four-engined airliners parked all about us, when suddenly there was a bang and a hiss of air. The wretched brake sack had chosen this moment to burst, and it could not have picked a worse moment.

We had just begun a turn into our parking space, then bang! hiss!

"Brakes gone," I called, shrinking back into my seat in dismay, while feverishly grabbing both fuel cut off levers and yanking them back to shut down the engines. The starboard brake was still working, and I now had my right foot trying to press it through the floor boards. It was swinging the aircraft, but might also help us stop. Mesmerized, I watched the left engine below my side window as it ran down. We were swinging in an arc towards a parked van. Would it stop in time? The windmilling four-bladed propeller seemed to be taking an eternity to run itself down. The van was practically underneath it, and passed through the arc of the blades just as they finally stopped.

My luck was really in that day, for the blades obligingly came to rest in the vertical and horizontal position. The wing only just scraped over the van, and finally stopped with the vehicle only a few feet from the fuselage. No one was more aware than me that I had escaped accident investigations and insurance interviews by a hair's breadth, and it all served to add extra elements of caution in later years.

Those days of flying the 'Horse Freighter' across the English Channel and elsewhere were an era that would never return, because of changing times. Modern ground radar surveillance, for example, now rules out the exquisite pulse quickening pleasures of flight at low level.

At Southend, one lovely summer's day, we set off to fly the

BRAKE FAILURE AT AN INOPPORTUNE MOMENT AT PARIS.... LE BOURGET......

Freighter empty across to Deauville to pick up six horses to be taken to Ireland. As we flew sedately across the south coast of England near the bleak flatlands of Dungeness, I said to the other two crew in the cockpit, "Too good an opportunity to miss — anyone mind if we go down for a bit?"

They both grinned, and the co-pilot gave me a 'thumbs up'. The column was eased forward, and the Freighter went into a shallow dive.

It was not long before we were skimming over the sparkling blue sea at a height of about 20 feet, banking occasionally to pass by ships and yachts. They were all magical moments: a Dutch yacht, being sailed down Channel by a couple, enjoying a fine following wind in their sails, waved enthusiastically as we passed; a ship's cook, in the middle of throwing a bucketful of slops over the stern of a merchant ship, looked up at us with a broad grin. A few more ships and fishing vessels later and the coast of France could be seen on the horizon, and it was not long before we were closing rapidly with it.

With the chalk cliffs of Normandy now looming above us, a turn to the right made climbing over the ramparts unnecessary as we continued to fly down the steeply sloping pebbly beach towards Le Havre. In the vicinity of Etretat some of the rock formations were of a most curious shape; wind and weather over thousands of years had done a strange sculpting job. Along a particularly deserted section, the Freighter was climbed up alongside the vertical chalk face and flown along the cliff top. It was most exhilarating flying as that spectacular scenery unwound below us, the proximity of the cliffs adding to the sense of movement.

Now getting closer to the built up areas near Le Havre and the mouth of the Seine, we zoomed up skyward before our approach to Deauville airfield. The stimulating effects of our flight so far was topped off with a really tight circuit before landing, which kept the pulse racing. It worked out just right as the old Bristol made her final swoop to earth over the trees surrounding the aerodrome. The steep turn was finally completed, and the wings levelled only seconds

A THOROUGHLY ENJOYABLE TRIP TO DEAUVILLE IN FRANCE... COMPLETELY UNKNOWN TO US AT THE TIME... WE HAD PASSENGERS IN THE AFT CABIN....

before the wheels brushed onto the ground. The three-point landing had been like a feather, and brought a feeling of immense satisfaction. The aircraft was taxied across the grass to the hard-standing in front of the club house and hangars, and the engines switched off.

Feeling quite pleased with myself, I relaxed in my seat and set about completing the necessary paperwork. Looking up from my writing, I became aware of a group of figures gathering below the cockpit window and gazing upwards. I recoiled back into my seat, out of their line of vision, and half hissed at the engineer behind, "Where the hell have they come from?"

He blandly replied, "They're our passengers, Skip — three owners and six grooms."

Seeing my look of complete astonishment, he added, "Didn't you know they were aboard, Cap'n?"

That was a question that needed no answering at all! I had completely overlooked that they were with us, as we had had no horses aboard, and assumed that we were empty. I experienced that awful sinking feeling again — this was not going to look good when the complaints rolled in.

I ventured back to the window and looked down; the little group was still there and still with heads upturned, but there was something else — they were all smiling! I gulped — this looked encouraging. Pulling back the sliding window and leaning out, I could even see one or two with thumbs up as I called down, "Gentlemen, I really am very sorry. I would never have subjected you all to that if I'd known we had passengers aboard."

I made a mental note to ask the traffic officer back at Southend how he had managed to keep these few heads so dark on the ship's papers. One of the group standing below us called up with a laugh, "It was very enjoyable, Captain. We were a bit concerned when we first went down, but the rest of the trip was terrific. Must fly with you again sometime!"

These indulgences were few and far between; it was a case of many factors having to come together at the same time, for example, having no passengers aboard and to be flying over an area remote enough not to cause disturbance, or for that matter to have one's number taken!

Another low flying visit, which I made to a friend's house in East Sussex during the summer of 1959, had long term connections for me because 25 years later, little did I know, I would buy and live in the

... AND MEETING A VERY SPORTING GROUP OF ENGLISH GENTLEMEN....

property myself. We were flying empty, again in the Bristol Freighter, and this time it really was empty, from Gatwick to Southend with just the co-pilot and myself at the controls. It was a beautiful summer's afternoon as we carefully map-read our way to Robertsbridge, and I soon spotted my old friend's house perched on a hill well away from the town.

The Freighter's nose went down and treetops were soon skimming by below us. We were aimed straight at the chimney top, the large oak tree in the centre of the paddock went past, and a last minute pull up into a steep turn to the left took us away over the beautiful Sussex countryside adjoining. I did not know it at the time, but the lady of the house was in the middle of feeding her baby daughter and she rushed to the window. Meanwhile we were headed back for a second pass round the house; treetops were rushing underneath the Freighter's stubby nose and, darting a glance downwards over the

DEEP IN THE SUSSEX COUNTRYSIDE, A VERY GOOD FRIEND'S WIFE, IS DISTURBED, WHILE FEEDING THE BABY........

massive bullet shaped propeller spinner along the wing arcing just above the trees, I thought I caught a glimpse of a figure looking out of a bedroom window.

Unknown to us, another drama was unfolding along a leafy lane below us, and I learned about this much later from my friend who had not been home at the time. The District Nurse had been riding sedately on her bicycle when she saw our Bristol Freighter pass overhead. In her very own words, she was absolutely positive that it was going to crash as she could distinctly see that the aeroplane had its wheels down! It was reported that she disappeared, cycling frantically after us over the brow of the hill. Indeed, how I had often wished that that noble aeroplane's wheels could have been retracted, as I had watched ice forming in massive chunks on its struts. I never did consider getting a message through to the District Nurse about all this.

When the winters came around and the fog, ice and snow returned, flying was often not quite so pleasant. It is well known that an aeroplane buzzing around inside clouds in freezing conditions will begin to collect ice on its propellers and front surfaces at a rate dependent on its shape and speed. The Freighter, with its huge bulk, thick wings and tail, proved to be a natural ice collecting device as we found out one day to our dismay. The aeroplane's anti-icing system was next to useless; alcohol was supposed to flow out of porous strips along the wing surfaces, similar to the Viking.

What I would have given to have had the designer with us as we passed Liverpool, having crossed the Irish Sea from Belfast. The weather had become progressively worse, as we flew through a frontal system with still quite some way to go to our destination, Cranfield, in Bedfordshire. As per the book and with tongue in cheek, we had already started to pump alcohol from the strips along the wing leading edge and tail surfaces. We kept this going, for it looked like we were in for a hard time as we entered the icing conditions. The engines were already spluttering occasionally with their carburettor heat fully on, and there were a continuous series of loud bangs from very close behind the cockpit as lumps of ice slammed into the sides of our machine, having been thrown from the propellers. However, it was the wings that were really worrying us as we ploughed on through the bumpy air and thickening cloud.

Looking out of the side window, through the propeller arc of the roaring Hercules just outside, could be seen an ominous white build-up of ice on the front edge of the wing which was growing and growing. Our antiquated alcohol system obviously was having no effect, as we progressively had to increase engine power to prevent our airspeed from falling off.

Unseen to our right, we passed Birmingham as we struggled on through the dense cloud — getting above it would be out of the question. Our only hope was to get down and land before we literally fell out of the sky.

"Ask Air Traffic Control for a descent," I said to the co-pilot, and this he promptly did. Easing the aircraft down gradually, we were just about able to hang on to our airspeed, still with the same high power set on our two straining engines.

After what seemed like an age, we were at last in radio contact with Cranfield, and they guided us down on radar. What a relief it was when the runway eventually came into view, as we came out through the bottom of the clouds. However our touch down was anything but normal. The controls felt like lead. Instinct warned me that we were perilously near stalling point so engine power was kept well up and only partial landing flap was lowered to help keep drag to a minimum. The Freighter flopped on to the runway at last, like a sack of potatoes, and we were relieved to get her off the strip and parked with the engines switched off.

The results could now be surveyed at leisure. Unloading had commenced as we climbed down the ladder from the cockpit and stretched our legs. First priority was a cup of tea, after which we would deal with our ice problem. The sun had just begun to break through occasionally and a slow thaw seemed to be setting in as the co-pilot and myself returned to our aeroplane. She would certainly not be flying again today until every last vistage of that killer ice was removed. De-icing an aircraft was always an expensive business as gallons and gallons of fluid were needed, and less money in the kitty meant a lesser chance of being paid promptly at the end of the month. However the ice was thawing steadily, so the sun therefore would be pressed into service on this occasion.

As I stood below the wing on that winter's morning the ice had begun to come off in chunks and slabs, with the process continuing until the outline of the aeroplane lay marked in ice debris on the ground where it had fallen from the wings, tail, bulbous nose and undercarriage legs.

Stooping down, I picked up a piece and it took me completely by

IN THE DEAD OF WINTER.... FEELING THE SHEER WEIGHT OF THE ICE, OUR LONG SUFFERING FREIGHTER HAD BEEN STAGGERING AROUND WITH.

surprise. I seemed to have based my previous judgement of the weight of ice entirely on the chunks in a glass of whisky, but this was something very different. It was so heavy that a second hand had to be brought into use to comfortably support the elongated block of ice. I looked at the rest of it, lying in a line, in awe and gulped. My God! — we had been carrying all that tremendous load of icy death around the sky for quite a while, thanks to a next to useless anti-icing system.

Flying this aerial ice collector around the winter skies of Europe had another big problem as well, and this was to do with keeping warm in the aeroplane itself. The best that some unknown, often reviled designer could offer was a fearsome burner, fed by petrol, and located below the cockpit floor inside the main cabin. This highly inflammable device was there to provide warmth for the occupants.

The only trouble was — it rarely worked.

Attempts to start the heater would invariably fail. A pilot or engineer would then climb down the ladder, withdraw the spark plug, dry it out and try again. With temperatures steadily plummeting as the aeroplane climbed, and with this performance repeated several times, defeat would eventually have to be admitted, with much cursing of the heater.

Freezing temperatures on the surface could well mean a very chilly minus 20 degrees at cruising height without special warm clothing, and the crew would have to put up with this misery for hour upon hour.

Human ingenuity, however, knows no bounds, and it was not long before some bright spark thought of using the very cargo we were carrying on regular contract from Luton to Northern Ireland, to help warm ourselves. The pilots would take it in turns to climb down the ladder into the main cabin, seat themselves in a car, start up, and it would not be long before the engine was thoroughly warmed up with the heater going full blast. With the car windows up, the exhaust fumes were soon dispersed in the Freighter's draughty cabin, and life-giving warmth would soon start flowing back through chilled limbs.

Pilots sitting in running cars in flight!

Such were the lengths to which we were often driven, just to keep warm in an aeroplane.

Progress fortunately brought more effective systems, but one of the greatest advances that came upon the aviation scene was the advent of the pressurized passenger and crew cabin. Here we could now climb and descend at previously undreamed of rates, without discomfort to the ears; we could soar high above mountains and fly in air so thin that human life could not be supported in it for more than seconds. Unfortunately, this great milestone had yet to be reached, when one day I fell victim to the results of a fairly rapid descent with a blocked ear in an unpressurized aircraft, which perforated my eardrum. It was a period of great personal crisis for me, because I knew that it might inevitably mean the loss of my Flying Licence and, consequently, the end of my aviation career, like so many other pilots I had known who had suffered the same ill fortune on flights.

A BURST EAR DRUM... THE CONSEQUENCES OF FLYIN G WHILE SUFFERING WITH A COLD......

CHAPTER 9

Ever since starting in aviation, I had occasionally had trouble in clearing my left ear on descent. One or two years might go by without experiencing any difficulty, and then it would suddenly recur. This was to be one of those times, on an autumn evening, as we descended into Cambridge carrying horses in the Bristol Freighter. Because of the excruciating pain, the rare occasions when it did happen had come to be dreaded, but this time it seemed to be worse than ever before. The lower the aeroplane descended, the worse the pain became. Clutching my ear, I called to the other Captain with whom I was flying, "Slow down the rate of descent, Ernie. Bloody hell! It feels like my ear's going to burst." My friend did his best, but we could not prolong our arrival back on the ground indefinitely.

By the time we were down, the pain was so great that I found myself staggering around in a daze. Medical attention was rapidly becoming a vital necessity as far as I was concerned and, it being a Sunday, this created further problems. Some urgent telephone calls made by our Agent revealed that our best bet was to divert the taxi, arranged to take us back to base, to a hospital in the East End of London, which was the only likely place capable of dealing with an ear problem on a Sunday evening. However, there seemed to be very little they could do, and at home a day later, the eardrum gave up the struggle and perforated. In severe pain, I dragged myself round to the local doctor, who confirmed this. My heart sank — it was a black day — desperation and secrecy now followed.

My only hope was that the drum might heal before the Ministry of Civil Aviation found out about it and withdrew my Flying Licence. The pain gradually diminished under treatment of antibiotics prescribed by the doctor, and I pestered him for information on the damage. He eventually drew a diagram for me showing the size of the perforation, and told me to come back in a week.

I was now on three weeks' sick leave, and I knew that if it had not healed by then I would not be able to keep events dark any longer and that my flying career would be at an end. Time dragged by as I lived in apprehension, and a week later the doctor again peered into my ear. The small hole was beginning to show faint signs of repairing itself, and a week after that my joy knew no bounds when the doctor informed me that tissue had re-formed over the damaged area.

Less than three weeks later I was back at work, and about a month afterwards, full of doubts, I presented myself before the official Ministry of Civil Aviation doctor for my bi-annual licence renewal medical. As the doctor peered into my ears in turn, I knew the moment of truth was at hand. When he completed his inspection, I asked expectantly, "Everything OK with the ears, Doctor?"

"Reasonably good," he replied, and then after a very slight hesitation he added, "one of the drums seems to look a bit scarred though, but I'd say they were OK."

This time I had got away with it — my flying licence had survived through luck and a lot of help from nature.

Such incidents were an example of the many pitfalls in an aviation career, and, then again, there were the many self-inflicted risks that pilots took in those times, because it was the general practice, unhindered by rules or the law. Bad weather on landing was the challenge, and the game often became one-upmanship to see which pilot could get down in the worst conditions.

Up until then, the company manuals had laid down minimum conditions for landing in reduced visibility and low cloud for their pilots, but there was absolutely nothing to prevent a crew, if they so wished, making an approach to see how circumstances looked to them. Nothing, that is, until there was a fatal accident involving a Vickers Vanguard landing one night in fog at Heathrow. A law was quickly passed, and after that a pilot could end up in Court, prosecuted for landing below certain visibility limits.

It seems strange by today's standards that this was so long in coming, but before this however there were not many pilots who did not bend the rules. Depending on one's familiarity with the aeroplane, local knowledge of the airfield, and nerve and skill, one came down through the murk as low as one cared or dared getting the crew's agreement beforehand. For a few brief months, London Airport provided a good example of this, no doubt, foolhardy competitiveness, of which I too was guilty.

The 'sixties was the decade of exciting new developments on the horizon, with automatic landings one of many revolutionary ideas being worked upon. Part of all this was the installation of powerful lines of lights set in the touch down area of the concrete itself, and it did not take us, other users of Heathrow with our older aeroplanes, long to realize that here was an excellent aid to get us down below limits.

One evening we were on our way back to London in an Ambassador with fifty-five passengers from the North of England. The Thames Valley was vanishing rapidly in fog as it got dark, and we waited impatiently for our turn to land while listening to radio reports of conditions becoming worse and worse by the minute.

When our turn finally came, chances looked very slim as I hand flew our old Ambassador down the ILS centre line and glide path of the runway. The fog had now become quite dense (it was being reported as less than 300 metres), but we informed the controller that we would like to exercise our option to come down and see how we fared. We had an admirable steed after all; the Ambassador with its high wing meant that the pilot's position was relatively close to the ground, for example it was perfectly easy to hand anything out of the cockpit window to someone standing on the ground outside, and this gave one a much better chance of seeing the runway lights on approaching them. It was the old story, if we did not make it into Heathrow that night, the extra bother of a diversion somewhere else would be most inconvenient.

With wing flaps set, we were now descending through the murk, as I devoted all my concentration on sensitive movements of the control column to keep the small cross needles on the Instrument Landing System centralized, and only daring a brief snap glance forward through the windscreen for any sign of runway lead-in lights. We were passing 200 feet and still going down. Outside there was now a diffused glow of lights, but nothing even remotely distinct and the glow was getting brighter almost to the point of mesmerizing us. I called to the co-pilot, "It's flat country around here — we'll continue down to 100 feet," adding, almost as an excuse, "no obstructions around."

We both knew very well that we were now contravening our company's orders by going below their recommended minimum height, and at 100 feet still nothing was clear — just the glow of the lights below us becoming brighter. By today's standards it was monstrous folly and, looking back on it, my co-pilot must have had immense faith, for as we sank blindly below 100 feet blurred glowing cross bar lighting came up through the gloom. It was the newly introduced high intensity bar illumination on the runway itself and, easing the power off, we flared on to the carpet of lights.

The wheels touched down on London Airport's concrete, with glowing runway centre line lights racing past beneath the seat of our pants and fog swirling about ahead of us. We braked gently to taxiing speed. A voice in my headset enquired, "Are you down?" And then, "When did you see the lights?"

But our recent clandestine activities were not for broadcast to incriminate ourselves, so tongue in cheek I replied, "Saw the lights at about 200 feet, a bit patchy though."

I consoled myself with the thought that it was not a complete lie; daft enough to take a chance but not quite dumb enough to admit we had bent the rules, and very badly at that. Looking back on our near blind landing, helped by advanced lighting, it was a good example of competitive foolhardiness which the law stepped in to end.

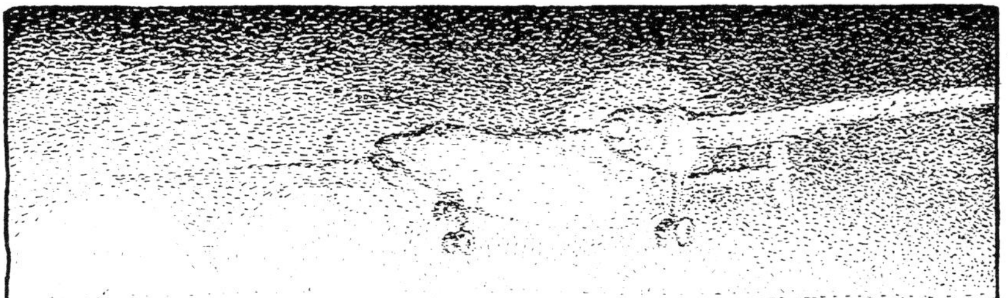

A NEARLY 'BLIND LANDING' IN FOG... LONG BEFORE 'AUTOLAND' HAD BEEN PERFECTED....

The newly installed runway bar lighting was part of the revolutionary new Autoland System being developed by several British companies working in conjunction with each other. Little did I dream that, less than twenty years later, I would find myself seated in the lofty flight deck of a wide bodied Tristar with 350 passengers aboard, while that 200 ton aeroplane set itself down on this very runway as gently as a feather, in the thickest of fogs, entirely without the help of human hand on controls or throttles. Gone into the realms of the past were those days of high risk, where only a pilot's skill and daring in adverse weather meant the difference between arriving at the destination or not.

Beautiful aircraft that the Ambassador was, she occasionally laid a trap for the unwary, and as events turned out a very painful one too. The device that could strike out at the unsuspecting pilot, if he did not adopt a set procedure, was the aircraft's control lock strap. To lock the control surfaces on the ground in windy conditions, a lever on the throttle pedestal between the two pilots was pulled up but, to remind them against making the deadly mistake of trying to take off with the locks in, a red tape in front of the pilot's face secured the lever. However, the snag was the hefty rubber loop, pierced by steel bolts and fixed on to the end of the red tape, which was rolled round a drum in the roof of the cockpit. In the heart of this drum, energized by a powerful spring coiled and lurking, lay the means of striking viciously at the unwary.

Flying an Ambassador, one day, was a notoriously absent-minded Captain who had started a take-off with the controls locked. The co-pilot, a long time friend of mine and now a Captain himself on 747 Jumbos, related how he had shouted a warning as the aircraft sped off down the runway. The Captain had left the locks in after the check list had been read, saying that he would do them later. Above the roar of the engines, the Captain in disarray shouted back, "Oh! release the locks then please Bryan."

This he had already started to do, for disaster was racing nearer. Grasping the lever on his side of the central pedestal with his right hand, he pulled it up, and then with his left hand slipped off the rubber loop on the end of the tape. The released locking lever was urgently slammed down, freeing the flying controls of the speeding aircraft, and none too soon for the moment of take-off was rapidly approaching. The Captain was now able to ease the control wheel back as the co-pilot released the tape.

Murphy must have been around because as the reel on the cockpit roof spun in the tape, it snaked upwards and the heavy end, which could have expended its force in a hundred other directions but did not do so this time, chose the luckless Captain's mouth as its target, smashing into his lips at the very moment he was in the act of lifting the airliner into the air. Blood spurted from the wound spattering his uniform shirt, and the pain caused the victim to let out a howl of agony. Fifty-five unsuspecting passengers would certainly have had a word or two to say had they been able to witness these strange goings on up front.

Word about such events must have filtered back to aeronautical designers, because cockpits, or 'flight decks' as they were becoming known, gradually became more foolproof. This applied to most aspects of Civil Aviation, and the passing of the petrol powered engine in passenger airliners greatly helped to reduce the hazard of fire. Petrol, that highly inflammable liquid, had been a bogey which

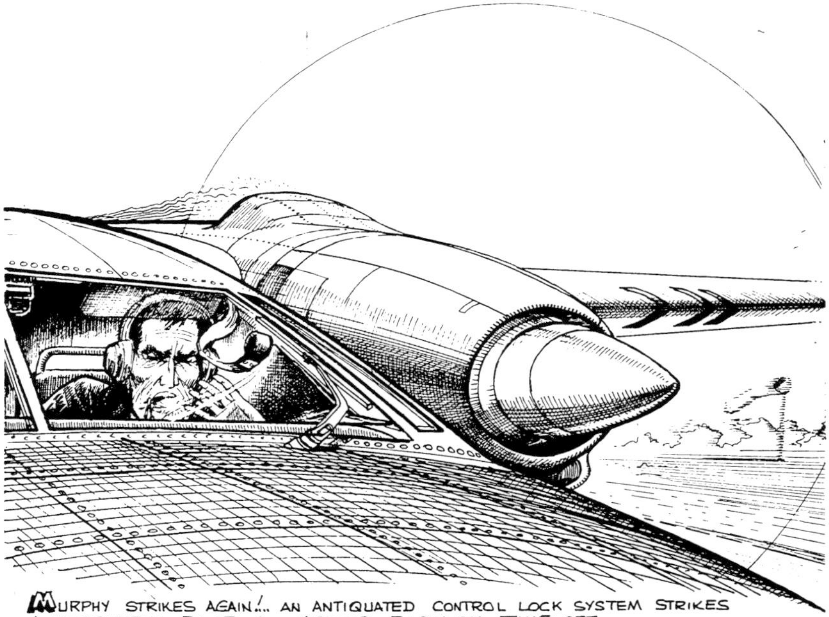

MURPHY STRIKES AGAIN!... AN ANTIQUATED CONTROL LOCK SYSTEM STRIKES A FORGETFUL PILOT A VICIOUS BLOW, ON TAKE-OFF......

had long hung over our heads; most pilots tried to dismiss the possibilities from their imaginations — fire would not happen to them. That spectre was farthest from my mind one winter's night at Newcastle-upon-Tyne as we prepared to depart with a full load of passengers for London.

Our Ambassador had been standing in the open for some while, and a heavy coating of frost and ice all over the top surfaces would have to be removed. The engineers set to work and the ice soon wilted before an onslaught of de-icer fluid applied hot to quicken the melting process.

We made ready to depart; all the passengers had been boarded and it was the co-pilot's turn to fly. Doors were closed, and I said, "OK, John, start her up."

My eyes dropped back down for a last minute check of the paperwork on my lap. The co-pilot had plenty of experience on the aircraft and could be relied on. The starter was engaged, and from outside I could hear the huge four bladed propeller on his side turning over. Both of his hands were stretched out in front of him, one hand operating the starter switch and the other pressing the fuel priming button to enrich the petrol air mixture to aid starting the stone cold engine. Pen in hand, my concentration raced over the paperwork, but a gut feeling prompted that all was not right. Glancing upwards from the papers, there seemed to be something strange about the floodlit tarmac outside; the lights seemed to be getting brighter, flickering and turning into a glowing orange rosiness.

My head shot forward, and at full stretch I could just see past the co-pilot's face out of the small rearmost cockpit window. He was still concentrating on the engine start, his silhouette being backlit by the reflected glow from the adjacent hangar doors. Fire! Our mighty Centaurus engine had been over-primed with fuel and was taking fire. The ground engineers, standing in view over the nose, were beginning to display great agitation, their white overalls now glowing orange. I could see the engineer-in-charge leaping high into the air to attract our attention, pointing at the engine while his other arm flailed round wildly in circles. I had drunk many a pint of beer with him off duty; he was an old timer, and I understood his gestures only too well indeed. We had all had these over rich starts many times before in our careers, and the standard drill was to keep the engine turning to try to draw the over-fuelled mixture through the engine.

"Stop priming! Keep her turning on the starter," I cried to the co-pilot. "We're going on fire out there!"

He turned his head and the sight of the flames above the wing from the engine exhausts, just visible from where he sat, must have shaken him badly.

"Christ!" he exclaimed, recoiling, and at the same time involuntarily released the starter switch, but the engine had to be kept turning, and there was no time for any delay. With the propeller blades slowing to a stop, the flames were now flickering upwards with no propwash to blow them away backwards.

My hand flashed over to the starter switch and frantically re-engaged it; the long suffering starter motor would just have to risk losing a few teeth. The big propeller began to turn again, in spite of the by now almost red-hot starter long past its time limit for continuous use. Salvation came none too soon; there was a half-hearted cough and then a splutter as one or two cylinders fired. A dexterous flick of the switch over to 'start and boost', with judicious movement of the throttle with my other hand, and our luck changed as the Centaurus burst into life.

"Even the de-icer fluid on top of the wing looked as if it had started to burn, but the prop blew it out — it was touch and go," said Bob, our engineer, the next day. There was possibly an element of guilty conscience in his voice too, for we had not been told that the engine had still been hot from a previous test run and hence the co-pilot's heavier than necessary fuel priming.

The stewardess told us how agitated our passengers had been as they sat powerless in the cabin, watching the flames licking around above them and even cascading down from the wing outside. This was the sort of event that the 'regulars' learned to live with, when travelling as passengers in the Ambassador, and certainly from the pilot's point of view no two engine starts on that aeroplane were ever the same. Depending on the season of the year, the most powerful radial piston engine ever built in Britain had to be treated just right, to burst into life.

ENGINE FIRE, DURING START-UP........

The lovely old aeroplane could hand out favours too, as a certain incorrigible co-pilot happily attested on a flight back from Portugal to London one night. It happened to be my turn to fly the sector.

"Put your head down if you wish," I said to the co-pilot, "I'll look after her for a bit."

But he obviously had other ideas as he replied, "Think I'll stretch my legs and chat up the birds."

With that he slipped through the cockpit door, leaving me in the company of the stars and making sure the autopilot continued to take us in a straight line across the Bay of Biscay in the darkness below us to our landfall at Quimper on the Finistere Peninsula of France.

He was absent from the cockpit for quite a while, and when he made his appearance again he had a trace of dishevelment about him and a hint of lingering female perfume. Sitting in his seat at the controls, he could no longer contain his sense of euphoria.

"How did it go?" I enquired, noting an unmistakable look of satisfaction on his face.

"I think I can claim a little record here," he said glancing at the altimeter on the lighted instrument panel. "Sixteen thousand feet," he added with a wry smile.

I knew exactly what he meant, and I realized also that I would get the full story before long as we had flown together for years and knew each other well.

I was not mistaken for by the time we were passing high above Jersey in the early light of dawn, the escapade unfolded. He was one of those characters who was always forthright, not given to exaggeration, and I had to give him full marks for ingenuity. One of the two stewardesses was a curvaceous young lady, who turned many an eye, and this was to be their night of magic.

In the darkened galley just behind the cockpit their bodies had touched; the signals were unmistakable as he whispered to her to follow him down to the tail of the aircraft after a few minutes. He made his way aft along the darkened cabin, past the rows of slumbering passengers to the far end, and entered the dimly lit starboard toilet, which was special as it had an access to the rear baggage hold behind it. The co-pilot knew his aircraft well; he quickly unclipped a layer of padded soundproofing material from the toilet bulkhead revealing a small door. It was designed for emergency crew access only, and the covering also served the purpose of concealing the door from the eyes of inquisitive passengers. He squeezed through the door into the baggage hold, and rearranged the jumble of suitcases into a flatter layer under the securing webbing. He had hardly completed this when there was a light knock and the stewardess entered the eagerly opened toilet door, which was then bolted. The passengers slumbered on in the sky above Biscay that night, and I was often to wonder what aircraft designers might say if they realized what other uses people can find for their products.

The lovely old Ambassador, in which we flew that night, was again by strange coincidence 'Alpha Delta'. Graceful as she was, her fate was soon to come when she plunged inescapably to her doom into Terminal One at Heathrow Airport, London.

As the decade of the 'sixties rolled on, passenger traffic was on the increase; thus expansion was necessary, and larger aircraft with better range were needed to carry the loads. As usual in those times, the option was cheaper secondhand aircraft that were coming onto the market when the State Airlines re-equipped with new generation jets.

'The Whispering Giant' was to be our firm's new acquisition and, having stuck with the company now for more than ten years, I had accumulated sufficient seniority to be one of the pilots selected to do a course.

After our Ambassador, the aircraft's sheer size was awesome; full of the usual initial doubts, I stood below gazing up at the ex-BOAC 'Britannia' which hopefully I would soon be flying. The four-engined monster towered above me; to step out of the main cabin door without the help of motorized steps would be a bit like launching out of a first floor window — broken bones a certainty. Each one of the four engines was a good deal more powerful than anything I had handled before; it was basically a jet engine driving a huge propeller through a turbine.

It was the coming of a new era in aviation for most of us in the company, together with some big changes too. We would be required to complete a full time Ministry approved classroom course; there would be no more need to go off hunting around for information on

ONE WAY OF KILLING TIME AND STAYING AWAKE ON A LONG FLIGHT...... TWO PILOTS PLAYING AT THE GAME ,OF, "WHO CAN LOOK THE DIMMEST" REFEREED BY THE FLIGHT ENGINEER. THE WINNER .... THE ONE WHO COULD REMAIN SERIOUS LONGEST.... THE HILARIOUS LAUGHTER WAS UNBELIEVABLY DIFFICULT TO RECOVER FROM TO REENTER THE CONTEST.....

a new aircraft, scrounging notes from here and there, and then trying one's luck at the Air Registration Board examination on the type. Starting one Monday morning, we found ourselves sitting in a proper classroom having it all dished out to us by a battery of instructors from nine until five — this was indeed a new world.

The big day of my start on flying training eventually came round; the aeroplane was parked on the tarmac at Shannon Airport, and I climbed into the left hand seat for my first training detail. It felt like a spotlight was on me and I was filled with a feeling of acute unease. In the co-pilot's seat sat a BOAC Training Captain, and behind me were two more instructors, one in the flight engineer's seat. I need not have nursed any such qualms for the Training Captain and his assistants turned out to be nothing like their awesome reputation as hatchet men. Instead a friendly voice, with a strong Geordie accent, talked me into relaxing and learning how to fly the big beast. The start was to be nice and gentle — the pressure stuff would follow later. She was enormous by comparison with anything I had ever flown before, and as the machine started to throb with life, when all four of the huge Proteus turboprop engines were lit up in turn, I tried to keep pace with the mass of instruments (twice as many as I had been used to before) that had come to life in front of me. They talked me round the first take-off and landing with plenty of encouragement handed out. Flying details continued at intervals for the next week, day and night.

Just over two weeks later, the first crews had been checked out; immediately we began flying passengers around in the new addition to the fleet, and the aircraft had already started to shrink in my imagination. It is widely accepted among aviators that however large an aircraft the smaller it becomes in time with handling. The Britannia proved to be no exception and, in spite of a few early problems mainly due to electrical troubles, we were soon flying her with increasing confidence.

The aeroplane was worked hard on routes for which it had never been designed. She had been intended to do long range flights with landings at big international airports. Instead it was now short sectors and many landings. One runway, which we used many times daily at Newcastle in the north of England, used to change its profile by the month. Coal-mining operations below ground were the cause of this and, before they were halted and a new runway built, the big aeroplane took fearful punishment. Dips and depressions hammered the heavy speeding aircraft's landing gear, wheels and brakes to the limit, while jolting and rocking passengers in their seats. However, the old Britannia was built solidly, and I had good reason to find this out one filthy black night at Teesside in Durham.

A very active weather front was sweeping through the area, and we were unlucky enough to arrive in the middle of it. We broke through ragged cloud to the south of the airfield, with rain beating on the windscreens and the prospect of having to put the aircraft down in a blustery crosswind, which was already blowing occasionally over our limit for landing. If we did not get in tonight, it would mean a diversion to far off Manchester, an all night coach ride for about 100 passengers, and worse still a ridiculously early start for our crew to get back to square one in the morning.

As the Britannia was turned on to base leg, the runway lights were barely visible through the rain. We were being bounced around in the cockpit as the controller's voice came through telling us that the wind was increasing. I was pinning my hope on being able to land during a decrease in the gusts; a quick discussion with the co-pilot and flight engineer, and they agreed that I give it a try.

We turned on to final approach and started down; the rain had slacked off a bit, but those north country winds had weight in them. Even though we were now lined up with the runway, the nose was pointing away over to the right. My white knuckled hands wrestled with the control column as I shouted to the co-pilot, "Land flap please."

The flight engineer reached between us and concentrated on handling the four throttles. As the speed decreased with the lowered flap, I found myself looking at the runway coming up towards us, not from ahead as normally but through the side window.

We were now swooping down towards the runway threshold with my left foot straining against the rudder pedal, probably at the limit of its travel. In the heat of the moment, the controller's voice again sounded in my ears as I lowered the right wing as much as I dared without striking the huge outer propeller blades on the ground. He had chosen the right second to deliver more bad news — the wind across the runway had increased still more in strength. Too late; the tyres had already made contact with the soaking wet runway, and it was only this that saved us from something much worse. There was a fearful scuffing sound from outside as the aircraft slid bodily sideways down the runway. Full rudder and brake on the left main wheels had no effect at all; it was only the streaming wet surface that saved the tyres and wheels from failing. I remember the landing lights shining, not down the runway but across the field towards the Control Tower as we skidded sideways along the runway.

As the propellers were put into reverse, we started to slow but still swinging about as the nose wheel steering began to be effective again. At last the aircraft came to rest and miraculously we were still on the runway. Even at a standstill she still shook and trembled as the howling gale buffeted her about. My heart seemed to be thumping away somewhere in my throat as I breathed a sigh of relief.

A CROSS WIND LANDING... COMPLETELY OUTSIDE LIMITS... THAT GOT A LITTLE OUT OF HAND.

"What did that landing seem like in the back?" I asked the senior stewardess when I got the chance.

"Nothing too unusual," she replied. "Perhaps rather bumpy on the way down."

When asked, she said, "No, I had not noticed the landing lights illuminating the airport buildings just after touch down!" and she gave me a strange look as well!

When I stepped out of the aircraft, with my uniform hat pulled well down over my ears, the body had to be leaned right forward to walk against the wind. I recall commenting on my heavy suitcase that refused to stand up unless it was faced exactly into the teeth of the gale.

We were pleased to have got the aircraft down in one piece; the only traces she carried of her ordeal were scuff marks on the tyres. However, we were all patently aware that we had broken the rules badly that night, and had been lucky to get away with it.

The Britannia's servo controls were her Achilles' heel when it came to crosswind take-offs or landings. All the wing and tail control surfaces were not linked to the cockpit at all, but were hinged to flap freely. What was linked to the pilot's controls was a narrow servo tab stretching along the length of each control surface's trailing edge, and to be effective this tab needed a good airflow over it before the main surface itself was moved by it to control the aeroplane. The system had weight and other advantages in a big aircraft, but brisk response to the controls was not one of them, and hence its poor performance in crosswinds.

I had an opportunity to appreciate the Britannia's control sluggishness one day flying empty to pick up return passengers from Bastia in Corsica. As we neared our destination, the weather was perfect. The beautiful island lay before us, and it was just too good an opportunity to miss. I pressed the call button, and one of our four stewardesses was soon leaning over our shoulders.

"Fancy doing a bit of low flying?" I said. "Ask the rest of the girls if they would like to come up front."

We were already in an early descent towards the rugged coastline, when we were joined by the rest of the girls, all raring to go. Down went the nose and off came the power as we dived earthwards. The scenery was really tremendous; seven pairs of eyes peered forward through the Britannia's cockpit windows as the sights sped past below under the nose. In some parts the cliffs were sheer and gaunt, and

the next moment we would suddenly come upon a remote fishing village built almost vertically up the cliff side. It was all very enjoyable, but somewhere along the coast the 'beat up' definitely became overcooked.

A small headland lay ahead of us and the nose was lifted gently to take the 'Whispering Giant' over it. For a split second my senses flashed a warning that the big mass of machinery was going to continue on its original path into the rocks, but she lifted in time and passed over the ridge. I do not think anyone of the spectators noticed me swallow hard, but it was a timely warning, and although the crew seemed to think it was a nicely judged pass the handler definitely did not. Perhaps it was those servo controls again, inertia, my imagination, or the driver just getting a little older and losing his nerve. However there was to be only one more occasion on which we would be able to indulge in this erstwhile sport, as the black box flight recorder was introduced, which would record everything the aeroplane did and be a great step forward in making aviation safer.

As the airline expanded, the classical series of changes crept in, more staff and less of the personal touch. Sadly, one of the first things to go was the spirit of co-operation that existed between the smaller circle of staff who knew each other well. No doubt there may be other disadvantages associated with a small friendly operation, but inefficiency is not usually one of them. A good example of close co-operation occurred on a very early morning start from the hotel in Darlington, where the crew had been staying the night.

We had all enjoyed a very sociable evening together, retired late, and slept soundly — too soundly in fact, for my first recollection was the flight engineer hammering on my door.

"My God! look at the time!" I cried in horror. "No hope of making a scheduled departure! Why wasn't I called?"

The answer to that would have to wait. I scrambled into my uniform, not bothering about toiletries, packed my bag, and dashed downstairs. The rest of the crew had finished breakfast, and had already been sitting in the crew minibus outside for about twenty minutes. Why had not someone else acted when I had not shown up for breakfast? The answer transpired that they thought I had ordered it in my room, and was just very late. The co-pilot was on loan from another firm operating Britannias, and so perhaps could be excused for not using his initiative. It added up to no points for co-operation so far, but a dramatic improvement was to follow when the early morning cobwebs had blown away.

"Call the airport, will you please?" I asked the night porter as I raced through the hotel lobby. "Tell them we're on our way."

My question to him, "Why wasn't I called?" trailed away on the wind as I ran out to our transport. We sped away across the early morning Durham countryside, with myself urging the driver for speed and more speed. During the mad drive, I learned that the night porter was brand new on the job, and had only given the faintest of taps on each of the doors. Our driver was doing well, and as we rounded into the airport entrance on two wheels, I said to him, "Well done! Straight out to the aircraft!"

The journey to the airport usually took about twenty minutes — we had made up a bit of time on the ride today, and as we pulled up near our Britannia we had only a few more minutes to the all important scheduled departure time. It could not be done. I thought of how this was all going to be explained at the inevitable enquiry, but I had not reckoned on our magnificent ground staff.

The senior engineer on duty, another long standing colleague with whom I had also drunk many a glass of ale, was the first to speak to me as I alighted from the crew transport.

"Everything's organized, Arthur — just climb into the kite!"

I almost got caught in the rush. The traffic officer had been speaking to the stewardesses, and they all made rapidly for the aircraft steps, followed by myself. As I mounted the steps I could see passengers' faces at the cabin windows, and at the entrance door the four stewardesses turned right to walk sedately to their positions in the cabin, relieving two ground traffic attendants who had been supervising the passengers.

I turned left towards the cockpit, and as I did so I heard the unmistakable whirring sound of one of our huge Proteus turbines being started. This was, of course, before the days of air traffic clearance being necessary to start engines, and the ground engineer, who had started the engine, handed over to our flight engineer as I entered the flight deck. The second engine on the starboard side was already being started as I climbed into my seat, and the traffic officer handed me the weather reports and the ship's papers to check and sign.

Hasty thanks all round, and the doors were closed on time. The flight engineer started the port engines. We completed the rest of the checks, and taxied out. As the Britannia lifted gracefully into the air a short while later, Derek, our irrepressible flight engineer, turned to me with a broad grin and, tapping his watch, exclaimed, "Why, that's got to be a record, Arthur! Twenty-seven minutes from head leaving the pillow to wheels up after take-off!"

Thinking about the fifteen fleeting minutes spent on the road journey, the hasty scramble into clothes, and all the rest, I could not see any reason at all to disagree with him!

Looking back on the operation, it was not as rushed as might first appear. The aeroplane had been refuelled the previous night, the engineers had done all the checks right up to pre-start, the ground hostesses had boarded the passengers (making sure two pairs of steps were in position in case of evacuation being necessary), and the traffic officer had loaded the aircraft correctly — we relied on them all having done what was done properly, because we knew their capabilities well.

'Small is beautiful' was proven that day in Teesside, with the stops being pulled out when necessary — an era that is perhaps vanishing from the aviation world.

Scarcely ever could such corner cutting be seen in airline operation, and to make sure it did not happen, or even the companies

LATE FOR WORK!.... BUT, AN 'ON SCHEDULE' TAKE-OFF... AFTER A NIGHT STOP.

themselves from skimping on expenditure at the price of safety, the Government founded Civil Aviation Authority had long since been taking an interest. To do this they were fielding an ever increasing number of inspectors, ex-pilots themselves, and, dressed in civilian clothes, they could swoop upon one without the slightest warning. Even being at the far corners of the earth did not guarantee immunity from being checked up on; an aircraft could arrive at some remote airfield to find an inspector on the ramp awaiting your pleasure to check all the crew and go through the aircraft, its documents and equipment with a fine toothed comb.

The inspector's powers were sweeping, but were rarely exercised to the limit; a writ, affixed to an offending aeroplane's windscreen grounding it, was the ultimate penalty if things were blatantly unsafe. Furthermore the man from the Ministry might also choose any flight at random and ride along in the cockpit just to check up in person on how procedures were being carried out. They had to pass the same flying tests as pilots themselves, and this policy made good sense because it could be all too easy for a non-flying man to sit behind and criticize an operating crew.

On the Britannia we had our regular inspector, and he happened to be aboard one day on a flight to Salzburg. It was not the very easiest of airfields, lying at the foothills of the Austrian Alps. A wall of sheer mountains rise rapidly from one end and encircle the other two sides in lesser degree. Some of the hills are topped with picturesque castles perched on them; indeed a lovely sight if seen on a clear day, but a very definite hazard to aviation when one could not see clearly.

As luck would have it on the day of our visit with the man from the Ministry, a thick misty haze blanketed the area. We had been expecting this as the airfield had been closed earlier in the morning due to fog. The proximity of the wall of rock lying just to the south meant that instrument approaches could only be made towards the mountains, and while we winged south-eastwards the weather was being reported as still below our landing limit. I could feel my stomach knotting itself up, and with the gentleman sitting behind me holding his little blacknote book matters were not improved one bit.

"You are cleared to make an approach," came the voice of the Salzburg controller. "Aircraft have been landing before you."

This was by no means assurance that we would get down because we could not actually see the runway at 800 feet on our run in, so we might have to turn immediately and climb away out of the clutches of the mountains.

With my eyes glued on the little cross needles of the ILS, I carefully hand flew the Britannia down the glide path. Automatic coupled approaches had not yet reached us, and the utmost concentration was required. With her three sets of wheels locked down and landing flap set, our Britannia continued down the glide path. The flight engineer crouched forward holding the four throttles, trimming them as I called the power settings required while flying the aeroplane and aware all the time of the man sitting behind us with notebook and pencil.

As we went through 1,000 feet just the ground directly below was all that was visible when I flicked my eyes sideways, away from the instruments, for a brief glimpse every now and then through my side window. My pulse was beginning to race. At 900 feet it was getting slightly better, but still nothing could be seen ahead. At the fateful

800 feet, faint details were just becoming visible, but certainly no runway.

I felt in my bones that in these conditions we would see it at any second. However the Ministry inspector would have no choice but to report an infringement of the rules if I went lower without sight of the runway. On an impulse I raised my right hand with a chopping motion of the palm in the direction of the front windscreen, and mustering as much confidence as I could called loudly, "I have the runway in sight."

At which point, so the flight engineer later on discreetly informed me, the Ministry man's head shot forward peering uncertainly ahead. Fortunately for me after we had descended another 100 feet, the runway floated dimly out of the murk.

"I must compliment you on your excellent eyesight, Captain," said the inspector as I walked with him to the terminal building after we had landed. There the matter ended, and I got the distinct impression that our inspector, being an experienced pilot himself, even approved of my tongue-in-cheek call earlier on. He had a job to do and his practical approach was commendable.

On another occasion I confess to a certain amount of guilt at the great amusement we had, at the same inspector's expense, on a long night flight, again in the Britannia.

Always the worst by far were the early morning hours on a night flight and struggling to keep weary eyeballs unshuttered — our Ministry man was no exception as the first light of dawn tinged the sky. Out of the corner of my eye, the movement of a nodding head did not pass unnoticed, and I looked as our erstwhile invigilator, seated behind us in the navigator's seat, gradually gave up the fight to keep awake. The head continued its sudden dips forward and, after a few near escapes from the embrace of Morpheus, he eventually succumbed to a deep sleep.

This in itself was perfectly OK as far as we were concerned; after all, if we had not been under inspection ourselves we would most likely be taking turns at resting too, but the fact was that the slumbering figure was becoming a major distraction.

It was one of the funniest sights I had seen in flight; the whole noble face gave the impression of slipping downwards. As sleep relaxed the muscles, the mouth sagged, the jaw dropped, and the lower lip curled outwards and downwards. From the now gaping mouth, sounds were building up that were beginning to be audible even above the steady surge of our four Proteus turboprops.

The co-pilot, flight engineer and myself were now literally creased up with laughter, made even more difficult by trying not to wake the sleeping figure. Surely a photograph would be in order? The camera was just being aimed, when a louder than usual snort nearly choked the sleeper into wakefulness. The idea of recording the spectacle on film was pegged because of the embarrassment of perhaps being caught *inflagrante delicto*. The inspector slept fitfully for most of the rest of the flight, little knowing how much he had helped sustain us during those weary hours; our laughter being all the more heightened because of our own fatigue.

Those five short years spent flying the Britannia were about the last of an era for a lot of us in our airline. There was more organization and orderliness, and excesses on night stops more controlled; not a little of the cause must have been the improved conditions of work and what we stood to lose, or maybe just the crews getting older and wiser. Nevertheless some night stops away from base still produced some wild activity, mainly spurred on by the 'demon' drink so easily available 'duty free' on the aircraft.

To help fill in the winter slack period, our company secured a contract to run a weekly tour using the Britannia, and for most of the crews they turned out to be a mammoth alcoholic endurance test. Every Saturday morning a crew would leave London and return a week later, when a fresh team would take over.

It was a case of 'ships that pass in the morning', as the crew and myself awaited the crew transport bringing in the incoming flight members. The Chief Pilot had been away for a week on this one, and I could hardly believe my eyes as he stepped out of the vehicle. He looked like death — dissipated was hardly the word — his eyes were sunken, the bags under them were bigger than ever, and most notable of all was a dreadful grey-green pallor to his face. As he trudged past with a muttered "Good-morning," his co-pilot said to me in a lowered voice, "My God! this has been one hell of a week-long party! I feel like death!"

I could only smile for I felt fairly certain that the coming week's flight would be no different.

Our first stop was always picturesque Seville in southern Spain with up to 112 passengers. The tours would get off to a swinging start shortly after arrival at the hotel, with a room party after everyone had changed out of uniform. Dinner-time was always a lavish affair as the company paid all meal bills in those days rather than pay out an eating allowance. Expense was therefore usually no object in our choice of restaurant, and naturally, as wine and spirits could not be billed, these were always shown as hors d'oeuvre or such like by arrangement with the head waiter. Two days in lovely Seville sped by with partying, sightseeing and gastronomic adventuring, followed by drinks and dancing in perhaps a Flamenco Night-Club or Disco, making our morning call to go back to work rather difficult.

Once in the air again and heading southwards towards Africa, leaving our winter further behind, the warmth and sunshine streaming through the Britannia's flight deck windows soon dispelled the cobwebs.

"How's the bottling work getting on back there?" I asked the flight engineer.

With a grin, he looked back over his shoulder, craning his neck to survey a hive of industry going on round the navigator's table. The co-pilot and two stewardesses had a mini production line assembled; several crates of Coca-Cola bottles were each having their caps levered off gingerly. Half of the contents were being poured away and then topped up from a seemingly endless supply of large Bacardi rum bottles grouped in another corner, before each Cola was re-capped.

"Keep up the good work," I said, "we're all shareholders."

We were bound for the walled city of Marrakesh at the foot of the Atlas Mountains, and the reason for all this unusual mid-air activity was a sudden change of heart by the local Customs officer. Word had come back that the hotel we used at Marrakesh had complained that crews were bringing in too much of their own supplies of liquor to sidestep the establishment's fancy bar prices. Our once friendly Customs officer, who had always before turned a blind eye to the crew's bottles, was now strictly banning any imports. It was strongly tipped that the hotel management had got to him. Therefore we had decided to make fresh arrangements as none of us had money to burn.

All was back to normal by the time we brought our Britannia down for her landing at Marrakesh; arid desert stretching away to the north, with splashes of greenery, palm and orange groves, giving way to the rising ground leading up to the high Atlas ranges. Our old friend, the Customs officer, after he had examined the crew's baggage, was all smiles as we walked away following our baggage trolley topped with cases of Coca-Cola.

However, it all turned out to be self-inflicted problems in the end, after a party I attended that night in the co-pilot's suite. Events started to warm up, and it did not take long for someone to suggest that his split level bedroom, reached by a staircase, would make an excellent jumping platform. There had been several well-oiled launch-offs from the upper floor level onto a large settee below. This was proclaimed as too tame, for the next round the participants would jump from the top of the balustrade itself. Everyone was having a marvellous time, and the jumping progressed accompanied by cheers from the crowd below in the lounge.

The co-pilot, somewhat more worse for wear than the rest, climbed atop the rail very unsteadily and peered down, while only just maintaining his balance.

"Christ! it doesn't half look high from up here!" he blurted, and his launch-off, when he had swayed round to it, was a disaster. He landed with a crash on the frame of the settee rather than in the centre; there was an extra loud splintering and rending noise, and after that things seemed to happen in slow motion.

Sitting very near the settee, I saw him reel sideways and fall bodily almost horizontally across a heavy plate glass table which was absolutely loaded down with bottles and glasses. The next second there was an almighty crash of shattering glass and bottles. The co-pilot now lay stretched out full length with piles of jagged glass under and over him — an Indian fakir on his sharpest bed of nails could not have done better. I looked down at him in horror, fully expecting to

see spurts of blood from a slashed jugular vein, but all was well. His eyes flicked open and, still somewhat dazed, he forced a trace of a smile, saying:

"Will you give me a hand up please Arthur?"

This I rapidly did, for I was never so pleased to hear a crew member speak.

The shambles that we were confronted with was a very sobering sight indeed; the thick plate glass table now lying in bits was going to be a big enough problem explaining away, besides the semi-demolished settee as well with which to contend. The thought of what all this could cost each of us, galvanized the revellers into action. Everyone present immediately set to work clearing up the glass and broken bottles.

We then turned our attention to the settee. The heavy tubular steel frame was buckled in the middle, the side mechanisms were adrift and distorted, and wooden parts splintered. Surreptitious repairs were going to be the only answer, and a plan was formulated for the next day. It was going to be essential that no hotel staff be let into the room. The co-pilot would remain there all morning, while the rest were detailed to scour Marrakesh for wire. Very fortunately, the flight engineer had a good selection of tools with him.

"See you all back here at midday," I said as we dispersed for the night.

At noon, the repair party reconvened in a much more sober condition, and a good harvest of assorted wire had been gathered as well. We immediately set to work. The settee was turned upside down and three of us, with linked arms standing on the bent frame and jumping in unison, finally got it straight. While all this had been going on, further splintering of wood had occurred, and it all had to be wired back together carefully. Lastly all the upholstery had to be put back into place.

"I think that's the job done," I said wearily, three hours later as we turned the settee back upright again and stood back to admire our handiwork.

"No one go near that settee," I said with a wry smile to the assembled workers. "The next party will have to be in someone else's room!"

I still had the problem of the broken table to settle with the manager. Attack would have to be the best form of defence I thought, as I sought him out that evening.

"These glass topped tables in some of the rooms are very dangerous," I said to the manager when I had tracked him down. "Last night the co-pilot slipped on the marble floor in his room — the table top is very precariously balanced — it broke, and he could have been seriously gashed."

The hotel manager looked back at me with a knowing smile and replied, "Ah, Captain, I know there was a big room party last night, no?"

Tongue in cheek, I debated and haggled over the breakage, and the manager agreed that we would settle the matter before we left in the morning, when he had checked on the price of the glass.

The price turned out to be fairly steep, and we stood in the lobby next morning in our uniforms ready to depart while further haggling commenced. A satisfactory result was negotiated; we would split the difference, which was billed to the company, and we departed for the airport on friendly terms. Still thinking of the settee I did not breath a sigh of relief until our Britannia was lifted into the air, climbing on course towards the Canary Islands. I can only hope our repair job is still holding out in old Marrakesh, for I never did get the chance of a return visit to check it out.

It was in the Canary Islands, on another trip of this series, that more than one drama occurred. On that occasion, our Britannia had just begun her climb out of Las Palmas bound for the nearby island of Tenerife, when an engine had to be rapidly shut down due to a fire warning, which proved to be a real one. The flight engineer closed down the engine, and very soon the huge four-bladed propeller came to a standstill in the feathered position. The sight of a stationary propeller through the cabin windows never failed to produce varying reactions and emotions among the passengers. These ranged from sarcastic comments to fear bordering on panic, all of which had to be dealt with by the crew using the appropriate approach. We could have quite easily returned to Las Palmas, which was still close by, but it was very definitely in the interests of the company and the passengers to get them to Tenerife where we were due to stay for two days. After a quick discussion, it was decided to continue, although that was easier said than done.

We set about coaxing the Britannia into a climb on only three engines, and we had a relatively short distance of about 50 miles to do it with the mountainous island of Tenerife ahead. On a clear day the airport can be seen at its spectacular best; at one end of the runway the terrain drops steeply from 2,000 feet almost abruptly to sea level, while at the other end a more gradual escarpment, dotted with picturesque Spanish villages and villas, rises in stages from the direction of the island's harbour below. Above all this towers the massive conical volcanic peak of Tiede (pronounced Tie-ee-day), rising to over 12,000 feet not many miles away and ever present in a pilot's mind when shrouded in cloud. Today the cloud was broken. When we had completed our engine-out landing and breathed a sigh of relief, it was quite interesting to note how many of our passengers offered to buy the crew drinks at the hotel!

Again one day, departing from this wild backdrop, we were faced with a sudden crisis caused by the foolish action of a passenger. Our old acquaintance, Murphy, was again lying cunningly in wait ready to throw in, not one but several, spanners into the works as we prepared to take off using the uphill runway towards the steep drop, weighed down with a full load of fuel and passengers.

We had a trainee flight engineer aboard, and he sat slightly rearwards and between the co-pilot and myself. His job would be to open up the four big Proteus turbines to-take off power, adjust the engine torque with the throttles, trim the propeller revolutions with the prop switches, and monitor all the various engine parameters. He had not been doing all that brilliantly so far on this tour, and we were therefore leaning over backwards to give him as much practice as possible. Hovering over our trainee, watching his every move and prompting him in a lowered voice, was our supervisory flight engineer, who knew the job inside out.

The engines were opened up, wheel brakes gently released while our heavily laden aircraft shook herself and started off uphill along the runway, with the speed building up painfully slowly. The needle of the airspeed indicator gauge still hovered below lift-off speed, and the runway continued to rush past. It had all been carefully calculated from our graphs and we knew it would be perfectly safe, but we were going to use an awful lot of concrete. The speeding Britannia was now going along like a train, and at that very second above the roar of the engines a shrill feminine screech reached my uncovered right ear, "Captain! an emergency exit window has fallen in."

Our trainee friend had heard it too! He had both hands stretched forward grasping the four throttles, but out of the corner of my eye I could see his face turned towards me in bewilderment.

"Stop?" he croaked.

This was no time for niceties. At the top of my lungs I bellowed, "Fuck the window! Full power!"

My urgently compelled shout was so loud that it was heard, embarrassingly for me, by passengers in the front rows of seats in the main cabin. However it achieved the desired results, but was a shaker nevertheless, for our friend under training had been on the very point of pulling back the throttles. They remained firmly opened, and the next second we lifted into the air with the runway end slipping past under the nose. Shortly afterwards, seemingly catapulted into space, we found ourselves looking down from well over 2,000 feet at the sparkling Atlantic Ocean below us.

I was still shuddering inwardly at the thought of what could have happened to us all, when the stalwart Derek, the flight engineer-in-charge, craned his neck past our trainee and spoke in my ear, "We'll delay pressurizing, Arthur. If you would keep her level for a bit, I'll go back and check the window." Saying this, he was away. As the Britannia cruised along in level flight, I could not help but reflect on the wonderful advantages of having an experienced crew aboard. He

DRAMA DURING TAKE OFF, FROM TENERIFE .... 1966.

was back in next to no time; the window had been successfully relocated and he commenced the pressurization of the aeroplane.

When all systems were back to normal again, we continued our climb to cruising altitude, steering towards southern Portugal, our first landfall. Time now permitted us to turn our attention to solving the mystery of the detached window. The panel containing the window was a sizeable chunk, and the couple into whose laps it had fallen were adamant that it had just flopped inwards on its own.

"Must have frightened them out of their wits," said Derek, describing the scene he had come upon when he had gone back to the cabin. "The noise of rushing air was like a hurricane in a wind-tunnel!" adding, "I secured it back in place without too much trouble though."

He went on to describe how baffled he had been, and just as he was about to leave an elderly lady, sitting in an adjoining row, had tugged at his uniform coat and said to him in a rich Geordie accent, "It was him Henny! I saw him playing with the catch, the silly bugger!" and then with a hearty laugh added, "and hasn't the Captain got a loud voice! We all heard him you know!"

That got a big laugh up front, but did not prevent a scathing lecture being delivered to the gentleman who had tampered with the catch, and after that we let the matter rest. Murphy had at least been successfully foiled at an attempt to scatter us all down the mountain-side.

We were bound for Heathrow and, as usual in those days, a large part of our efforts went towards making sure that on arrival we successfully avoided any problems with Customs. This is hardly a consideration nowadays among crews, because good pay, conditions of work and pensions make smuggling no longer worth while. It was a different story in the 'fifties and 'sixties. Finding ways of getting a bottle or two of spirits or cigarettes for smokers past HM Customs was generally considered to be a bit of a game. With half bottles all duly tucked away in inside pockets and elsewhere, we awaited the onslaught after the passengers had left the Britannia and been coached away to the terminal. The Revenue men were soon on the scene, but this time without a rummage squad to go through the aeroplane with a fine toothed comb — just an ordinary search of briefcases and bags today. The search was completed. The Customs officers gave their permission for the crew to leave, and they now turned their attention to sealing up the duty free aircraft bar boxes in the midship section.

The crew were filing past them on their way to the Britannia's centre door, when it happened — Murphy could not have shown more impeccable timing! I heard an ominous thud from ahead of me in the queue. There on the floor for all to see, right next to the kneeling Customs officer, lay a half bottle of gin. The owner, a girl named Felicity, who was a bit of a character, could only look down

in blank amazement. Silence followed, broken by the Revenue man's slow deliberate tones, "And where did that come from?" he enquired.

Felicity stared back at him, "From between my legs," she replied in a defiant tone.

The embarrassed officer, still kneeling, flushed a scarlet red and could only splutter, "Please go," adding, "and take it with you."

The cabin staff at this time did not enjoy the same good conditions that most do today. In spite of this, loyalty and dedication to the airline seemed to be just that little bit greater then, and the company sometimes were quick to take unfair advantage of it. This was amply demonstrated before a very early departure one morning on the Britannia.

Outside our building, transport was all set to take the crew into the centre of London Airport to Flight Planning, and then out to the aircraft. But a small crisis had developed. One of the stewardesses had failed to turn up, and we needed all four this particular morning as we had a full load of passengers. A hasty telephone call had been made to the missing girl's flat, but she was not there. Someone then suggested trying her boyfriend's place. This time the duty officer was lucky; she was there, had overslept, but, he added, she would not be able to make it as her uniform was back at her flat. The duty officer had no alternative but to quickly telephone her boss, the Cabin Services Superintendent. This man was made of much sterner stuff, and was in addition not at all pleased at being awakened at this unearthly hour. The telephone lines soon burned, and it was not long before we learned the results.

Within about 15 minutes, the unfortunate girl arrived looking fairly dishevelled, clambered aboard through the rear door of the transport, and we roared away. Sitting in front of the vehicle, I had been aware of some tittering and whispering from the rear seats, but the sight we were treated to on alighting was something our jaded eyes had not counted on being treated to that early in the morning. The lady was wearing virtually nothing under her uniform overcoat! It turned out that she had been given an old-fashioned ultimatum by her boss: either turn up for the flight or be fired forthwith.

"Get your boyfriend to collect your clothes," he had been reported as saying, "and deliver them to the airport." As events turned out, her clothes arrived about five minutes before the passengers boarded, and one of the toilets provided a makeshift as well as very

cramped dressing room.

A Union official today, of course, would have had a fit at the thought of such coercement. Nowadays vast numbers of cabin staff, as well as pilots, are kept at the airport on standby duties to cover for those who, for one reason or the other, fail to show up for duty. It was not considered necessary back in those times.

The Britannia was a tough aeroplane, and in particular her very strong undercarriage proved invaluable on many an occasion. In the depths of winter, an early morning flight had prepared to depart from Newcastle, with the runway ice- and snowbound. In those days the airport did not have its own snow ploughs; the city bus routes had first priority on the city's available equipment, so as a result aeroplanes had to make do. The Britannia slithered and slid its way to the take-off point, and the crew went through their take-off checks. While the flight engineer varied the engine power doing the propeller 'stops check', the aircraft was sliding forward on the packed snow as the Captain applied the parking brake with his feet. The Skipper then ordered take-off power but, while he had been distracted keeping an eye on the checks and the slipping aircraft, he forgot to release the parking brake. The Britannia roared off down the runway with all its eight main wheels locked solid, then completing the take-off run she lifted off the packed snow and was pointed south for London. There, however, the runway was as dry as a bone, and the parking brake remained forgotten for some strange reason, perhaps because it was not one of the items included on the company's pre-landing check list. As the big four-engined machine touched down, there was a sudden squeal, multiple bangs, and all the main wheel tyres burst. The aircraft continued on its wheel rims until it came to a standstill and later, after a thorough inspection, eight new wheels were fitted making the aeroplane soon ready for service.

Not all was grim drama where the 'Whispering Giant' was concerned. She did steady work over the next few years, and at that time the Ministry of Civil Aviation permitted our crews to fly two dissimilar types of aircraft. There were some mutterings about this among the pilots, as the Britannia was a very different kettle of fish to the Ambassador. The main difficulty was judging height when landing — from a cockpit which one day might be very close to the ground if flying the Ambassador, to being seated perhaps the next day as high as the roof of a double decker bus.

It so happened that I had just finished my stint flying the horse freighter, and was back for a spell of operating passenger services on the Britannia — this time it was to be a night flight out of Newcastle. Fast asleep that afternoon in my hotel room and long before my wake up call had been booked, the door suddenly boomed with someone pounding on it. Sluggishly I made my way to the door and opened it. Outside stood the co-pilot.

"Christ!" he said, "Turn on your TV set and watch the news repeats. It looks as though our Ambassador has just gone in at Heathrow."

I immediately switched on the set. The news item was such a dramatic scoop that I did not have long to wait. By some million to one chance a cine photographer had been standing on the north side of the runway with his camera pointing in the right direction, and had recorded the whole nightmare crash sequence. Horrified, I saw the chilling spectacle happening almost in slow motion, before my very eyes. The doomed aircraft drifted across the screen at a bizarre angle with the wings tilting steeper and steeper; then right into its path floated a line of parked aircraft and the main terminal building. How I willed them to make it — inside the aircraft, I knew, were friends

THE CATASTROPHIC RESULT, OF THE FAILURE OF A SMALL SCRAP OF METAL, IN A WING FLAP LINKAGE..........

and colleagues, and had the chilling thought that it could be one of us.

The Ambassador, our faithful long serving 'Alpha Delta', now clearly out of control, her wings very nearly vertical, plunged to destruction. She sliced the top of the tail off the first parked Trident jet in her path, then demolished the whole of the rear section of the next, before smashing into a steel barrier and the terminal building. There was a horrific blast of metal against metal, bricks, dust, masonry, and fuel which rose in a mushroom cloud, and that was the end. There was no fire in the final wreckage, and only two persons survived the terrible impact — two of the grooms in the tail of the aircraft were pulled from the debris barely alive.

The next day I was again at Heathrow, after completing my night flight, and I stood beside the great mass of twisted metal with memories flooding back. It was a numbed feeling to think of friends who had met their deaths in this once beautiful aeroplane which was now a shambles.

Both engines had been at maximum power right until the end; one had been torn completely loose and was embedded deep into a wall, with the propellers folded back round the engine like the petals of some huge flower, blooming from the wall high above our heads, suspended in smashed brickwork in spite of its tremendous weight.

Just a small strap of metal had broken in the linkage of the flap mechanism, as full flap had been lowered for the landing, and from that moment on the fate of 'Alpha Delta' had been sealed. The pilot had felt the left wing drop away from under him as the whole of the port side flap had collapsed, and because of a balancing device that went haywire, the other side had lowered still further beyond its maximum right down to the vertical position. No aircraft could have lived with that amount of drag on one side only, and we could not escape the fearful thought that it could have happened on any of the thousands of flights done with passengers aboard.

The tragedy was that this had all been forecast by one conscientious man. Sitting in a small lean-to shack adjoining the hangar at the company's engineering base at Southend, the Chief Inspector had often been seen mulling over drawings of the Ambassador's flap system. He was one of the old school, who knew well the meaning of honest to goodness attention to detail. His instincts had led him to put his finger right on the weak link in the flap design; the exact spot where the failure did in fact occur. He had duly notified his superiors of his fears, and had followed up with memorandums as reminders. Down through the system had come vague answers: modifications would be too expensive, there had never been any trouble to date so the system must be sound enough.

The Chief Inspector had still remained troubled, and had sent on his report to De Havilland's at Hatfield, who had inherited responsibility for the designs of the old firm of Airspeed, the original makers. The matter rested there, while inside the wing that small flange of metal pierced by several bolt holes, which even further reduced its strength, continued to be stretched and stretched again. Finally it reached its limit; the flange tore apart as predicted, unable any more to support the immense weight hanging on the two barn door sized flaps, each time the aircraft droned in to land.

It did not take the accident investigators long to trace the villain of the piece, and after all they even had a film sequence of the whole tragedy to call upon. Eight horses and seven crew and grooms perished.

Our company Chief Pilot and Operations Manager was in his office at Heathrow Airport when the horrific news came through. He was rushed to the scene and found himself picking his way through the wreckage, it being necessary for him to identify the crew members. As he made his way towards where the crushed remains of the cockpit lay, a burly fireman barred his way.

"And where do you think you're going mate?" he said with his asbestos gloved hand held against the other's chest.

Our Operations Manager explained the purpose of his visit to the fireman, who gazed back at him almost with compassion.

"You're a pilot, aren't you?" he enquired. And added, "For your own good, I'm not going to let you see what's in there. If you want identification, the Captain has a large gold ring on his middle finger."

He understood the fireman's concern very well, and appreciated it because he had had this awful job to do before on the slopes of mountainous Croglin Fell in Cumberland just seven years previously.

The sad business of the burials followed, and the last to go was our engineer, John Moody. A more well loved man it would be difficult to find; he had become so much a part of the horse transport scene that a year or two before they had even named the company's Bristol Freighter after him. On the last flight of the day, wherever their journeys might have taken them, he would invariably remain behind at the airfield doing maintenance jobs and 'putting the aircraft to bed' as he would say. No job was too much trouble, and always it would be done with a joke or a laugh. The hours, which he put in, should have made him a lot of money, but he was one of a generation gone who worked for the love of the job.

Midday found a group of us aircrew and stewardesses as passengers by road from Heathrow to Southend with a bottle being passed around, for we were all bone weary and in need of fortification. We had been flying all night long and dawn found us landing in the far north of England, from there we had caught the early flight to London, and now we were on the last lap. A melancholy chain, that had started many years before on an aircraft designer's drawing board and was soon to conclude at a small Essex church.

How well the Priest, who conducted the service for John Moody, summed it all up when he said, "This man must have been greatly loved by all — I know this as I look around at the great many faces gathered here in sorrow."

The church was indeed packed to capacity, and the overflow was so great that the churchyard was full of people as well. Even to those standing outside among the tombstones, the service came across the hushed summer air from the open windows of the church.

Later, near the graveside, I happened to be standing beside my friend, Keith, the Chief Inspector. He stood with shoulders jerking as he sobbed with grief. I laid my hand on his shoulder as I offered what consolation I could — he had certainly done his share to try to avert this tragedy.

This seemed to be the way of aviation, with poor designs sometimes having to wait until the next generation of aircraft to be corrected. Flaps would no longer be forcibly pulled down on hinges like a door, but run out and downwards on fixed tracks on later aircraft.

The shadow of the accident had hung over the company like a cloud, and sitting with a group of our pilots some while afterwards, I listened as another Captain recounted an incident, which had happened in Spain, that so fully summed up our departed colleague's good humoured character.

The bulbous shaped Bristol Freighter, with 'John Moody' painted in large letters on the side, was standing in the noonday heat of midsummer on the tarmac of Barcelona Airport. Standing atop the wing in oil stained scruffy clothes was the man himself, administering fuel to his aeroplane. Six horses were on board, but it had been necessary to off-load a lot of excess weight including baggage and gear that would have to be sent on another flight. On completing the refuelling, John climbed down off the wing and reported to the Captain, with his usual infectious chuckle, that all had been done and that the fuel in the tanks had been 'well stamped down' as requested. At this there was further merriment, knowing winks and nodding of heads among the group below for they knew he meant that a little extra fuel had been put aboard for eventualities. They were oblivious of Murphy at work behind the scene building up for another performance.

As they were about to clamber up the ladder to the cockpit, the Spanish Agent dashed up to the aircraft.

"So sorry Commandante, but eet ees no posseeble to take baggage on Iberia — they are full up as well!"

To make matters worse, the Captain was also informed that the charterers were insisting the full load should go on this flight. They were trapped as they could not get fuel taken off. So many pilots had been confronted with this situation. The Captain went back to his load sheet and did some hasty calculations, mindful that he could not endanger the Freighter's safety by overloading her. He reckoned they could just about legally manage the extra weight.

The gear was thrown back on board in the nose doors, and the engines were finally started. A slight sea breeze had sprung up, and the Captain reasoned that this would help reduce the adverse effect of the midday heat. The engines were run up and checked, and the Freighter lumbered on to the runway. Then with their characteristic crackling roar, the two Hercules radials were opened up and the aircraft gathered speed down the concrete strip, with the Mediterranean shimmering beyond. A few final bumps and she was airborne, crossing the shoreline and climbing.

They had barely reached 300 feet and were now over the sea, when one of the engines faltered and died. The Captain rammed the good engine wide open, and quickly pulled back the propeller pitch lever and throttle on the failed engine. Then with his foot straining on the rudder pedal, he stretched forward and pressed the feathering button to bring the propeller to a standstill. (Countless aircraft had crashed in the past because of pilot error in not doing this drill.) It was a sequence which had to be got right and quickly. Already the heavily loaded Freighter was sinking down towards the water. After agonizing seconds the uselessly windmilling propeller, with all the drag it was producing, finally stopped as the blades were forced round edge-on to the airstream by the feathering pump. It was none too soon. The overburdened aircraft continued to stagger along, but the loss of height was reduced.

The Captain shot a glance at the other two as he struggled to keep the Freighter flying.

"Looks like we might have to go into the water chaps, but I'm going to attempt a shallow turn and try to make the other runway."

We stood listening as the tale was being told. We all knew that the Skipper, who was telling it, was one of the best, and many another pilot might not have got the aeroplane back down again safely.

As the Bristol Freighter recrossed the coastline still sinking lower, the other runway came into view. John Moody was at this time sitting behind the two frantic pilots and rolling a cigarette, which he very sensibly continued with as there was really very little he could do to help at the moment. The ground was getting ever closer, and when at last the aircraft started down the cigarette was still being smoked. The jolt and squeal of the wheels as they contacted the concrete again was music in their ears. With some difficulty they got the machine clear of the runway and shut down the remaining engine with a sigh of relief.

"Must be ready for a nice cup of tea chaps?"

The two pilots could hardly believe their ears, but turning round there it was before their very eyes. The thermos flask had been opened, and the cups of tea were being steadied by an oily hand while sugar lumps were stirred in with his screwdriver. Tea never tasted so

good.

Following the funerals, we had not been back at work many days when word got around of the disgracefully inadequate compensation that had been paid to the widow and her children. So we were reduced to getting a collection going all round the company network and various bases, but the results were very disappointing; the collection, which should never have been necessary in the first place, had got off to a woeful start and it was flagging miserably. I gave the matter further thought that evening, and soon an idea came to me. I disappeared into my darkroom and got to work. It was not long before I had produced six big enlargements of a photograph which I remembered taking years previously. It had always been my practice to carry a camera with me when I was flying, and during a spell on the ground with the Freighter I had been sitting in the cockpit waiting for loading to be completed on a beautiful sunny afternoon. I had turned to John, who was filling in some paperwork, and said, "Say, John, have you had a photograph of yourself taken with 'your' aeroplane?"

With his usual chuckle, he had replied, "No Cap'n, never have."

Reaching for my camera, I had climbed out of my seat and made my way through the cockpit hatch, which was open, and walked out along the wing. He had been absolutely delighted when I later presented him with the result — a photograph showing the name 'John Moody' painted in large letters on the side of the nose section with himself standing above it.

Now that old picture would earn its keep. The photographs, with attached black bordered appeals, were placed at various bases and had dramatic effects on the collection.

CHAPTER 10

The end of that year approached, and with very little warning some of us suddenly found ourselves being whisked into the jet age — undeniably somewhat later than most, but nevertheless we were arriving at last.

The famous De Havilland Aircraft Company at Hatfield had merged to become Hawker Sydeley, and tucked away in the corner of one of the hangars lay three uncompleted aircraft shells, on which a previous purchaser had gone bankrupt. In spite of just having come out of another financial crisis following the accident at Heathrow, our Company became the new owners of these machines after some very hard bargaining. They were Trident IEs, and in the opinion of the makers they were the best of the Trident variants which had been made. Admittedly they lacked the Automatic Landing Systems fitted to the others, but their simplicity was also a big advantage. Furthermore, they had much greater range and could carry up to 139 passengers, although ours were to have 123 passenger seats.

My aviation vocabulary was about to be enlarged with many new words: 'leading edge slats', 'lift dump', 'spoilers', 'speed brakes', 'Dutch rolls' and 'yaw dampers', being but a few.

After completing the engine course with Rolls-Royce at Derby and the Maker's course at Hatfield, the big day finally came to start flying training. Little did I know what a mindboggling experience this was to be, as I strapped myself into the left hand seat with a Hawker Sydeley test pilot in the co-pilot's position on my right. Engines were started — there were no longer any propellers buzzing near by the cockpit — with just a faint whistling sound coming from somewhere far behind us. I released the brakes very cautiously, and the brand new jet liner moved forward; we commenced taxiing round the airfield perimeter track so that I could get the feel of the machine.

Then to get the maximum length of runway for our take-off, the test pilot instructed me to taxi along a narrow strip of concrete ending in a dumb-bell. So incredulous was I, at the request, that I slowed the Trident to a stop and said with a nervous laugh, "But surely we'll never be able to turn right round on that small circle of concrete?"

My instructor was patient when I further asked him if he was pulling my leg. I edged the aircraft forward and commenced turning when he told me to; if we were going to sink in up to our axles, then it would not be my fault. The nose wheel was far behind the cockpit, and I found myself in the entirely new position of sitting with grass moving past underneath me but with all the wheels still firmly on concrete behind us. Duly impressed, we finished up facing exactly down the runway, and after checks had been completed I grasped the three throttle levers pushing them forward under the watchful eyes of the Hawker Sydeley men.

The jets behind us built up speed to a full-throated roar at a tremendous rate, making the aeroplane seem as though it were rocket propelled. I experienced a continual pressure in the small of my back, and there seemed to be no holding the beast back. The Trident positively leapt into the air and zoomed skyward; almost immediately she had to be throttled right back to prevent shooting right through our circuit altitude.

I was never more grateful to have someone sitting beside me to talk me round and when the runway, which was not very long by normal standards, came into view ahead of us it looked like the size of a postage stamp. As the jetliner screamed down to the runway threshold, all my previous flying judgement, built up on years of experience, was having to be instantly overridden. Thoughts raced through my mind as we hurtled down towards the runway: 'What madness is this?' 'We're not going to make it!' 'We're certain to finish up in the houses at the far end!'

Out of the corner of my eye I could see the test pilot, who was handling the throttles while I flew the machine, lift the engine reverse levers even before the wheels were anywhere near the ground, and there was a massive roaring noise from the jets in the tail. I could see his left hand cramming on full reverse power with the throttles, and we were amazingly still in the air but beginning to use up runway when the wheels contacted the ground at last. Pushing the control column forward brought the nose wheel down, and I started to apply the brakes while we seemed to be still hammering along at a fantastic speed. The runway end was approaching fast when the test pilot's voice, in an almost conversational tone, suggested, "That's right, keep the braking going."

The deceleration had been fierce; unbelievably there was still actually some runway left when we had at last slowed down.

It had all been such an experience, like nothing I had had before. A 'hot ship' she was indeed — one of the few, if not the only civil airliner, that was certificated to use reverse engine power in flight, while on the rest it was only possible to use reverse on the ground to decelerate. This facility we would soon learn to use to great advantage when we gained experience on the aircraft.

It was a sunny spring afternoon in 1969 at Hatfield when our test pilot instructor came to see us off. I had been granted the privilege of flying the first aircraft to Heathrow to commence the next day's schedules. This was our big day; after all the weeks of training, the co-pilot, flight engineer and myself would for the first time not have anyone looking over our shoulders. Ron Clear, the test pilot, stood behind the three of us strapped into our seats, "Goodbye chaps — have a good flight," and he added, "try not to bend it — she cost one and three-quarter million quid!"

Just over nine years were to follow flying the Trident, but big changes were in store for us. There was a marked decline of problems on the aeroplanes themselves and they were more reliable on all counts. Admittedly events did happen a lot faster in the air, but to balance this some controls were a lot easier. For example, to increase power for a climb on the old piston-engined aeroplanes, the mixture control would have to be reset, the propeller revs increased, the throttles opened, the cowl gills adjusted, perhaps the carburettor heat controls reset too, and each of these had their own limitations to be watched. The jet engine was by comparison simplicity in itself — just one lever, the throttle, to push or pull. The new aeroplane served excellently — a tribute to the craftsmen of Hatfield who built her, and a terrific morale booster for those of us who operated the machine.

New frontiers had been opened to us; we were now flying in the substratosphere, high above most of the weather which we had once ploughed through hour after hour with airsick passengers. However, we still had to face the music like before, when there was bad weather in the lower levels during take off and landing.

One afternoon in Spain, we had the rare opportunity to be actually looking at the very spot where lightning struck. There had been a lot of thundery activity around Alicante, and as the day wore on the clouds became more and more menacing. A full load of 123 passengers sat cooling off in the air-conditioned cabin as we waited our turn to enter the runway for take off. The co-pilot was flying this sector, and I was becoming most anxious to be away as a huge black thunderstorm, getting blacker by the minute, was approaching the airfield of Alicante, threatening to block our way out. As our Trident lifted off, the storm was almost upon us. I was surprised that the co-pilot had not started a turn away, as we had discussed on the ground just previously.

"Start your left turn," I called, but he still hesitated and replied, "There is high ground on that side."

Not a second more could be wasted.

"We know about it — I have the mountains in sight. Start turning now!"

FIRST HAND WITNESSES TO THE TREMENDOUS POWER OF A LIGHTNING STRIKE..

He immediately put the Trident into a fairly steep bank, and from the very spot, for which we had been heading, came an enormous flash that lit up the blackness of the cloud. Blinking my eyes, I saw over the nose a vicious fork of lightning scorch down towards the earth. It seemed to remain suspended in the air for seconds, a zigzag stream of vivid light, and where it met the earth there was an eruption like a bomb burst. A lurid flash sent dust and rocks flying into the air. The arid field, where the strike occurred, was fortunately deserted otherwise there must surely have been casualties. We had been privileged to witness a spectacular display laid on by nature for our benefit, from exclusive ringside seats, and all the more appreciated having just evaded it. Minutes later we were climbing past the jagged crags to the north and into clear blue sky above the clouds, safely homeward bound.

They happen in threes, so the saying goes, and I have often found this very true in aviation. Two mid-air collisions had recently occurred, and that afternoon our Trident was in exactly the same position near Nantes in France, a week after the last accident had happened. It had been a bad one — both aircraft had collided and gone down, one nose diving into the ground, killing all aboard, while the other had force landed. The memory was still fresh in our minds as we flew along just above a cloud layer. Sipping a cup of tea, I happened to glance out of my side window, and there, converging on us, was another aeroplane still some distance away. Jabbing a finger in its direction, I called to the co-pilot, who was flying the sector, "Aircraft — looks like it's at the same height."

The relative bearing was remaining the same, which meant we were on a collision course, and it was very rapidly getting bigger.

"It is at our height!" I exclaimed urgently, "disengage autopilot and start turning right quickly."

While he was doing this, I grasped the throttles and pushed them forward.

The other machine was a Boeing 707, and we could quite clearly see the TAP livery painted on its side. We were now flying parallel, and while our speed was increasing I called up the French controller to let him know what was happening. The Portuguese pilot had also seen us and was letting forth a stream of words, while our Trident, being much faster, began to pull ahead.

It turned out to have been a genuine mistake on the part of the Air Traffic Controller and, coming so close on the heels of the previous tragedy, I felt even slightly sympathetic. When the outraged demands for an explanation from the pilot of the other aircraft had subsided somewhat, we were directed by French radar onto our original tracks that had converged over Nantes.

While I was filling in a 'Near Miss Report' to be handed in when we returned to base, one of the stewardesses appeared at my shoulder and when I looked up she said, "Captain, a lady passenger has just asked me to tell you that she was able to see someone waving from one of the back windows of the aeroplane we've just passed!"

The incident was becoming ancient history, when about a month later the enquiry report from France was received by the company. It turned out that we had each been under different Sector Controllers and there had been a lapse in liaison between them. Would it happen again? Possibly not, thanks to the corrective procedures set up to deal with just this sort of event. There must be few pilots who would not appreciate the difficulty of a controller's job, especially at night and in the very early morning when air traffic is sometimes at its busiest, making a super alert mind necessary for the safety of hundreds in avoiding collisions.

However, there is always a first time for everything, and we had an unique experience one winter's day at Munich, which highlighted possible language difficulties and the need for instant contact between controllers in the same building. The three of us were sitting in the Trident's flight deck, having just finished our breakfasts and

A MID AIR COLLISION, CAUGHT IN THE NICK OF TIME.........

waiting for our return passengers to board. It was a moment to relax briefly, and I was absently looking out of the cockpit window across the airfield dotted with patches of snow. A small aeroplane had just come into view below the fairly low cloud base. Something was not quite right. I blinked and looked again, "He hasn't got his wheels down, has he?" I announced to the other two.

In answer to my half question, the co-pilot and flight engineer immediately looked out, but even before they uttered confirmation I had grabbed my radio headset and was transmitting.

"Munich, the aircraft on short finals here has not got its wheels down!"

The controller's voice came back, "Station calling Munich, say again please."

Frantically I repeated the message, for the light aeroplane was getting closer and closer to the ground, but it was no good because although I was speaking to a controller on the airfield he was not the actual one in touch with the landing aircraft and the message did not make any sense to him. Right in front of our eyes the machine, with its wheels neatly tucked into the wings, was now hovering above the runway about to smash itself into the ground.

Unbelievably I had time for one last desperate call, "Munich, the aircraft about to crash on the main runway has not got its wheels down. Fire a red flare!"

But time had run out, the next second we saw a vivid shower of sparks fanning out behind the machine as it settled gracefully on to the concrete. It was the sort of event that happens in a dream with some strange scene and a desperate warning shouted out that the victim never hears. The stricken aeroplane, its unfortunate pilot and his passengers slithered down the runway until it ground to a standstill, luckily without a fire starting.

In due course three people stepped out of the machine lying ignominiously on its belly on the runway.

"Poor bugger," I commented to the other two, "and you know what this means, don't you?"

There was silence and, as there were no takers to my question, I continued, "We're in for a two hour delay while they clear the runway."

I had hardly uttered these words when our headsets cracked into life.

"All aircraft, this is Munich Control — airport closed until further notice awaiting clearance of blocked runway with lifting equipment."

There followed a little hilarity in our cockpit following a remark by the flight engineer on his Captain's apparent clairvoyance.

While all this was going on, I had been thinking about the last words of Munich's broadcast. I said to the co-pilot, "Say, you're an expert on light aircraft, what do you reckon that one weighs?"

He thought for a moment, "I'd say about 2,500 pounds."

I scribbled this down on a piece of paper and did some quick division.

"Twenty men ought to do the trick! Do I take it you'll volunteer with me, Gents?" I asked the other two with a laugh.

I called up Munich advising them we estimated that about twenty men ought to be able to lift the aircraft manually, and I added that three of us were willing to help along with perhaps some of our able bodied passengers. The reply was a non-committal "Thank you," and I was left with the distinct impression that we should leave it to them. There seemed nothing for it but to resign ourselves to the wait, so I broke the bad news to our passengers. We pulled out our newspapers and settled down with a cup of tea.

A quarter of an hour must have slipped by, when I glanced up over the newspaper having caught a sign of movement. My jaw dropped in amazement. There, trooping across the snow was a party of about twenty burly airport workers! The aircraft was soon hoisted up, and placed atop a large freight trolley. It was all over and being wheeled away within 15 minutes. A short while later we were on our way, leaving me with a distinct feeling of satisfaction at having more than played my part in events, albeit without any recognition at all.

Along with our new aeroplane, we found ourselves introduced to a training device that had been in regular use with the bigger airlines already for many years. It was an artificial airliner flight deck, anchored permanently on the ground, correct to every last detail of controls and instruments. The whole capsule, in which the crew sat to be trained and tested, even reproduced motion, and it was known as a Simulator, although at other times irreverently it was called 'The Stimulator', 'The Box' or 'The Sweatbox'. Up until that time we had done all our periodic checks and tests during special training flights on the aircraft itself, but this had become increasingly expensive as larger aircraft came into service. The Simulator could do a much wider range of tests and training at a fraction of the cost, and we therefore had to resign ourselves to learn to live with it. There was

ACTUAL PILOT COMMENT AFTER AN INADVERTANT WHEELS UP LANDING ON TRAINING....

obviously a limit to how long a candidate could be allowed to continue on a real aeroplane after he had started making mistakes, but in the Simulator he could crash the box into a mountainside if necessary to learn a lesson.

The trials and tribulations of the Simulator were suffered by many pilots, not because of the machine itself, but due to the great contrast among the examiners or instructors who ran it. There were some Training Captains who did the job wonderfully well; they would set everyone concerned at ease, and the pilot would come away after his two days of tests and training feeling that he had learned a great deal. Then there were others who conducted the sessions, of which they were in charge, on the lines of 'the night of the long knives' — Training Captains with sinister nicknames such as 'The Smiling Assassin', 'The Poison Dwarf' and 'Trapper Jack'.

There was another who failed a complete crew on Christmas Eve and is reported to have told the three dispirited men, whose jobs were now on the line, "You've all failed, Gentlemen. Don't worry about it too much — go back to your families, enjoy the festive season, and you can come back to do a retake in the New Year."

They all knew that this failure would now be on their records for the rest of their careers, and that if they failed again there would only be one more final chance before the sack.

I was unlucky enough to have done two checks with this particular Training Captain on separate occasions, and both times had an extremely uneasy passage. On the last of these, the pilot who was acting as the third member of our crew under check had been failed. He had been so badly victimized that I said to him afterwards I would support him if he wished to complain to the Training Flight Manager, but he decided later to let the matter drop.

Standing in huge purpose built rooms, the Simulators would be perched atop long hydraulic rams, and were entered from a platform high above. Loaded with advanced electronics, they had come a long way from the little old Link Trainers, and because they were so enormously expensive were utilized virtually round the clock. Essential maintenance was done during night shifts, and pilots often found themselves reporting for Simulator details at ungodly early morning hours or late at night. Most found it a disagreeable prospect at the best of times without the difficulties and drama that sometimes occurred within.

Thus it happened that I found myself reporting at the Simulator block one winter's morning at 6 a.m., having listened to my alarm clock and its backup jangling at 4.30 a.m. In these early hours, the life force is at its lowest ebb, and the adrenalin was being called upon to do overtime as I started my detail under a particularly dour Training Captain. This one was not going to be an easy ride — the name of the game would depend a lot on the other crew members under check and how well we could co-operate with each other. The co-pilot, although a most willing and affable fellow, was not among the best and our examiner, being a gruff man of few words, was not going to help matters. I had expected a bad time, but the miserable experience we were all in for that morning, to see a grown man nearly completely destroyed, I would most gladly have done without.

Breathing a sigh of relief at having completed the worst of my tests, it was now the co-pilot's turn. He got off to a reasonable start, but it was not long before he was beginning to get a bit frayed at the edges. I had already been reprimanded for doing more than usual in trying to assist him. He had come into flying late in life after having flown with the company for years as a radio operator, and when that had been phased out he had learned how to fly on borrowed money.

"You'll have to do that last radio beacon let down again," growled a voice from behind us.

While the Simulator was being set up to commence another take-off, the thought went through my mind that what the co-pilot really needed was some good instruction on how to do it properly, but from behind us there was only a deathly silence. With the tension mounting, the unhappy co-pilot prepared to take-off yet again.

We started and were just lifting off the runway when an engine was stopped dead. As our box staggered drunkenly into the sky, it all began to turn into a can of worms. I very much doubted if the co-pilot had ever been trained to perform and practise this manoeuvre, for all of us in the company were newcomers to this form of testing, and had largely been left to find out for ourselves the hard way.

I felt great sympathy for my old colleague, but I was powerless in this situation to aid him. He had by now reached about 1,000 feet, and alas nearly everything was wrong. He suddenly just gave up, and with a choke he let go of the control column. His shoulders sagged, his head slumped forward, and his whole frame became racked with uncontrollable sobbing. Now to further exacerbate the unfortunate man's misery, a stentorian voice from behind said, "Pull yourself to-bloody-gether man!"

This only seemed to serve to make the pitiful sobbing worse. Not a word more had been spoken, nor looked likely to be. 'Christ!' I thought to myself, 'it's time I did something if no other bugger is going to.'

The sobbing was coming across loudly through the co-pilot's open intercom switch and would not be making a very good impression on the consul operator sitting outside at his desk. I stretched across the cockpit and flicked off the switch on the right hand control column. The weeping ceased to echo directly into our headsets, which was a start, but there was still no sign of action from our Examiner sitting behind. I waited, but still there was no word spoken while the sobbing continued. Was there no spark of human compassion in the man? I therefore decided to continue; stretching across once again I laid my hand on the co-pilot's shoulder to draw his attention, and with the other I pointed to the card clipped on the instrument panel in front of him.

"Look," I began, "when the engine is failed, concentrate on keeping her straight, then just fly these speeds."

While I was speaking a noticeable change had come over my old colleague. He had begun to pull himself together and was listening.

With finger still pointing at the Vital Data Card in front of him, I continued, "Start your climb after the engine failure at this speed here."

He was now listening keenly, and it looked like I was winning. The thought crossed my mind that I was doing someone else's job for him, but nevertheless I persevered.

"When you get to the height shown here, level off, and when the speed builds to this figure," my finger tapping the line above, "pull the flaps in, and then climb at this next speed to your safety height. No problem, you can do it easily."

I ran through the whole procedure once again, and could now only hope the Training Captain, still sitting in silence behind me, would give the co-pilot another chance. Reluctantly, with a grunt of approval, permission to do another take-off was granted.

Away we went again. The old radio operator had his engine fail as expected and performed a classic engine out climb, with me pulling silently for him from the other seat. It proved all he really needed was a little relaxed instruction and less of the heavy hand. A feeling of some satisfaction was inescapable.

Our friend's recent traumatic breakdown was nothing new. It had been seen many times before in one form or the other in the Simulator. It had got so bad in one well-known airline corporation with so many pilots being failed and harassed by a particularly tyrannical training branch that matters came to a head. There was a major rebellion involving the pilots' Union in protest, and as a result sweeping reforms were introduced. Simulator 'checks' became known as 'refreshers', and the Training Branch became a separate unit so that pilots could no longer be victimized by management — an era of enlightenment had dawned. High standards were nevertheless demanded, but the accent was more on training and this applied equally to operating crew as well as the cabin staff. The vast majority of stewards and stewardesses were of the highest professional calibre, although only female cabin staff were employed by the company during most of the time that I spent flying the Trident. Only just once in a blue moon, the wrong one will be there at the wrong time, and inevitably that will be the time when the wily Murphy looks in on the scene too.

Just such a combination came up one afternoon flying southwards towards the holiday island of Majorca. The young lady in charge of the cabin that day happened to be somewhat highly strung;

perhaps it was because of her, never admitted, humble northern background that she always found it necessary to compensate with a very ostentatious accent, but we had learned to live with all this.

We were now flying high in a clear blue sky with the snow clad mountains of the Pyrenees stretching across our path under the Trident's nose. All was peaceful, just air noise round the cockpit that the three of us sat in as the jet rushed along.

Suddenly a piercing scream rent the air very close to my ear, and there stood our senior stewardess transfixed between the co-pilot and myself, each hand frantically clutching the backs of our seats for support. The two of us, turning from the controls, looked at her in complete amazement. Her wide open eyes reflected terror, and were accentuated by protruding veins and tightened tendons in her neck. She was trying to speak, but it was more like she was choking — finally the words started to flow.

"Ca-Ca-Captain! A wo-wo-woman has j-just had her finger cut off in the toilet door!"

She had got it out at last, and the sentence was finished in a rather

high pitched screech.

"W-what can we do?"

I looked across the cockpit at the co-pilot's bulging eyes. It would have been funny if it hadn't been a crisis. What can we do? Obviously in her present distraught state, this would not be the time to remind her that taking care of such emergencies in the cabin were part of the job.

Turning in my seat, I said firmly to her, "Bring the lady up to the flight deck, sit her in the spare crew seat, and ask if there's a doctor on board please."

While we waited for the storm to break over our heads, I glanced at the co-pilot; his face was as white as a sheet — not much hope there.

"How are you on first aid, John?" I enquired of our flight engineer sitting behind us.

His answering snort, I knew from past experience, could mean anything, as he was a man of few words — he had been in aviation since the year dot and was now nearing retirement. However there was no time to go into further details because the cockpit door opened and our casualty was brought in.

One of the stewardesses was holding the unfortunate woman's hand high, the finger end wrapped in a serviette, and a second later the senior stewardess flounced in, still in a very agitated state. In a rather shrill tone she enquired, "Shall I give her a large brandy?"

The answer came, boomed across the flight deck, in a rich Irish brogue, "Don't be fartin' stupid woman! Can't you see she's in shock? Bring her some hot sweet tea!"

The number one stewardess just vanished, and I glanced round to see our stalwart flight engineer, John, swing into action. Skilfully he applied a tourniquet. The patient stared fixedly ahead with the very faintest trace of a sickly smile on her lips as beads of perspiration covered her forehead.

The mountain range of the Pyrenees was now behind us. Ahead we could just see Barcelona as a smudge on the coast and the airport's runways standing out with the Mediterranean shimmering beyond. Palma de Majorca, our destination, was not much more than a further twenty minutes'flying time so I decided to continue. A brief radio call to Spanish Air Traffic Control advised them of our problem. They commenced making arrangements for a priority approach for us and alerting the medical services.

The first officer had been behaving strangely. I noticed that he was studiously averting his gaze, and was definitely not his usual self. I learned later that he had been worried that he might have fainted at the sight of blood as he had done in the past.

Offering what words of comfort I could, the lady had gazed fixedly ahead with just a barely perceptible nod when I had told her we would soon have her down and in good hands.

While I was occupied flying the aeroplane, memory was stirring on what little I knew on the subject of severed bits. Pressing the call button above my seat soon brought another stewardess into the flight deck. Beckoning her closer with a quick motion of my head, I whispered in her ear when she was near enough, "Would you mind going back to the rear of the aircraft and try to find the fingertip? Wrap it in a tissue, and keep it safe until we see the doctor."

It transpired that the accident had happened after our passenger had just left the toilet and another lady had entered. Our patient had put her hand up near the door hinge to steady herself, while inside the toilet, feeling some resistance, the other lady had reportedly put her foot up against the door and forced it shut. The door hinge trim had been designed to provide a flush fitting, but in actual fact, the U-section metal channelling made a perfect guillotine for stray misplaced fingers. Possible lawsuits in mind, the trim from the company's Tridents was removed almost overnight when the aircraft returned to base, too late unfortunately to help the suffering lady passenger seated behind me.

The island of Majorca was now in clear view ahead, as we had been travelling fast, using extra power to keep the airspeed on the maximum limit. As we prepared to descend, there was a hint of perfume and then a whisper in my ear, "We've found the finger end, but it's covered in dust — it's been lying on the floor."

"Doesn't matter," I said to the stewardess in a lowered voice, "keep it wrapped up somewhere safe."

The Trident was started down — the Spanish controller had given us a free hand to come in as quickly as we could and it was too good an opportunity to miss. With full air brake and reverse power, our aeroplane dropped down from high altitude like a stone. Once across the island's mountain range, a tight landing circuit and we were down. No arrival of ours at Palma had ever been quicker than on that afternoon. No time was lost taxiing in. The Spanish had indeed pulled out all the stops. An ambulance was waiting on the tarmac, and a doctor strode up the steps as soon as they were in position. On entering the front passenger door, the first thing the Spanish doctor asked for was the severed fingertip. Within minutes the patient had been bundled into the waiting ambulance and the party sped away.

The surgeons of Palma must have known their business well, for some while later we received news that the surgical repair had been successful. The lady had the use of her finger again.

The year 1974 was drawing to a close, when a heaven-sent opportunity presented itself that was seized upon while the going was good. The sheer pleasure of flying our hot ship at a much lower level

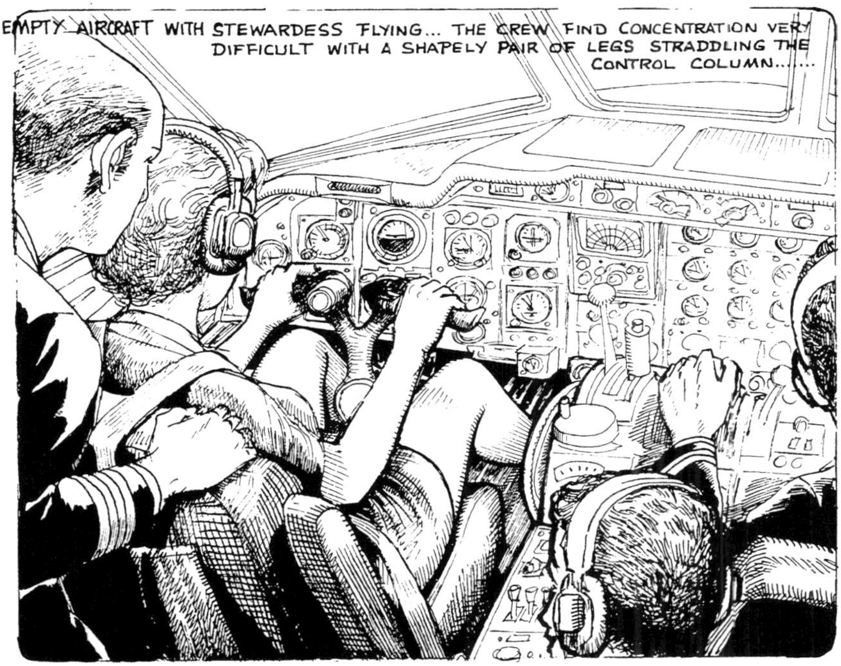

than normal was too much to resist. This would probably be the very last opportunity, and so it turned out to be. Our four Trident IEs were the only ones not yet fitted with Quick Access Flight Recorders, whose tapes were fed back through computers after each flight, instantly highlighting any irregularities during a flight. In addition, there was another device which had not yet been fitted — the Ground Proximity Warning System. If one got too near danger, this would sound off a loud 'whoop-whoop' and an eerie voice above the pilot's head would say, "Pull up — pull up," a call that would chill a pilot's blood, but would be a great step forward in air safety.

The Mediterranean island of Ibiza lay ahead on the horizon, the sea sparkled below us, and we were flying empty to pick up a load of passengers. It was the same old drill, four stewardesses called forward — yes: they would all like a little recreation break. Down went the nose and we dived towards the sea below. Once again that feeling of exhilaration as we skimmed across the wave tops, banking now and again as boats came into view, and we flashed past several at mast top height.

Moving relatively to nearby objects, the manoeuvrability of the Trident was admirably noticeable, as had once been demonstrated to me by the test pilot during my training. We had been conditioned by books and notes warning of the turning limits on handling swept wing jet liners, and on returning to Hatfield one evening after a day's training, I had asked my instructor, "Any chance of demonstrating a split arse circuit, Ron?"

His eyes positively lit up at the thought of enjoying himself doing a really tight circuit.

"Would you really, Arthur? — certainly."

He had called up the tower to advise them what he was going to do, and away we went. That day I witnessed a demonstration by a pastmaster I would not have missed for anything. I remember seeing the airfield boundary arcing round through the side window, and a final turn completed at about 50 feet before landing back on the runway. It was one of the most perfect and inspiring pieces of flying I had ever seen, and before that I would not have thought it possible.

Now, as we raced along, muffled exclamations of enjoyment came from behind the crew seats as the island of Ibiza loomed ahead. Staying below the level of the rocky cliffs, we rounded a bluff and found ourselves looking into the front windows of an hotel nestling among the rocks above its own sandy beach. It was delightful scenery but it flashed past too quickly, and soon, further down the coast, we could see the town of Santa Eulalia coming up. Time to call a halt! Putting on power, we zoomed skyward. There was no other traffic approaching the airport, and we were once again at a respectable height as the airfield came into sight.

On the ground, after shutting down engines, parked outside the delightful flowering creeper bedecked pergolas of old Ibiza's airport, I glanced across at the co-pilot. He had a strange look in his eye which I could not readily interpret, even though I knew him well as he was an old sailing buddy.

"Well, how did you enjoy it?"

"Very much indeed," he replied, "but what am I going to say to Biggles when I go for the interview about this, and me with a possible first command coming up?"

He was, of course, referring to the Flight Manager who, we all knew, would not even in his wildest moment of magnanimity protect anyone if it came to the crunch.

"Very important to always have a good excuse ready," I said to him. "Didn't you see the red flare fired up by that fishing vessel? It was our duty to go down to investigate."

There was a general round of laughter from those in the cockpit. "Yes," said the co-pilot, "it would be delightful to see a Trident fly past my hotel window provided it didn't come in."

In my ever changing aviation world, it had been the last 'beat up'.

IBIZA.... 'THE LAST BEAT UP.'

MILESTONES
OVER FOUR DECADES.

CHAPTER 11

Sitting in an Isle of Wight pub during the summer of 1977 with my veteran sloop moored just below in Cowes, a message, which proved to be momentous, was delivered to me by one of our group.

"Just been in touch with operations about my next week's programme. Lynn wants to know if you'll accept a Tristar course in December? Will you ring her back."

I recoiled in my seat, and took a deep draught from my pint of beer. Several months before and with tongue in cheek, I had filled out the Pilot's Yearly 'Bid' Form selecting Tristar as my choice. Now, it appeared, my seniority had won me a place. It was a sobering moment of truth, for it would mean a dramatic change in my secure niche and great risk if failure resulted, that being always a possibility.

"I'm going to jump in with both feet," I said to those listening. "Word has it they're waiting to carve outsiders up. I'll put a hundred quid into the kitty for drinks all round if I get through." But I kept coming back to thoughts of 'Trapper Jack', the 'Smiling Assasin' and the 'Poison Dwarf' lurking in ambush in the training establishment.

Such were my feelings at the time, because since our merger within the State Airline our small group had been dubbed variously as 'Cling-ons', 'Parasites', and an assortment of other names so that a real feeling of being inferior outsiders had been generated. However, when I eventually got into the course on this enormous new aircraft, I came to acknowledge nothing but heartfelt praise for the impartial treatment we received.

The warm classroom was the best place to be while the winter snow fell outside, and we hardly had time to spare to glance through the windows at the stream of others battling against the elements in the sky to land at nearby Heathrow. Totally dedicated concentration was necessary every second of our working day in the classroom, while hours of homework were absolutely essential to keep head above water. It was the hardest work I had ever had to face in my life. At the end of four weeks came testing time, and I was mighty relieved to find my name among those that had passed the examination.

Next followed 45 hours of Tristar Simulator time which, I thought, was where the hatchet men would descend on me. It was like being in the real aeroplane seated in a spacious cockpit. The first four hour session with a Senior Training Captain was relaxed and interesting. I was mystified. Why hadn't they started putting the knife in? Obviously just lulling me into a false sense of security.

The next day's detail, with a different Training Captain, was equally instructive and I was equally on guard, but surprisingly it all went smoothly. They must be just softening me up for the kill.

So the details progressed until it eventually dawned that my fears were completely groundless. That part of the course ended when each one of us twelve Captains had completed our Tristar Instrument Rating Test and Base Check. Now I was really on my way. The next stage would be actually flying the real Tristar.

When I came to do my first flight from Prestwick, the night was black with snow flurries. It was just the way the busy programme had worked out being a night rather than a day flight. First impressions, of the height that the pilots sat above the ground, were breathtaking, although like everything seen often it would eventually become commonplace.

Coming in for my first landing, this impression of height was even more mind-boggling; all my natural instincts screamed out that we were miles too high. While in the co-pilot's seat next to me, the Training Captain was beginning to sound extremely agitated as the third crew member called the giant aeroplane's main wheel height above the runway.

"One hundred feet!" came the crisp call from behind, read from the radio altimeter, followed rapidly by "Fifty feet!"

The Training Captain cut in, "Start checking, Arthur!" His voice was rising in pitch. "Check, check."

So I did what I was told, easing back on the control wheel, but thinking, 'This is sheer madness. We're going to drop out of the sky from hundreds of feet!'

"Thirty feet," called the voice from behind, and then unbelievably the main wheels, far to the rear of us, made contact with the runway. Sitting up front, we were still suspended high about the runway, and because of this an optical illusion gave the impression that not a lot of runway remained, but the nose was lowered and we slowed amid patches of snow with the landing lights showing plenty of space to spare. Old landing techniques had to be put behind, and new trust placed in this device called the Radio Altimeter which bounced signals off the ground to take a lot of the guesswork out of judging landings, especially in this new generation with mighty aero-

planes of huge proportions.

"It will take about a year to really get to know the aeroplane," said an experienced Tristar Captain in conversation with me over a beer one day, and I did not find any pilot thereafter who disagreed with this opinion. The aircraft was beautiful in every respect; it looked good from any angle one could choose, it handled wonderfully just like a big Dakota, but above all she lifted me with her on to a higher plane. Like nothing else which had happened so far in my life, the big beauty started shedding my complexes that had been a burden to me on and off for many a moon. Pilots flying older or smaller aeroplanes down the scale often suffer from them.

An entirely new era seemed to have dawned in the skies for me. Everything was now done properly; air safety was more paramount than ever, conditions of service and a wonderful crowd of colleagues made going to work a real pleasure, and as a final bonus reviewing the bank balance was very much more satisfying than it had been in the past.

'Let loose' on the routes, some of my landings in those early days on the new aeroplane, far from satisfied me. I had always prided myself on the major proportion of my touch downs being smooth, but the old 'greasers' somehow seemed to be eluding me. I remember a particularly heavy arrival on the short runway at Brussels one afternoon, and a very red neck as I hastily apologized to my fellow crew.

"Sorry about that chaps."

However, it prompted me to make a long and hard review and in a moment of contemplation it all came back to me.

I had been forgetting the advice that had been given to me so many years before, when I started off as a co-pilot on Dakotas.

Flying in Assam a veteran 'Dak' Captain had once said to me as I struggled to get it right:

"Try putting on a little tail trim, Whit."

What he had meant was that I should use the elevator trim wheel to make the tail slightly heavy, and of course this would mean exerting a forward pressure on the control column on final approach. Then, as the aeroplane floated down towards the ground, she was in a natural trimmed state, a gentle rearwards pressure on the stick would invariably produce a smooth touch down. The technique also had another spin-off benefit — that if a 'go around' became necessary, that was fine, for the aircraft was then in trim for the climb away. It has always been generally accepted that an automatic pilot could fly an aeroplane infinitely better than the human variety, and it was most edifying to watch the autopilot using this very same trimming back technique while doing faultlessly smooth autolands.

Reawakening to my old Captain's advice, followed all my flying life, soon had me back in the groove, and this huge aeroplane, that had overawed me into a temporary lapse, soon began arriving back on the ground in a much smoother manner when I was at the controls. This trimming tail down was a 'seat of the pants' practice, well known to the old timers, but sadly it got lost somewhere along the line as a younger generation of pilots came into aviation.

Problems, when they did occur, were predominantly concerned with passengers, not that we had not had our share of difficult travellers in the past, but now it was magnified with up to 350 people aboard.

The Cabin Services Director with his pursers and his many cabin staff were adequately trained in dealing with the occasional passengers who found themselves in a strange environment, had drunk a little too much, or even worse were on drugs — any of which brought out the worst in their characters. It had to be really bad before the Captain was drawn into trouble in the cabin, but drawn in I was, and at a time when I could ill afford to be.

We had a long night left ahead of us. Already 900 miles across the ocean from Bermuda had been covered and now, preparing to depart from Nassau, we still had the tricky night sector to the mountainous island of Jamaica, then continuing on to Panama, before we could have a beer or two and rest for the night.

"Captain, we're having a great deal of trouble with a passenger in the rear cabin. Will you come back and speak to him, Sir? He's getting out of control."

It was the Cabin Services Director, along with his purser, looking unusually harassed who leant over the three of us as we did our pre-flight checks. I turned in my seat, "If he's drunk, we'll have him off-loaded here in Nassau."

We both knew very well that this action was only taken in extreme cases, and the CSD responded by putting the ball back in my court.

"I think if you had a word with him, Sir, that might do the trick."

Inwardly cursing at having to become involved, I said to the other four in the flight deck, "I can well do without this sort of aggravation on a difficult sector like tonight's."

The one and a half hour's flight would take us right across Cuba, finishing with a tricky let down into Kingston with its nearby mountains and poor radio aids. However, I had a duty to back up the CSD.

"Bring him up here — I'll speak to him," I said, carrying on with our checks. I would be flying this sector, and was in the middle of going over our let down procedure at our destination with the co-pilot and flight engineer, when the flight deck door opened and in came our problem passenger.

He was a powerfully built black man, standing over six feet high, with a straggly moustache and beard, and the hair style of a Rastafarian. He was finding it necessary to stoop slightly to prevent his oversized woolly hat from coming into contact with the roof above him.

"What's the problem, man?" he boomed at me, while his arms moved curiously at his side as though trying to keep time with imaginary music.

"To start off with you can cut out referring to me as MAN! I am the Captain of this aeroplane, and I am doing my best to get you to Kingston, while you seem to be doing your best to disrupt the flight."

I went on to read the riot act to him, quoting from the Air Navigation Regulations on the powers of the pilot to off-load any passenger who created a disturbance. Our passenger did not give me the impression of being too concerned, so after a further brisk exchange of words he did agree that he would rather continue to his destination, Jamaica, and that he would not cause any further disturbance.

I took a deep breath and tried to settle myself back down again to the job in hand. Departure time was approaching as we carried on working our way through the pre-start-up checks. We had not got very far when the flight deck door opened and the CSD stepped back in again.

"So sorry to trouble you again, Skipper, but he's at it again. As soon as he returned to his seat, he announced to the whole of the rear cabin in a loud voice: I've just told the fucking Captain what he can do with himself."

There had apparently been an accompaniment of loud cheers from friends of his sitting near by. The gauntlet had been thrown down. I would far rather have been allowed to get on with our flight into the night, but this could not be let pass — the good name of my airline was at stake.

Snapping off my harness release and throwing off the shoulder straps together with the seat belt, I motored the seat backwards with the electrical control, giving me room to extricate myself.

"Here we go," I said to the co-pilot and flight engineer, slipping on my uniform jacket, while the CSD waited beside me. Reaching for the 'scrambled egg' hat from the shelf and jamming it on my head, I remarked resignedly to the others, "Don't know why I'm bothering putting this on — it will probably end up being knocked off my head!"

I made my way to the rear of the cabin along the left hand aisle saying "Good-evening" to passengers. The majority of the passengers were Jamaicans returning to their homeland for a visit. They were happy and well behaved. Why could not some folk just relax and enjoy a flight like everyone else?

Our troublesome passenger must have seen me coming for he stood up as I approached and stepped forward, towering over me as I came into the rear cabin. It could well have been called an eyeball to eyeball confrontation. Raising my voice, I shot at him, "It's just been reported to me that you referred to me as 'the fucking Captain'!"

This he immediately denied with a laugh, and I then moved past him and went round the cabin asking if anyone had any complaints. I was met by silence and shaken heads. Three white passengers, sitting together among the 45 in the rear cabin, were rolling their eyes and seemed to be trying to tell me something, but they remained silent. However, I was satisfied with what the cabin staff had reported, and I returned to our passenger who stood looking at me with a derisive smirk.

"Please take your seat," I said. "If the cabin staff report any further disturbance by you, I will have you arrested on arrival at Kingston."

If he had been playing to an audience before, I think he now realized that the price of further baiting of the crew would have to be paid for at a price. After a few words with the Cabin Services Director and the purser, I returned ruffled to my seat up front. Still shaking somewhat over my recent battle of words, it took considerable concentration to get back into the groove of the job in hand. Fortunately our passenger decided to keep the peace, and when we had got back down on the ground at Kingston it was gratifying to receive a message of thanks from some passengers for restoring order in the cabin.

Seeking reassurance, I happened to mention the incident to a good friend, also a Tristar Captain.

"I'd have off-loaded him straight away Mate," came his cheery comment, and he went on to relate an episode which had occurred on a flight to Paris that he had been flying. They were taxiing out for take off to Charles de Gaulle, when the senior stewardess popped her head over his shoulder.

"Sorry Skip, but we've got a passenger, Diplomatic Corps, who won't fasten his seat belt."

"That's OK luv," said my friend as he steered the Tristar along the taxi track.

She stood back thinking, 'That's strange. What's he going to do about it?'

She had not noticed that the huge aircraft, with its 350 passengers, had been turned on to an opposite direction track and was now headed back from where they had come. The pilot had been busy on the radio, and when the door was opened on arrival back at the jetty, Security men hurried aboard. The onerous CD man changed instantly from bratty behaviour to a model of co-operation when he realized he was going to be off-loaded from the flight. OK, he would fasten his seat belt. But it was too late. He was removed protesting from the aeroplane, and away to face serious trouble.

So grave a view had a Judge in Holland taken some years before that he had sentenced a passenger to four years imprisonment for refusing to fasten his seat belt prior to landing. The Captain on the flight in question had been forced to abort his landing approach, and hence the heavy hand of justice.

The aeroplane was superb; because of her size, the Tristar seemed to be able to shrug off most of the elements that had previously given us such a hard time in bygone years. However, having been struck by lightning many times during my flying career, a comparison of the severity of strikes was easier to make. But there was always a first time for others, as I witnessed to my amusement coming in to land at Heathrow one thundery afternoon.

The up and coming junior members of a crew have since the year dot often looked upon their Captain, in times of crisis or even normally, as one going into his dotage. Certainly one of the two pilots flying with me that day fitted into this category. Over-impatiently, he was just waiting to step into my shoes, which was fair enough, but as we settled down on final approach into Heathrow with the beautiful aircraft looking her best, nose held high, wheels and flaps set, I was looking with jaundiced eye at an extremely big black cloud sweeping up on our left.

With the runway in sight and judging the drift of the surrounding cloud, I reckoned we would just about clip the edge of it. I did not anticipate any problems, although conditions were getting a little murkier and some rain was beginning to splatter on the windscreen as the Tristar continued down the glide path locked on to the ILS and being flown by the two automatic pilots. They would be discon-

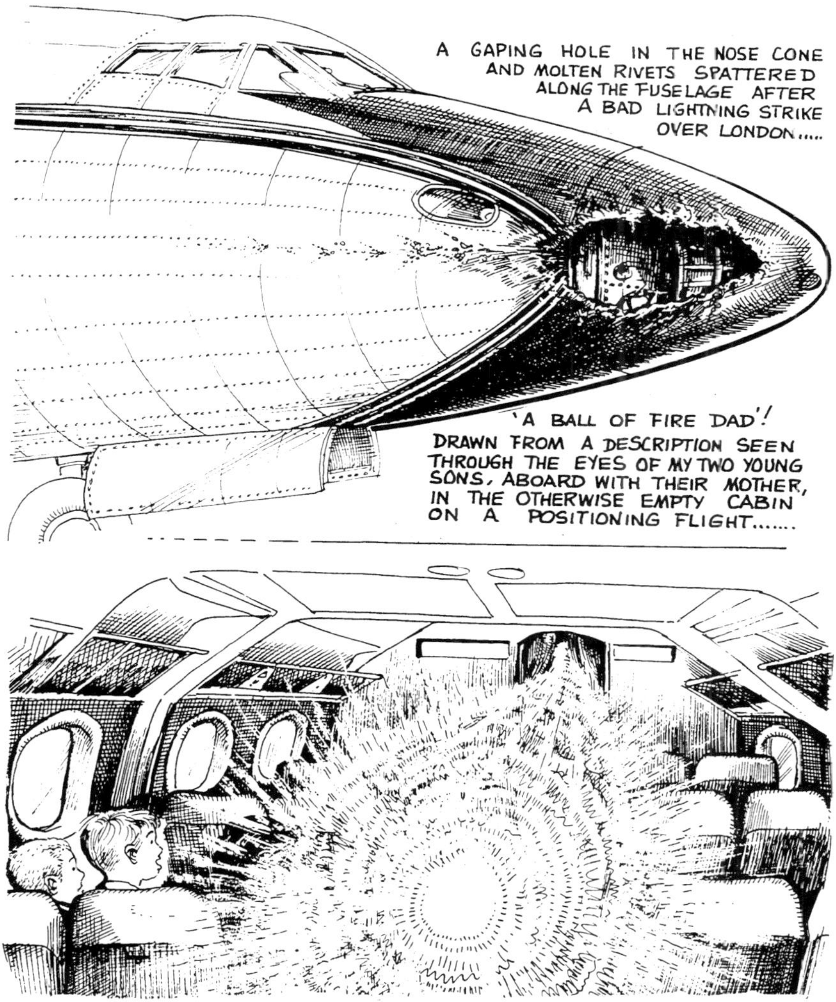

nected as we got lower and nearer the runway, and I would land the aeroplane manually.

Meanwhile as we completed our landing checks and continued monitoring the automatics, I noticed a pink glow, at first barely discernible, enveloping the windscreens.

"I think we're going to be struck by lightning!" I announced to the other two.

Glancing across at the two to whom I was speaking, it became patently obvious from that look in their eyes that their reaction was: 'Our Captain is cracking up'. That old familiar pink glow was getting brighter and beginning to turn yellow. It would come any split second now.

"We're going to be struck!" I exclaimed in a voice rising several notes higher, and instinctively ducking my head. The other two pilots were now looking at me in unabashed amazement when an ear-splitting crash rent the air. Head down and still looking across at them, I now had a broad smile on my face. They were sitting bolt upright with nostrils twitching at the scorched smell still lingering on the air. There was absolutely no need to say, 'I told you so' — their expressions said it all.

The Control Tower at Heathrow must have seen the flash too for our headphones came alive.

"Are you OK Speedbird?"

The co-pilot, whose job it was to do the R/T, was so overawed that he replied completely spontaneously, "Yes, but I've just heard the biggest bang I've ever heard in my life!"

Later, on the ground, we looked up at the aeroplane's nose which had just a patch of burnt paint and some dents. The same intensity of strike had once blasted a gaping hole in the nose of an Ambassador, which I had been flying over London with my family on board, while approaching to land on the very same runway used today. On that occasion, nearly fifteen years previously, a metal clipboard on the windscreen coaming had been blown rearwards, narrowly missing the co-pilot and myself and putting a dent in the bulkhead behind us. A fireball, a phenomenon sometimes accompanying lightning strikes, had travelled down the length of the cabin.

To be once again flying on routes beyond the skies of Europe made a marvellous change. It was tiring work, mainly night flying, but to have a few days off, for example, enjoying the exotic atmosphere of Bangkok, more than compensated. To sit in shirt sleeved comfort in an aeroplane at 35,000 feet, watching the Aurora Borealis over Northern Canada at night is some experience, as the multicoloured waves of light play about the aeroplane seeming to touch those inside. During daylight, looking down from over 30,000 feet, towering icebergs looked like blocks of pure white set on the blue sea with waves crashing against their bases. Circling high over Delhi in the morning sunlight, waiting for the fog to lift, the high Himalayas stretching across our horizon to the north, sparkling in the clear air, were a sight that could never be forgotten. Worldwide shopping, swimming off the snow-white beaches of Bermuda or Mauritius, and visiting so many new places made it all so very worth while. Our stopover hotels and the food we ate were the best, the work loads were reasonable at that time, and it was a wonderful way to approach the end of a flying career.

Cup of tea in hand and sunk deep into the padding of a comfortable armchair, I listened to the chatter about me. This was the extensive crew restroom in Queen's Building, at the heart of London's Heathrow Airport. Pilots and more pilots, mostly sitting around on airport stand-by duty. In a very few moments the three of us would be gathering up our briefcases, coats and hats and leaving to transport another few hundred customers on their way.

Our bright-faced co-pilot, ever seeking fresh knowledge, amiably addressed me over our table.

"Say, Arthur, just how many flying hours have you done?"

It was a question that pleased me — a chance for a little one-upmanship — for I knew very well that pilots of my vintage had an advantage here over this younger generation.

"Nothing too exceptional," I replied. "More than one of the blokes I started flying with back in India have clocked up nearly 30,000 hours but, myself, only 21,000 I'm afraid."

"WOW!" he exclaimed, "no chance of any of us ever getting up to anything like that!"

He was right, I thought, for the days of overworked pilots had long gone.

Meanwhile, my young friend had taken on a studious expression, and he reached into his uniform pocket and pulled out his calculator.

"8,760 hours in a year. That means you've spent nearly two and a half years continuously, day and night, up there!" he said, with an upwards jab of a sinewy finger.

Never before had I heard it put like that. He had suddenly added a new dimension to my eight million odd miles!

A flight in Concorde to Washington and Miami as extra crew introduced me to the supersonic age, albeit somewhat late but nevertheless a terrific experience. To clearly see the curvature of the earth from 60,000 feet and the blue sky turned to the blue-black of outer space was something new for me.

After a night stopover with the crew in Miami, we started on the return flight in our Concorde back to London. By now we were all on easier terms with each other and, as I sat in the narrow confines of the magnificent machine's cockpit powering skywards on our last sector, Tom, our good natured flight engineer, nudged my elbow, while working at his panel.

"There you are," he said, "blasé about it already after only a couple of trips," adding with a chuckle, "don't worry, everyone does it."

He was referring to the fact that we had just gone supersonic; we were through the so-called sound barrier and I had not even noticed it this time. Not altogether surprising though, for not the slightest tremor had been detectable, just a flicker of one small needle on the instrument panel and the steady increase on the Machmeter above Mach one.

"Bit different to the old Dakota," I said to Tom, and we got talking about old times and the subject of smoking in the cockpit came up.

"Not many aircrew smoke nowadays — they've got more sense." I nodded agreement as he went on. "Reminds me of the time I was flying with a certain Captain F. in a DC 7C freighter years and years ago. He wasn't half a heavy smoker. We were down Djibouti way when he discovered he had no matches, so the Skipper asked the rest of the crew in turn whether anybody had a light. Unfortunately we were all non-smokers. He was by now beginning to show signs of agitation. There were no passengers aboard, but we were carrying a steward who was his last hope as he pressed the Captain's call button. The steward appeared, but "No", he did not have any matches either. The Skipper muttered and went back to fidgeting in his seat, the thought of that elusive cigarette now foremost in his mind."

"Say Tom," he said suddenly, turning to his flight engineer, "stick this flight plan in one of your circuit breakers and see if you can get it to flame."

Tom looked at him in amazement at the thought of possibly setting their aeroplane on fire, but the Commander was quite serious. He gave the idea a try, just to humour him along, but it was no use, the paper refused to burst into flames.

The Captain brooded for a while longer, then suddenly he let out a shout of glee. "We'll go up through this layer of cloud and see if we can find some sunlight." They increased power on the four massive 3,400 horse power Wright Turbo Compound engines, eased back on the control column, and up they went.

"No need to tell Djibouti," said the Skipper, "there's no other traffic in the air and this shouldn't take too long."

The DC 'Seven Sea' was soon flying along above the cloud layer in strong sunlight as Captain F. reached feverishly into his briefcase and withdrew a magnifying glass. Placing a piece of paper on one of the cockpit window coamings he soon had it alight under the concentrated spot of light. As the paper flared up below the window the cigarette was thrust into it and sucked at rapaciously, as the Skipper finished off by swatting out the flames and scattering the smouldering ash about.

He pulled on the cigarette in deep satisfaction, dusting off the remains of the ash from his uniform and the aeroplane was on its way back down under the cloud to her assigned altitude before the dust had settled.

The story left us both creased up in laughter as the Concorde sped on. There are no two ways about it though — nowadays some questions would have been asked about such antics.

CHAPTER 12

REMINISCENCES

Just before transferring to the Tristar, having not revisited India for some twenty years, nostalgia called. The feeling was too powerful to be denied, and having some leave due I was soon on my way. Bombay was the first port of call and from there, after a brief reunion with some old pilot friends, I was in the air once again, heading south towards Bangalore. Here I had done most of my schooling in the far off days of the British Raj. It was a beautiful cantonment city of parks and shady avenues, situated on the Deccan plateau, and although not many degrees of latitude away from the Equator its elevation of some 2,000 feet considerably tempered the climate. Those who wish to escape the fierce heat of India's plains travel here during the hot season. Under British Rule, Bangalore was a garrison town with the roads and buildings kept in first rate order. Cool verandahed houses, each set in their own high walled gardens, lined the roads. Most of these residences had tall pillared porticos and driveways at their fronts to receive horse-drawn carriages and cars. It was altogether a delightful town, truly deserving of being known as a 'garden city', or at least that is how I remembered it. I was to find the present day reality somewhat different.

The basic change that had come upon India over the last 30 years since I had lived there was an approximate tripling of the 250 million population. The old school reflected this; most of the playing-fields had been built upon to accommodate extra pupils. The immaculate warden's garden was now a sandy waste and so many magnificent shady trees had been totally decimated. It was all very sad; however, I did learn, while chatting with a couple of the Masters, that a friend of mine from flying days, who had retired early because of ill health, lived near by.

Resolving to pay the family a visit, I set out that evening from the hotel along the old familiar roads which now alas were no longer in the fine condition that they had been under British Rule. The huge granite slabs of the pavements, hewn by forgotten convicts of an age long gone, were now in an exceedingly bad condition; many were cracked, a lot were missing, and some lay collapsed into the drainage channels which ran beneath them. Because of this pedestrians were forced to take to the roads, carefully avoiding piles of rubbish, sleeping bodies, wandering cows, cyclists, rickshaws and other traffic using what remained of the roads. Walking down that cantonment road with the last traces of a lovely still Indian sunset turning to night, boyhood memories of long ago stirred strongly. Familiar smells drifted on the evening air, wood fires, exotic cooking smells, sandalwood and jasmine, blended with the baser odours. However, warts and all, they were moments to be relished as nostalgic memories of old India came flooding back. I was glad I had come.

At last I arrived at the address which I was seeking. Standing before a large iron gate, I peered into a lighted courtyard, and saw to my amazement that the figure within, even though facing away from me, could not have been anyone else than my old friend. "Quinn!" I called tentatively. The tired looking figure slowly turned, and recognition was immediate in spite of such a long passage of time. We shook hands warmly. My old Flying Club buddy did not look in good shape at all, and before we had exchanged many words he had begun to tell me about his problems. He had been forced to give up flying quite recently because of heart trouble, and he now had to rely heavily on drugs to help him keep going. He had spent four terrible years in a Japanese POW camp, which had taken its toll on his health.

I cast my mind back to our first meeting at the Flying Club where we had both learned to fly. He had just been released after nearly dying while working on the notorious Burma/Siam railway, and was skin and bone. Quinton had gradually recovered but permanent damage to his health unfortunately remained. Over a bottle or two of beer we sat and talked of old times. Our meeting was to be a stark reminder of how two paths in aviation, once very similar, can diverge to become poles apart. Fate had dictated that my old friend had remained employed for the best part of the last 25 years doing what was sometimes almost suicidal bush flying.

He warmed as he went on to recount an experience that had occurred not long before he had been forced to give up flying. His destination had been an airstrip in the mountainous foothills of the Himalayas, and he had decided that it would be an interesting trip for his wife also. So it was that the Dakota with four persons aboard droned in towards the mountains to complete its assignment. They were to fly out a small bulldozer, which would be loaded next morning, and in the meantime accommodation had been arranged so they were free to enjoy the wild beauty of their surroundings.

The work started bright and early, and by midday the heavy chunk of machinery had been manhandled aboard, then securely lashed into position in the centre of the cabin. The Dakota visibly sagged under the weight, and the Captain, when he arrived, viewed it all with a jaundiced eye. Native loaders stood back from their labours, wiping the sweat from their brows as the noon sun scorched down, and not a breath of wind stirred on the strip. It did not take Quinn long to size up the situation. To begin with someone must have been trying to pull a fast one because the bulldozer was heavier than expected. The heat, lack of wind and extra weight precluded any thought of attempting a take-off. The engineer-in-charge was told that the take-off would have to be delayed until the cool of early next morning and weight taken off. This statement put the cat among the pigeons. The engineer-in-charge blew his top.

"Captain, if you don't depart today, the whole bloody load will have to come off," he heatedly shouted. "The aircraft cannot stand overnight with a bulldozer aboard; the landing gear, the hydraulics and the seals will not stand the continuous compression," he added loudly.

Then came the squeeze.

"I will have to have your decision soon, Captain, to allow time for the gang to off-load."

Quinn listened as countless other pilots before him had listened to ground personnel with little knowledge of aviation attempting to pressurize pilots into decisions. Silently he cursed the engineer and went back to his load calculations, then gave instructions for fuel to be drained from the Dakota's tanks back into fuel drums. This would leave him only sufficient fuel to get to a larger nearby airfield at a lower elevation where he could pick up some more. In addition to this he set about getting rid of as much extra weight as he could. Equipment and baggage was taken off and his wife and the radio operator were to be left behind. There was only one way out of the airstrip and that was away from the mountains. Quinn reckoned in the absence of any means of calculating the aeroplane's performance that with a good measure of luck they might just make it. After all, other arrangements had been made.

The Captain and his co-pilot climbed aboard, belted themselves in, and started the engines. They positioned the aircraft so as to take advantage of every inch of the airstrip, and the two Pratt and Whitney radial engines roared up to full power as Quinn's white knuckled hand pushed both throttles wide open. The old Dakota shook and vibrated under the strain, and she lumbered forward sluggishly as the brakes were released. Right from the start their rate of acceleration was nothing like it should have been, and nearly half-way down the runway to their dismay the tail wheel was still firmly on the ground. With the control wheel desperately pressed fully forward practically hard up against the instrument panel, the tail of the struggling aeroplane had just begun to rise. The screaming propellers clawed hopelessly at the thin hot still air, but by now they had used up three-quarters of the strip and had passed their point of no return. They had now absolutely no alternative but to keep on going.

As the Dakota reached the end of the runway, its tail in the air and both engines flat out, she was still firmly on the ground. Quinn's wife and the small group of spectators watched in horror as the aeroplane overran the strip and continued downhill, bumping over the rough slopping ground. As it disappeared from sight, the watchers looked in frozen dread, expecting at any minute to hear a crash and see a pall of smoke.

Aboard the gravely endangered Dakota, Quinton was nursing the control column as their bones were jarred by the vicious bumping. Just as it seemed as though their fate was sealed, the aircraft lifted momentarily, came back down again, bounced and mushed up into the air. They were flying at last, but only just. Putting the nose gently down, they built up a little extra speed, and then were able to ease the power off of the overheated engines. Quinn and his co-pilot were able to breath a sigh of relief, only too well aware of how very lucky they were to be alive.

Sitting on that hospitable veranda in the cool of an Indian evening in far off Bangalore, starting another chilled beer, I reflected thankfully on the sharp contrast between our two different worlds of flying.

Sadly, I was never to see my old friend again. His immense sufferings of the past as a half-starved captive, building forgotten railways in distant jungles, finally caught up with him and all too prematurely by the next year he was gone.

Holding in my hand an old group photograph with the white-washed hangar of the Madras Flying Club as a background, I looked at the rows of young hopefuls all turned out smartly wearing ties. It was to mark the occasion of the retirement in 1948 of our Chief Flying Instructor, Mr Harold Tyndale-Biscoe, and he would be laying aside at last his topee which he wore for flying. The rest of his days were to be spent in the Seychelles.

A youthful Quinn was there in the photograph, and he was one of the few who had not been subsequently killed in flying accidents. A mental dossier unfolded as my eye scanned the photograph again. This one was killed on a gusty day when his Dakota hit a high stone wall built right across the end of a runway in Mysore. There was the co-pilot who tried to walk out of the Nubian Desert. Another, further along the row, was a colleague who whilst working for the same company as myself disappeared in the trackless jungles of Assam. A good friend from my teenage years smiled forth, a close image of the film star Gregory Peck in his prime. He would perish only a year later on high ground landing a night mail flight during the monsoon, at an airfield with poor radio aids. Still further down the row was a co-pilot who was aboard the Dakota that flew into the ground after a night take-off from Calcutta because of a locked gyro horizon without warning flags on the instrument. Along the row a young face looked from that old photograph, little knowing the misadventure that awaited him within a year. He would attempt to put out a baggage hold fire in flight with the methyl bromide extinguisher provided and be fatally overcome along with a passenger by the toxic fumes. The Captain would do a good job force landing the Dakota on a dried river bed, but it would be years before this type of fire extinguisher was withdrawn. As my eyes scanned further, the sad roll went on and on, yet this was no wartime casualty list. They were among the many who had gone during this difficult era of Civil Aviation. It had not been in vain though, for they had each done a share for the rest of us who were to follow across skies made safer after those many tragic lessons.

THE END

CARTOON BY THE AUTHOR, PUBLISHED IN AN AVIATION JOURNAL, ATTACKING THE QUANTITY OF PAPERWORK REQUIRED OF AIRCREW.

AERODROMES VISITED DURING FLYING CAREER

Note: Places and countries are named as they were at date of author's landing.

1946	1	St Thomas's Mount, Madras — S.India
	2	Jakkur, Bangalore, Mysore — S. India
1947	3	Hindustan Aircraft Ltd., Bangalore, Mysore — S. India
	4	Ulundurpet — S. India
	5	Vellore — S. India
	6	Trichinopoly — S. India
1948	7	Panagar, Bihar — India
	8	Dum Dum, Calcutta, Bengal — India
1949	9	Bhubaneshwar, Orissa — India
	10	Vizagapatam — India
	11	Bezwada — India
	12	Cudapah — India
	13	Donakonda — India
	14	Hyderabad — India
	15	Bidar — India
	16	Sholapur — India
	17	Poona — India
	18	Santa Cruz, Bombay — India
	19	Cooch-Behar (Maharaja's Polo Ground) — India
1950	20	Rupsi, Assam — India
	21	Agartala, Bengal — India
	22	Kowai, Bengal — India
	23	Balurghat, Bengal — India
	24	Hasimara, Assam — India
	25	Grassmore, Assam — India
	26	Barrackpore, Calcutta — India
	27	Bagdogra, Darjeeling — India
	28	Gauhati, Assam — India
	29	Joorhat, Assam — India
	30	Talcher, Orissa — India

	31	Rampur Hat, Bengal — India
	32	Newlands, Assam — India
	33	Tezpur, Assam — India
	34	Benares, United Provinces — India
	35	Lucknow, United Provinces — India
1951	36	Patna — India
	37	Mingaladon, Rangoon — Burma
	38	Don Muang, Bangkok — Siam
	39	Tourane — Indo-China
	40	Kai Tek, Hong Kong — Hong Kong
	41	Nichols Field, Manila — Philipines
	42	Sookerating, Assam —India
	43	Mohan Bari, Assam —India
	44	Juhu, Bombay — India
	45	Porbandar, Kathiawar — India
	46	Sharjah — Trucial Oman
	47	Bahrain — Bahrain Island
	48	Port Sudan — Sudan
	49	Wadi Seidna, Khartoum — Sudan
	50	El Geneina — Sudan
	51	El Fasher — Sudan
	52	Kano — British West Africa
	53	Lagos — British West Africa
1952	54	Asmara — Eritrea
	55	Aden — Aden Protectorate
	56	Masirah Island — Muscat and Oman
	57	Maidugri — British West Africa
	58	Karachi — Pakistan
	59	Jiddah — Arabia
1953	60	Stansted, Essex — UK
	61	Northolt, Middlesex — UK
	62	Denham, Buckinghamshire — UK
	63	Southend, Rochford, Essex — UK
	64	Hamburg — West Germany
	65	Tempelhof, Berlin — West Germany
	66	Hannover — West Germany
	67	Kirkbride, Carlisle, Cumberland — UK
	68	West Hartlepool, Greatham, Durham — UK
	69	Innsbruck — Austria
	70	Pau, Lourdes, — S. France
	71	Kuwait — Kuwait

	72	Marignan, Marseilles — S. France
	73	Luqa —Malta
	74	Benina, Benghazi — Libya
	75	Tripoli, Kleiat — Lebanon
	76	Nice — S. France
	77	Jersey — Channel Islands
	78	Ronaldsway, Isle of Man — UK
	79	Woolsington, Newcastle-on-Tyne — UK
	80	Aldergrove, Belfast — Northern Ireland
	81	Manston, Kent — UK
	82	Le Bourget, Paris — France
	83	Nicosia — Cyprus
	84	Basrah — Iraq
	85	Heathrow, London — UK
	86	Kastrup, Copenhagen — Denmark
	87	Basle — Switzerland
	88	Bremen — West Germany
	89	Ouston, Northumberland — UK
	90	Fassberg — West Germany
	91	Coltishall, Norfolk — UK
	92	Cologne — West Germany
	93	Malpensa, Milan — Italy
	94	Brussels — Belgium
	95	El Adem — Libya
	96	Fayid, Canal Zone — Egypt
	97	Eastleigh, Southampton — UK
	98	Toulouse — France
	99	Mafraq — Jordan
	100	Chiampino, Rome — Italy
	101	Athens — Greece
	102	Istanbul — Turkey
	103	Jerusalem — Jordan
1954	104	Luxor — Egypt
	105	Almaza, Cairo — Egypt
	106	Beirut — Lebanon
	107	Bari — Italy
	108	Stuttgart — West Germany
	109	Dusseldorf — West Germany
	110	Amsterdam — Holland
	111	Lyneham, Wiltshire — UK
	112	Ahmedabad — India
	113	Penang — Malaya
	114	Changi, Singapore — Malaya

	115	Ratmalana, Colombo — Ceylon
	116	Jiwani — Baluchistan
	117	Baghdad — Iraq
	118	Frankfurt — West Germany
	119	Damascus — Syria
	120	Mersa Matrouh — Egypt
	121	Dublin — Eire
	122	Lyons — France
	123	Calvi, Corsica — France
	124	Son Bonet, Palma, Balearic Is. — Spain
	125	Salzburg — West Germany
	126	Tarbes, Lourdes — France
	127	Bembridge, Isle of Wight — UK
	128	Bairitz — France
	129	Blackbush, Hampshire — UK
	130	Wadi Halfa — Sudan
	131	Khartoum — Sudan
	132	Juba — Sudan
	133	Eastleigh, Nairobi — Kenya
	134	Antwerp — Belgium
	135	Zurich — Switzerland
	136	Tel Aviv — Israel
1955	137	Enugu — Nigeria
	138	Makurdi — Nigeria
	139	Jos — Nigeria
	140	Benin — Nigeria
	141	Castel Benito, Tripoli — Libya
	142	Gao — Algeria
	143	Aoulef Oasis — Algeria
	144	Algiers — Algeria
	145	Yeadon, Leeds, Yorkshire — UK
	146	Nutts Corner, Belfast — UK
	147	Ferryfield, Kent — UK
	148	Geneva — Switzerland
	149	Guernsey — Channel Islands
	150	Bournemouth, Hampshire — UK
	151	Ostend — Belgium
	152	Perth, Perthshire — Scotland
	153	Renfrew, Glasgow — Scotland
	154	Manchester, Ringway — UK
	155	Munich — West Germany
	156	Brindisi — Italy
	157	Creil Senlis — France

1956	158	Madrid — Spain
	159	Tangiers — Morocco
	160	Sidi Ifni — Spanish Morocco
	161	Villa Cisneros — Spanish West Africa
	162	Bathurst — Gambia
	163	Freetown — Sierra Leone
	164	Accra — Ghana
	165	Dakar — Senegal
	166	Gran Canary, Las Palmas — Canary Islands
	167	Lisbon — Portugal
	168	Orly, Paris — France
	169	Malmo — Sweden
	170	Bergen — Norway
	171	Vienna — Austria
	172	Klagenfurt — Austria
	173	Edinburgh — Scotland
	174	Elmdon, Birmingham — UK
	175	Dishforth, Yorkshire — UK
	176	Caen — France
	177	Ajaccio, Corsica — France
	178	Barcelona — Spain
	179	Bilbao — Spain
	180	Niamey — Niger
	181	Douala — Cameroon
	182	Leopoldville — Belgian Congo
	183	Elizabethville — Belgian Congo
	184	Livingstone — Northern Rhodesia
	185	Johannesburg — South Africa
	186	Cape Town — South Africa
	187	Windhoek — South West Africa
	188	Luanda — Angola
	189	El Golea, Sahara — Algeria
1957	190	Ankara — Turkey
	191	Habaniya — Iraq
	192	Palam, Delhi — India
	193	Nagpur — India
	194	Lasham, Hampshire — UK
	195	Shannon — Eire
	196	Palermo (City) — Sicily
	197	Rotterdam — Holland
	198	Bordeaux — France
	199	Oporto — Portugal

1958	200	Bastia, Corsica — France
	201	Swanton Morley, Norfolk — UK
	202	Santander — Spain
	203	Stockholm — Sweden
	204	Dinard — France
	205	Le Touquet — France
1959	206	Luton, Bedfordshire — UK
	207	Gatwick, W. Sussex — UK
	208	Woensdrecht — Holland
	209	Aberdeen — Scotland
	210	Belgrade — Jugoslavia
	211	Cranfield, Bedfordshire — UK
1960	212	Pisa — Italy
	213	Liverpool, Speke — UK
	214	Lille — France
	215	Stavanger — Norway
	216	Palma, San Juan, Balearic Is. — Spain
1961	217	Cambridge — UK
	218	Wymeswold, Leicestershire —UK
	219	East Fortune, Edinburgh — Scotland
	220	Hatfield, Hertfordshire — UK
	221	Deauville — France
1962	222	Zagreb — Jugoslavia
	223	Rimini — Italy
	224	Luxembourg — Luxembourg
	225	Middleton-St George, Durham — UK
1963	226	Prestwick, Ayrshire — Scotland
	227	Bristol, Avon — UK
1964	228	Venice — Italy
	229	Ljubljana — Jugoslavia
	230	Genoa — Italy
	231	Tenerife — Canary Islands
1965	232	Malaga — Spain
	233	Perpignan — France
1966	234	Seville — Spain
	235	Marrakesh — Morocco

1967	236	Turin — Italy
	237	White Waltham, Berkshire — UK
	238	Al Hoceima — Morocco
	239	Titograd — Jugoslavia
	240	Beauvais — France
1968	241	Ibiza, Balaeric Is. — Spain
	242	Alicante — Spain
	243	Gerona — Spain
	244	Pula — Jugoslavia
1969	245	Trieste — Italy
	246	Dubrovnik — Jugoslavia
1970	247	Burgas — Bulgaria
	248	Madeira — Portugal
	249	Fuerteventura, Canary Islands — Spain
1971	250	Tunis — Tunisia
1972	251	Minorca, Balearic Is. — Spain
	252	Los Angeles — USA
	253	San Francisco — USA
	254	Salisbury — Rhodesia
	255	Abbotsinch, Glasgow — Scotland
	256	New York — USA
	257	Antigua — West Indies
	258	Barbados — West Indies
1973	259	Metz — France
	260	Valencia — Spain
	261	East Midlands, Leicestershire — UK
1974	262	Helsinki — Finland
1975	263	Inverness — Scotland
	264	Monastir — Tunisia
	265	Faro — Portugal
	266	Almeria — Spain
1976	267	Cardiff — UK
	268	Fiumicino, Rome — Italy
	269	Cork — Eire
	270	Raisi, Palermo — Sicily

	271	Arlanda, Stockholm — Sweden
1977	272	Charles De Gaulle, Paris — France
	273	Naples — Italy
	274	Oslo — Norway
	275	Gothenburg — Sweden
1978	276	Larnaca — Cyprus
1979	277	Cairo — Egypt
1981	278	Baragwanath — South Africa
	279	Rhodes — Greece
	280	Linate, Milan — Italy
	281	Seychelles — Seychelles
1982	282	Biggin Hill, Kent — UK
	283	Dharan — Saudi Arabia
	284	Hong Kong International — Hong Kong
	285	Dubai — United Arab Emirates
	286	Abu-Dhabi — United Arab Emirates
	287	Toronto — Canada
	288	Bermuda — Bermuda
	289	Nassau — Bahamas
	290	Kingston — Jamaica
	291	Panama — Panama
	292	Mexico City — Mexico
1983	293	Kuwait — Kuwait
	294	Doha — Qatar
	295	Colombo — Sri Lanka
	296	Grand Central — South Africa
	297	Praslin — Seychelles
	298	Rawalpindi — Pakistan
	299	Dacca — Bangladesh
	300	Llongwe — Malawi
	301	Mauritius — Mauritius
1984	302	Nairobi, Kenya — E. Africa
	303	Abdul-Aziz, Jeddah — Saudi Arabia
	304	Rose Bay, Sydney — Australia
	305	Perth — Western Australia
	306	Kuala-Lumpur — Malaysia
	307	Philadelphia — USA

	308	Montreal — Canada
	309	Baltimore — USA
	310	Tehran — Iran
	311	Washington — USA
	312	Miami — USA
	313	Lahore — Pakistan
1985	314	Spilsted Farm, Sussex — UK
	315	Headcorn, Kent — UK
	316	Goodwood, Sussex — UK
	317	Rochester, Kent — UK
	318	Ringmer, Sussex — UK
	319	Heathfield, Sussex — UK
1986	320	Ripe, Sussex — UK
	321	Shoreham, Sussex — UK
	322	Felthorpe, Norfolk — UK
	323	Tangmere, Sussex — UK
	324	Sandown, Isle-of-Wight — UK
	325	Bognor Regis, Sussex — UK
	326	Dunkeswell, Devon — UK
	327	Shipmeadow Farm, Beccles, Suffolk — UK
	328	Kingsmead, Surrey — UK
1987	329	Parham, Sussex — UK
	330	Vancouver Harbour — Canada
	331	Nanaimo, Vancouver Island — Canada
	332	Goudhurst, Kent — UK
	333	Audley End, Essex — UK
	334	North Weald, Essex — UK
	335	Duxford, Cambridgeshire — UK
	336	Rand, Johannesburg — RSA
1988	337	Fairoaks, Surrey — UK
	338	Stapleford Tawney, Essex — UK
	339	Van Sant, PA. — USA
	340	Challock, Kent, — UK
	341	Redhill, Surrey — UK
	342	Lancaster, TX. — USA
	343	Pilansburg, Bophuthatswana — RSA
	344	Maypole Farm, Kent — UK
1989	345	Andrews Field, Essex — UK
	346	Old Warden, Bedfordshire — UK

	347	Gransden, Beds. — UK
	348	Popham, Hants. — UK
	349	Compton Abbas, Dorset — UK
	350	Calais — France
	351	Thruxton, Hants. — UK
	352	Old Sarum, Wilts. — UK
	353	Henstridge, Somerset — UK
	354	Addison, Dallas, TX. — USA
	355	Pretoria, Wonderboom Airport — RSA
	356	Lanseria, Tvl. — RSA
	357	Krugersdorp (Jack Taylor), Tvl. — RSA
1990	358	Brits, Tvl. — RSA
	359	Warmbad, Tvl. — RSA
	360	Ludham, Norfolk — UK
	361	West Malling, Kent — UK
	362	Dallas/Fort Worth, TX. — USA
	363	Ennis, TX. — USA
	364	Aero Valley (N.W. Regional), TX. — USA
	365	Flying 'S', TX. — USA
	366	Picayune, MISS. — USA
	367	Mobile (Bates Field), ALAB. — USA
	368	Crystal River, FL. — USA
	369	Lakeland, FL. — USA
	370	Troy, ALAB. — USA
	371	Delhi, LA. — USA
	372	Monroe, LA. — USA
	373	Corsicana, TX. — USA.
	374	Booker, Bucks. — UK
	375	Panshangar, Herts. — UK
	376	Wickenby, Lincs. — UK
	377	Fiskerton, Lincs. — UK
	378	Chilbolton, Hants. — UK
	379	Half-Penny Green, Staffs. — UK
	380	Danehill, Sussex — UK
	381	Salisbury, MD. — USA
	382	Ennis, MD. — USA
	383	Teneriffe South, Canary Isles — Spain
1991	384	Piltdown, Sussex. UK
	385	Tallulah (Hopkins Dusting) LA. — USA
	386	Vicksburg MS. — USA
	387	Clacton, Essex — UK

	388	Langham, Norfolk — UK
	389	Swanborough, Sussex — UK
	390	Woodchurch, Kent — UK
	391	Earls Colne, Essex — UK
	392	Ipswich, Suffolk — UK
1992	393	Cuxwold, Lincs — UK
	394	Old Hay, Kent — UK
	395	Leavesden, Herts — UK
	396	Elstree, Herts — UK
	397	Canterbury, Kent — UK
	398	Mesquite, Texas — USA
	399	Rockwall, Texas — USA
	400	McKinney, Texas — USA
	401	Lakeview, Texas — USA
	402	Goode, Texas — USA
	403	Arlington, Texas — USA
	404	Grand Prairie, Texas — USA
	405	Georgetown, Texas — USA
	406	Corpus-Christi, Texas — USA
	407	Aero Country, Texas — USA
	408	Stellenbosch, Cape — RSA
1993	409	Pent Farm, Kent — UK
	410	Slinfold, Sussex — UK
	411	St. Omer — France
1994	412	Waxahachie, Texas — USA
	413	Odessa, Texas — USA
	414	Deming, New Mexico — USA
	415	Tucson, Arizona — USA
	416	El Paso, Texas — USA
	417	Sweatwater, Texas — USA
	418	Mineola, Texas — USA
	419	Abbeville — France
	420	Dieppe — France
	421	Merville — France
	422	Fly-in, Tvl. — RSA
	423	Heidelberg, Tvl. — RSA
	424	Savanna Lodge, Tvl. — RSA

1995	425	O'Brien (Tx) — USA
	426	Eagle's Nest (TX) — USA
	427	Chanute (Kan.) — USA
	428	Redwood Falls (Min.) — USA
	429	Baudette (Min.) — USA
	430	White Moose Lake — Can.
	431	Bo Ship Farm (Sussex) — UK
	432	Covey Trails (Tx.) — USA
1996	433	Vereeniging (TVL) — RSA
	434	Springs (TVL) — RSA
	435	Laddingford (Kent) — UK
	436	Binstead (IOW) — UK
	437	Chilsfold Farm (Surrey) — UK
	438	Thurrock (Essex) — UK

Madras Harbour,
The Year 1934.
MY FATHER PROVIDING FOOD AND BEER FOR TWO GERMAN AIRMEN LEFT ABOARD THEIR FLYING BOAT, WHILE THEIR OFFICERS ARE ENTERTAINED ASHORE. THE FOLLOWING DAY THE SEAPLANE DEPARTED EASTWARDS INTO BAD WEATHER COVERING THE BAY OF BENGAL AND WAS NEVER SEEN AGAIN ....